You may be reading the

WRONG WAY!!

IT'S TRUE: In keeping with the original Japanese comic format, this book reads from right to left—so action, sound effects and word balloons are completely reversed. This preserves the orientation of the original artwork—plus, it's fun! Check out the diagram shown here to get the hang of things, and then turn to the other side of the book to get started!

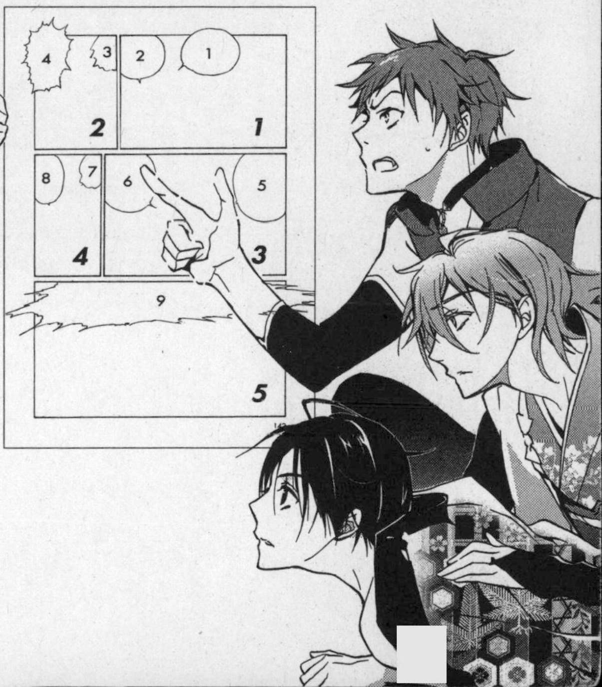

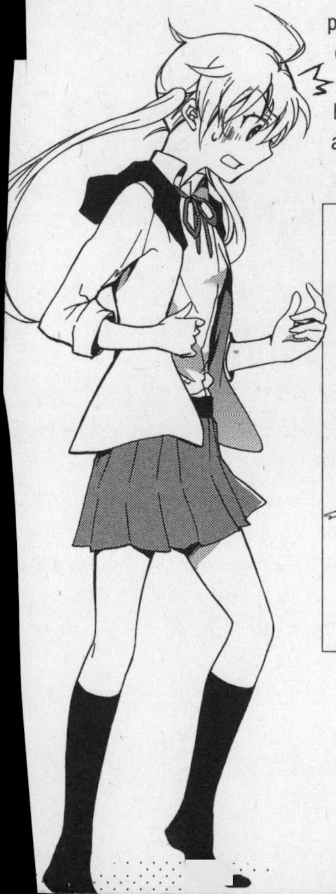

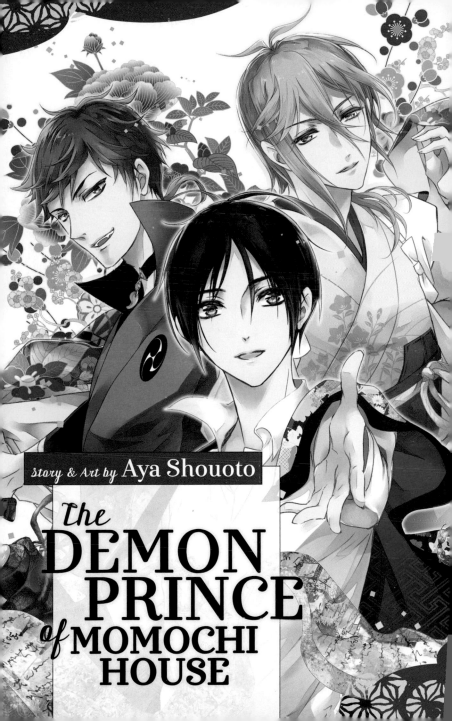

Story & Art by Aya Shouoto

The DEMON PRINCE of MOMOCHI HOUSE

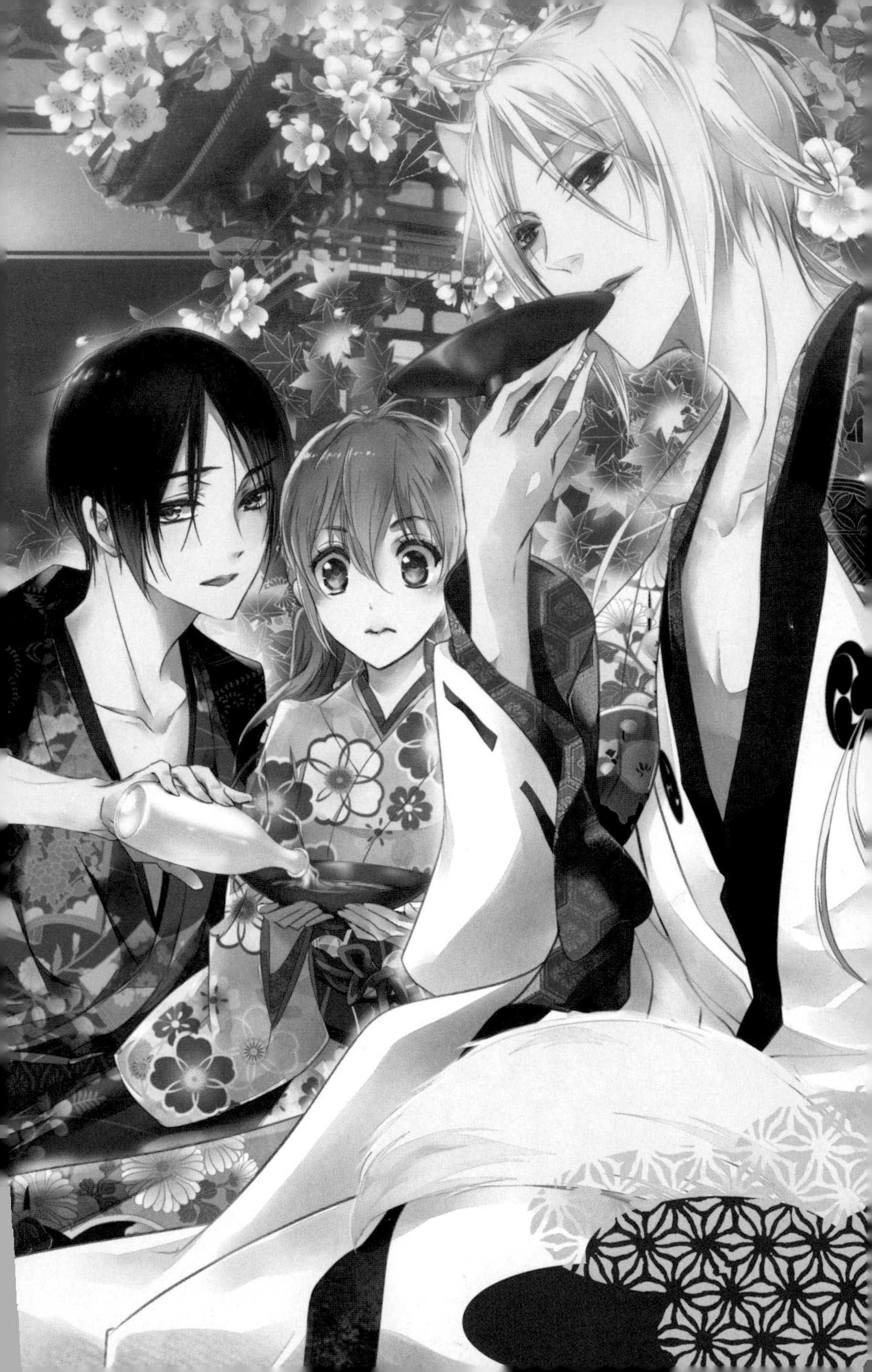

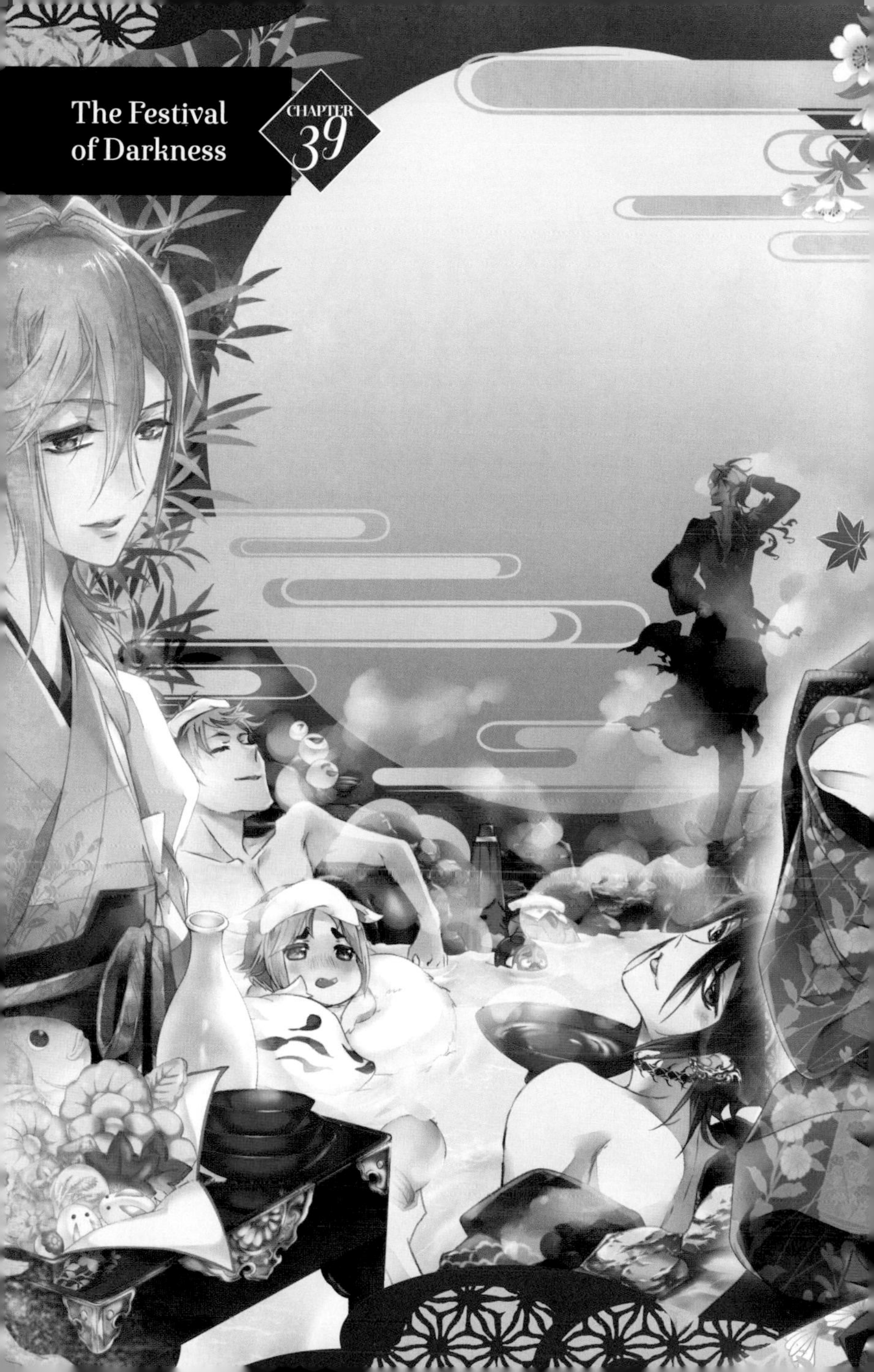
The Festival of Darkness
CHAPTER 39

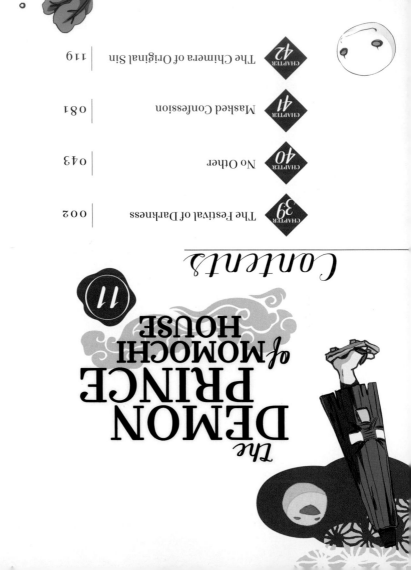

The DEMON PRINCE of MOMOCHI HOUSE

11

Contents

The Mysterious Residents of Momochi House

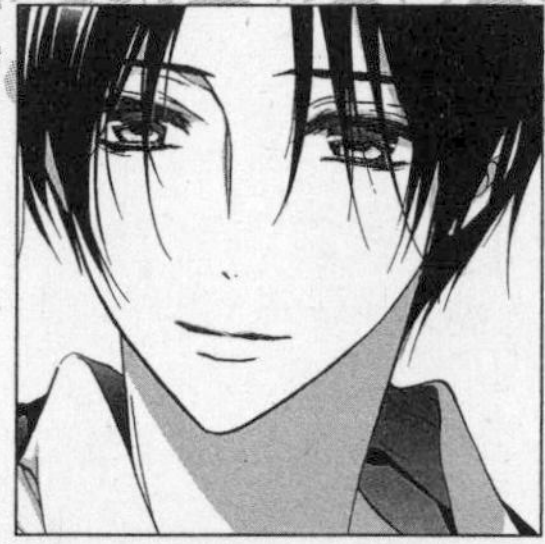

Aoi Nanamori

When he was 7 years old, he wandered into Momochi House and was chosen as the Omamori-sama. He transforms into a nue to perform his duties, but it seems this role was meant for Himari.

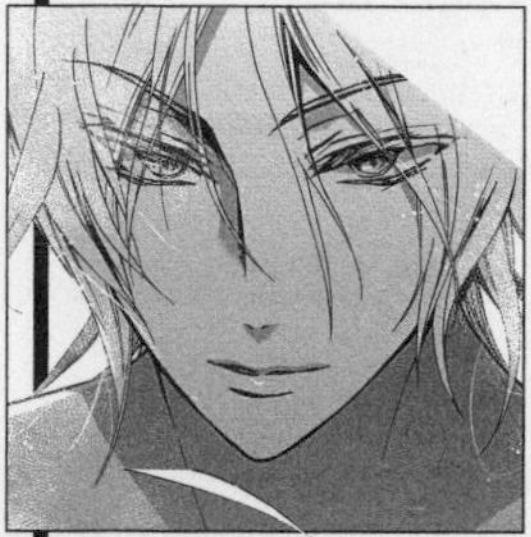

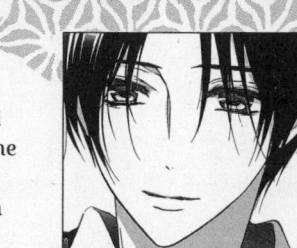

Omamori-sama (Nue)

An ayakashi, or demon, with the ears of a cat, the wings of a bird, and the tail of a fox. As the Omamori-sama, the nue protects Momochi House and eliminates demons who make their way in from the spiritual realm.

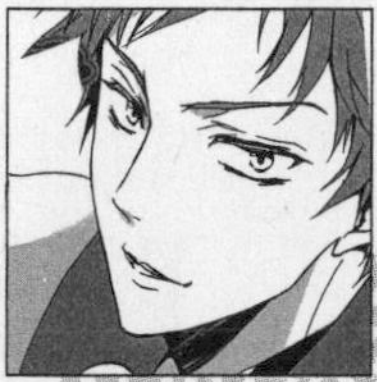

Ise

One of Omamori-sama's shikigami. He's an orangutan.

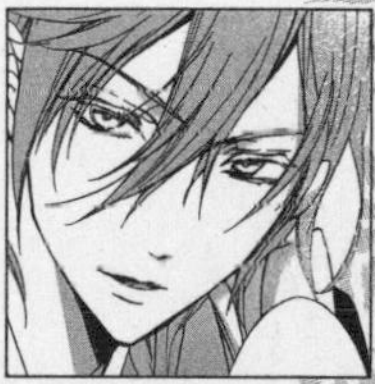

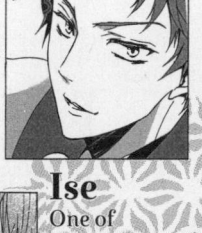

Yukari

One of Omamori-sama's shikigami. He's a water serpent.

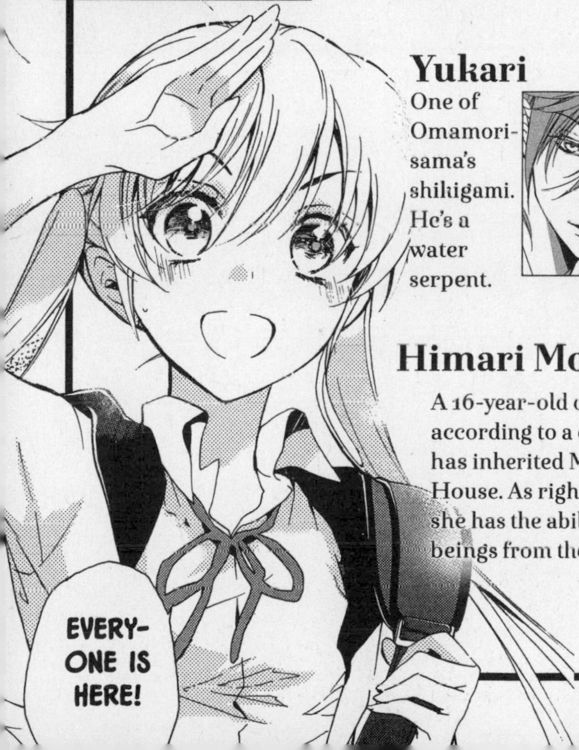
EVERY-ONE IS HERE!

Himari Momochi

A 16-year-old orphan who, according to a certain will, has inherited Momochi House. As rightful owner, she has the ability to expel beings from the house.

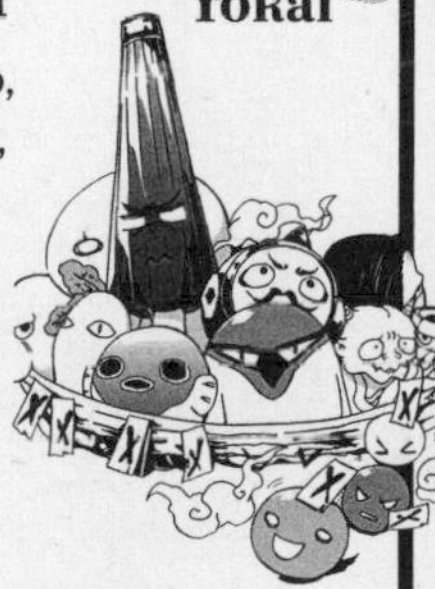

Lesser Yokai

Momochi House: Story Thus Far

"I do love you."

After Aoi confesses his feelings for her, Himari tries to continue on as normal, but Aoi's words and actions make her feel restless. While exploring Momochi House, Himari runs into the Guardian of the Gate once again. He tells Himari that if she'll marry him, he'll reveal information about the former nue. He explains that if the Momochi name passes to him, he will become the Omamori-sama. Himari becomes trapped within an iro oni dama, an ayakashi that absorbs colors it likes. Aoi must take on the Guardian of the Gate to rescue her and retain his position as the Omamori-sama. It is a difficult battle, but Aoi figures out the Guardian of the Gate's true identity and saves Himari. Aoi performs a shikigami contract with the Guardian of the Gate and restrains him with his commands. Aoi names his new shikigami Hakka. Now that Aoi has a shikigami who wants to become the Omamori-sama, it looks like there will be many more incidents to come.

Meanwhile, something disturbing is happening deep within the depths of Momochi House...

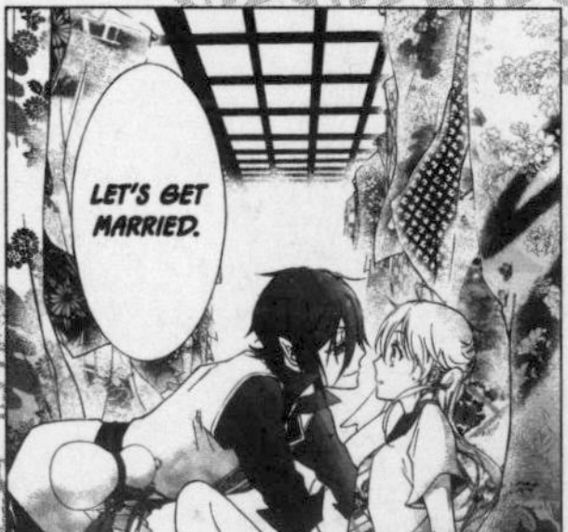
LET'S GET MARRIED.

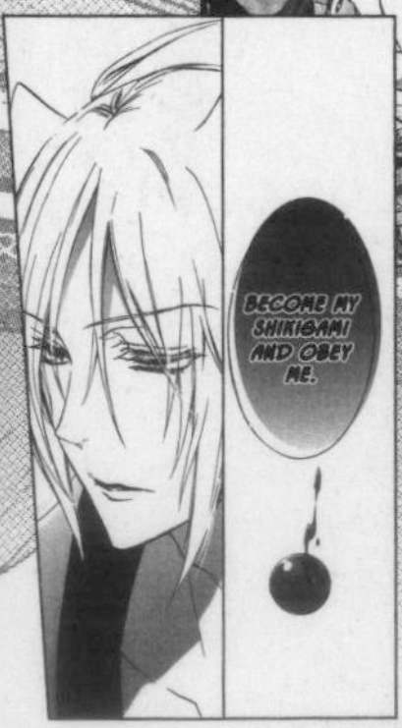
BECOME MY SHIKIGAMI AND OBEY ME.

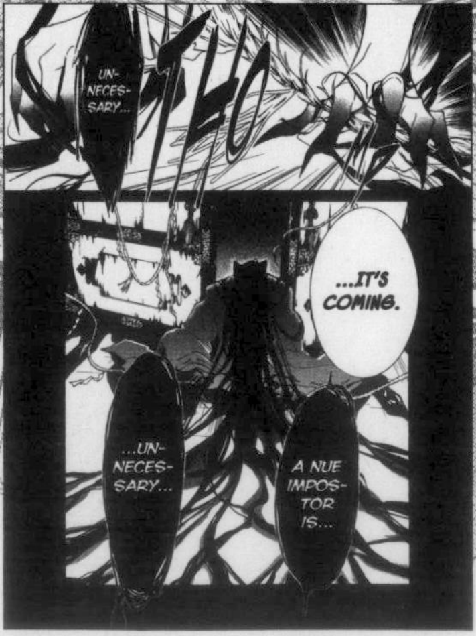
UN-NECES-SARY...
...IT'S COMING.
A NUE IMPOS-TOR IS...
...UN-NECES-SARY...

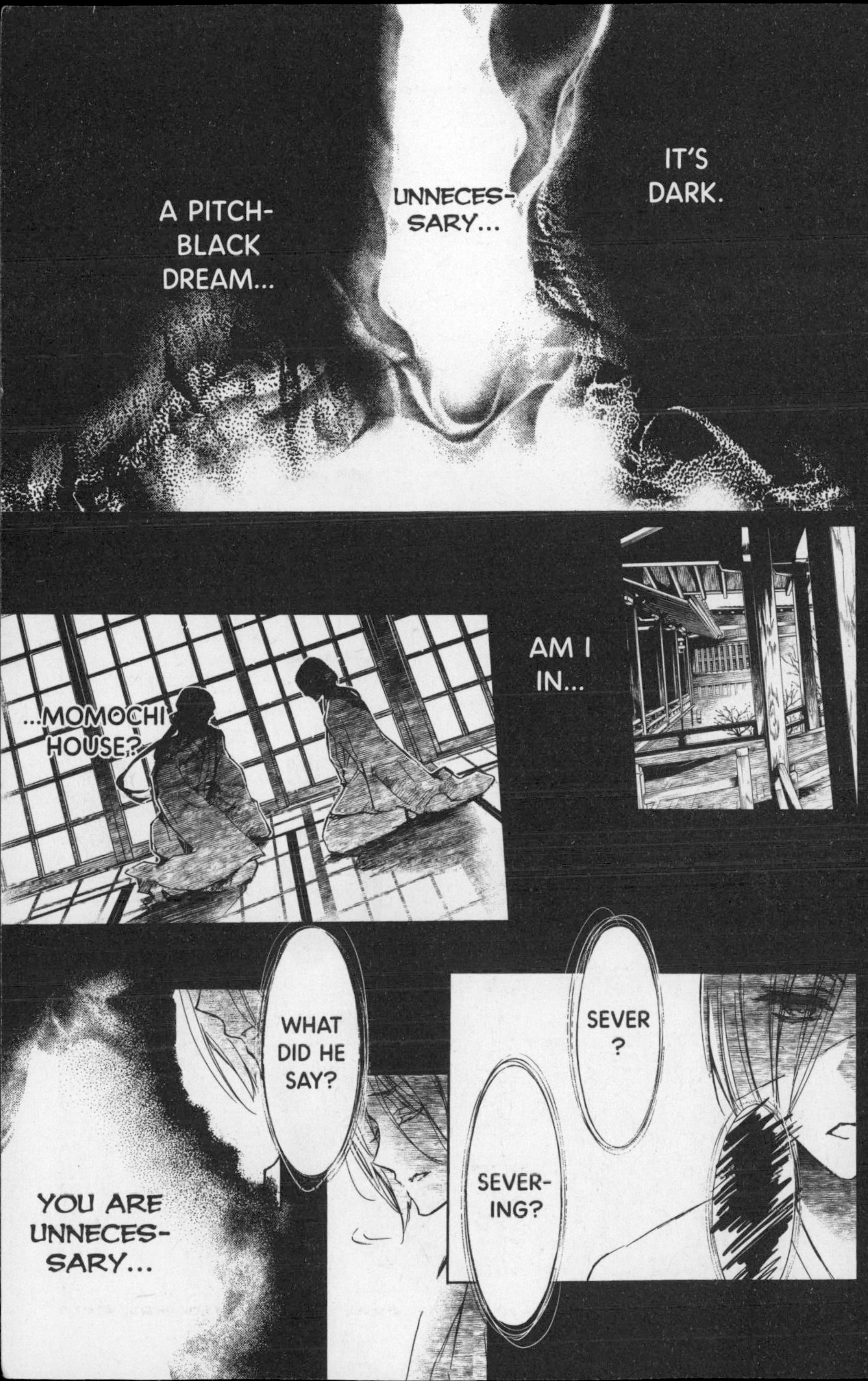
IT'S DARK.
UNNECES-SARY...
A PITCH-BLACK DREAM...
AM I IN...
...MOMOCHI HOUSE?
SEVER ?
SEVER-ING?
WHAT DID HE SAY?
YOU ARE UNNECES-SARY...

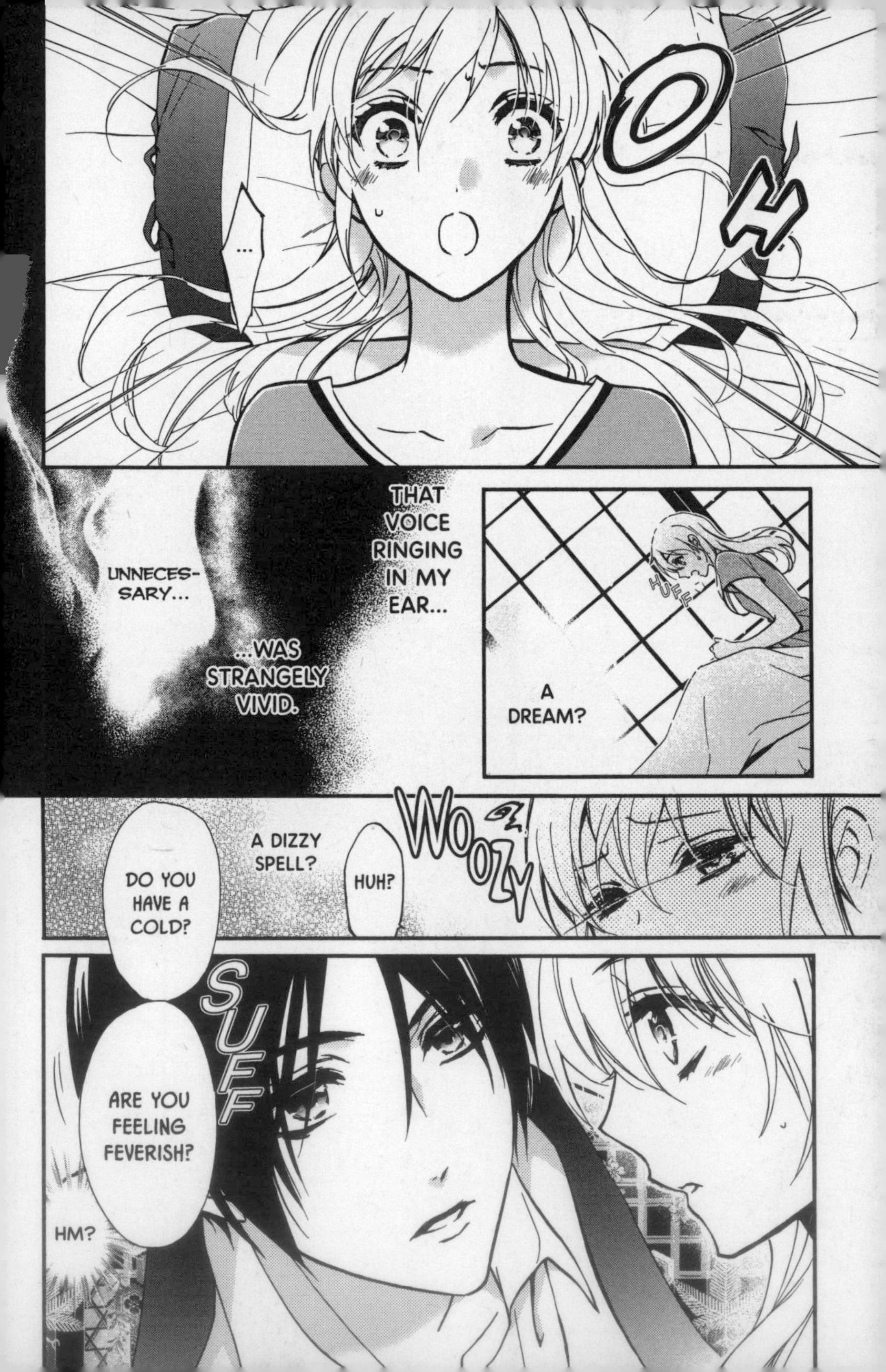
OH
...
THAT VOICE RINGING IN MY EAR...
UNNECES-SARY...
...WAS STRANGELY VIVID.
HUFF
A DREAM?
WOOZY
HUH?
A DIZZY SPELL?
DO YOU HAVE A COLD?
SUFF
ARE YOU FEELING FEVERISH?
HM?

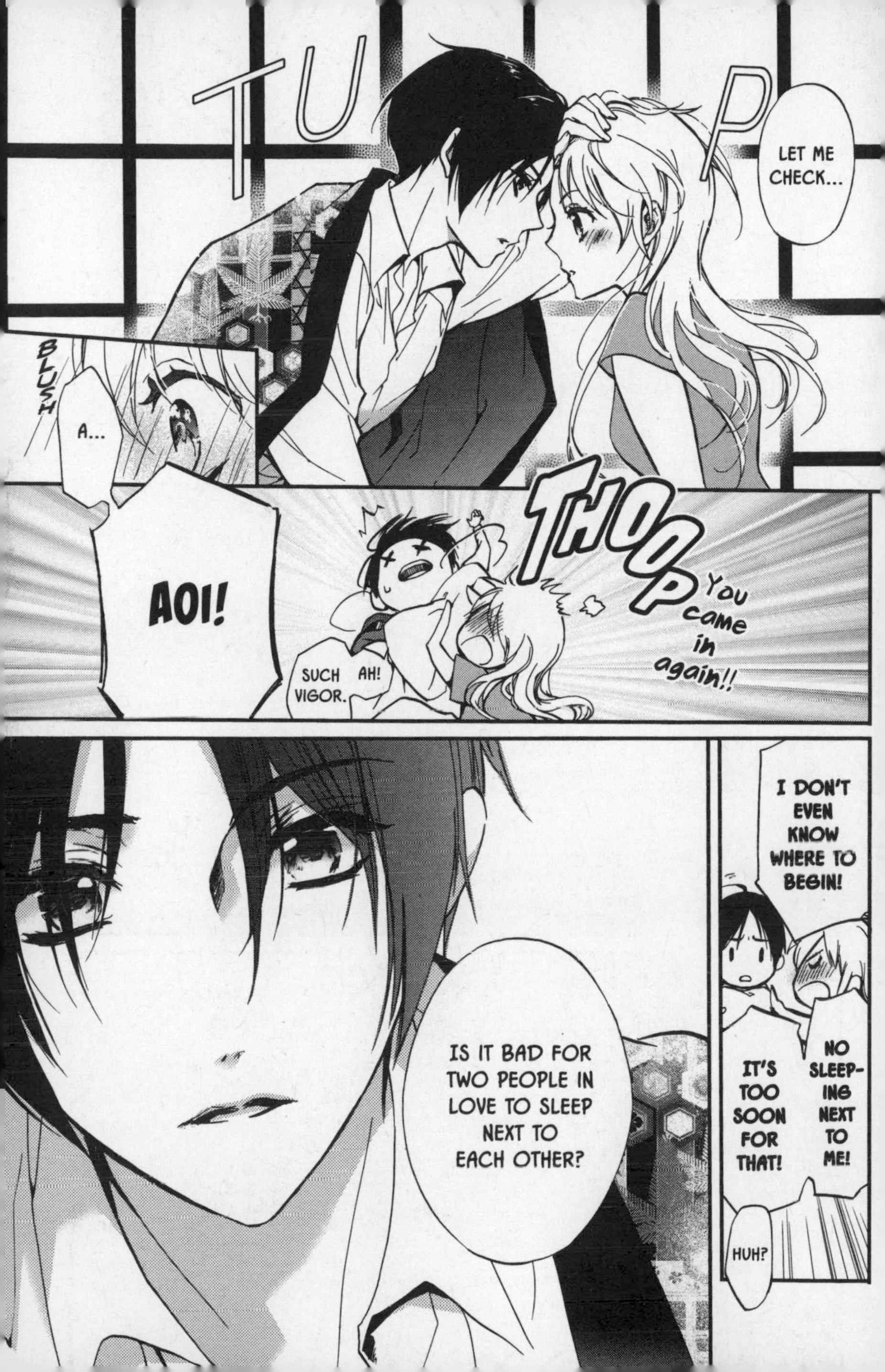
LET ME CHECK...
TUP
BLUSH
A...
AOI!
THOOP
You came in again!!
AH!
SUCH VIGOR.
I DON'T EVEN KNOW WHERE TO BEGIN!
NO SLEEPING NEXT TO ME!
IT'S TOO SOON FOR THAT!
HUH?
IS IT BAD FOR TWO PEOPLE IN LOVE TO SLEEP NEXT TO EACH OTHER?

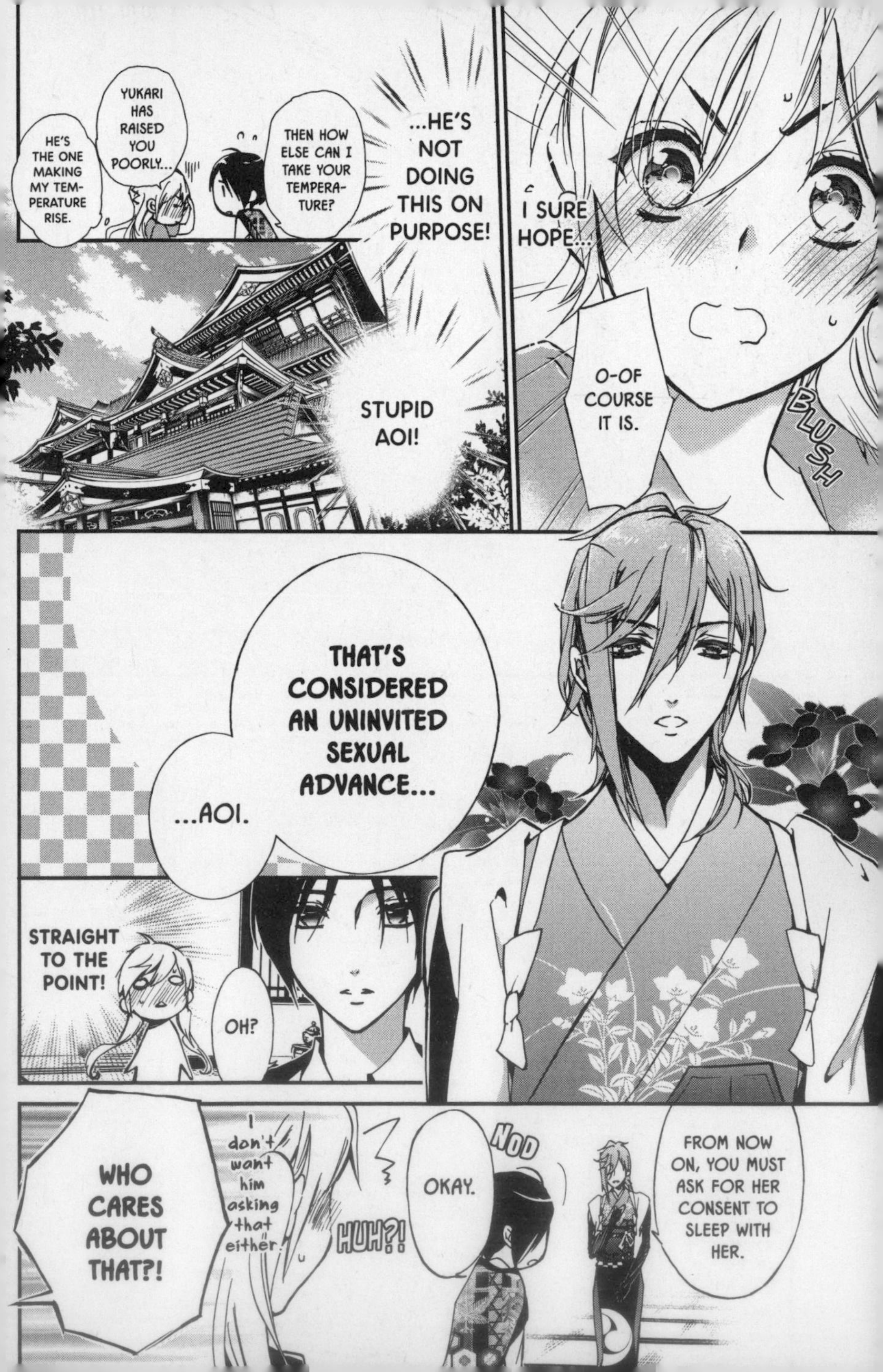
I SURE HOPE...
O-OF COURSE IT IS.
BLUSH
THEN HOW ELSE CAN I TAKE YOUR TEMPERA-TURE?
YUKARI HAS RAISED YOU POORLY...
HE'S THE ONE MAKING MY TEM-PERATURE RISE.
...HE'S NOT DOING THIS ON PURPOSE!
STUPID AOI!
THAT'S CONSIDERED AN UNINVITED SEXUAL ADVANCE...
...AOI.
OH?
STRAIGHT TO THE POINT!
FROM NOW ON, YOU MUST ASK FOR HER CONSENT TO SLEEP WITH HER.
NOD
OKAY.
HUH?!
I don't want him asking that either.
WHO CARES ABOUT THAT?!

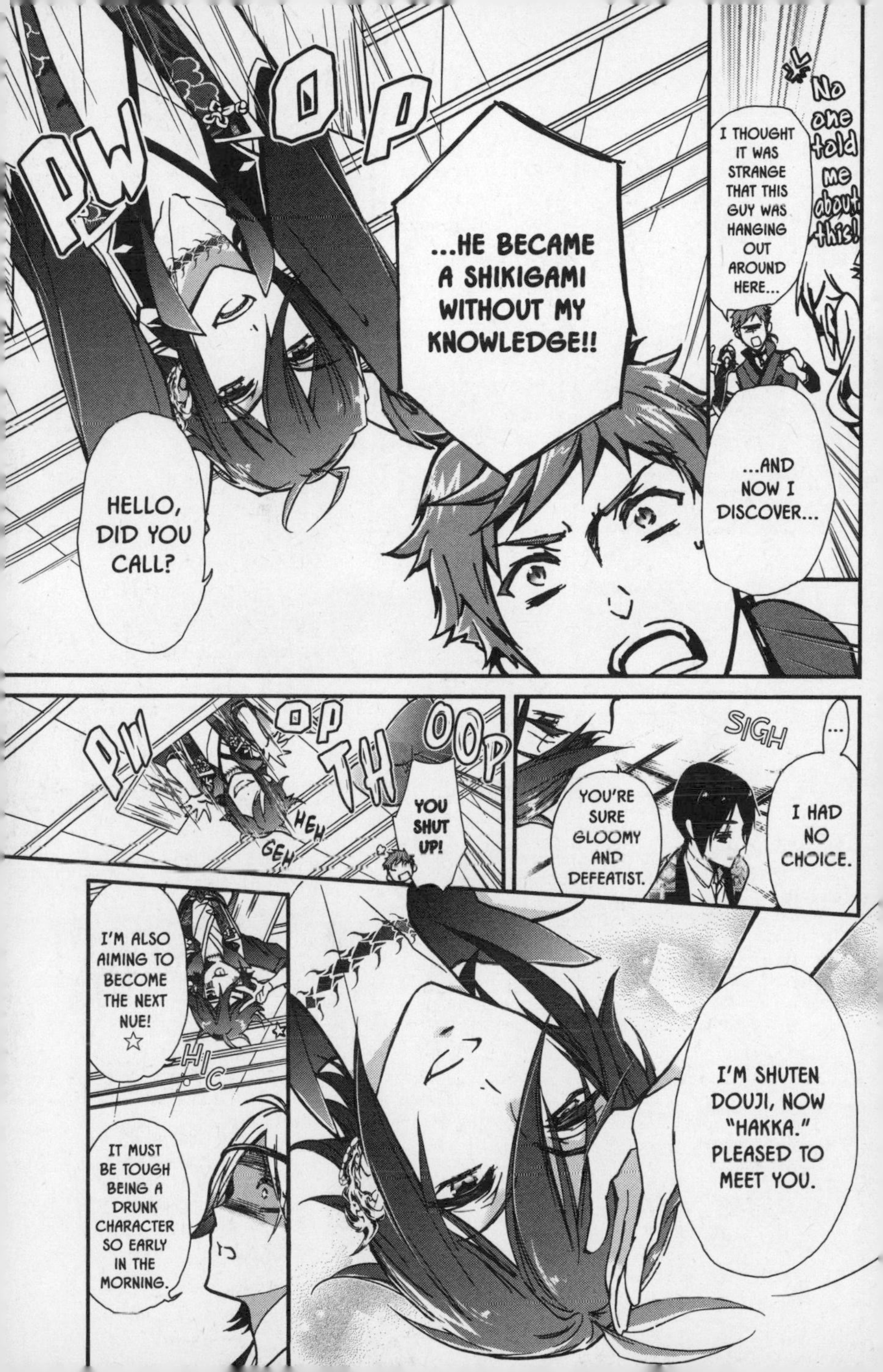
I THOUGHT IT WAS STRANGE THAT THIS GUY WAS HANGING OUT AROUND HERE...
No one told me about this!
...AND NOW I DISCOVER...
...HE BECAME A SHIKIGAMI WITHOUT MY KNOWLEDGE!!
HELLO, DID YOU CALL?
PW O OP
...
SIGH
I HAD NO CHOICE.
YOU'RE SURE GLOOMY AND DEFEATIST.
OOP
TH
OP
PW
YOU SHUT UP!
HEH
GEH
I'M SHUTEN DOUJI, NOW "HAKKA." PLEASED TO MEET YOU.
I'M ALSO AIMING TO BECOME THE NEXT NUE! ☆
HIC
IT MUST BE TOUGH BEING A DRUNK CHARACTER SO EARLY IN THE MORNING.

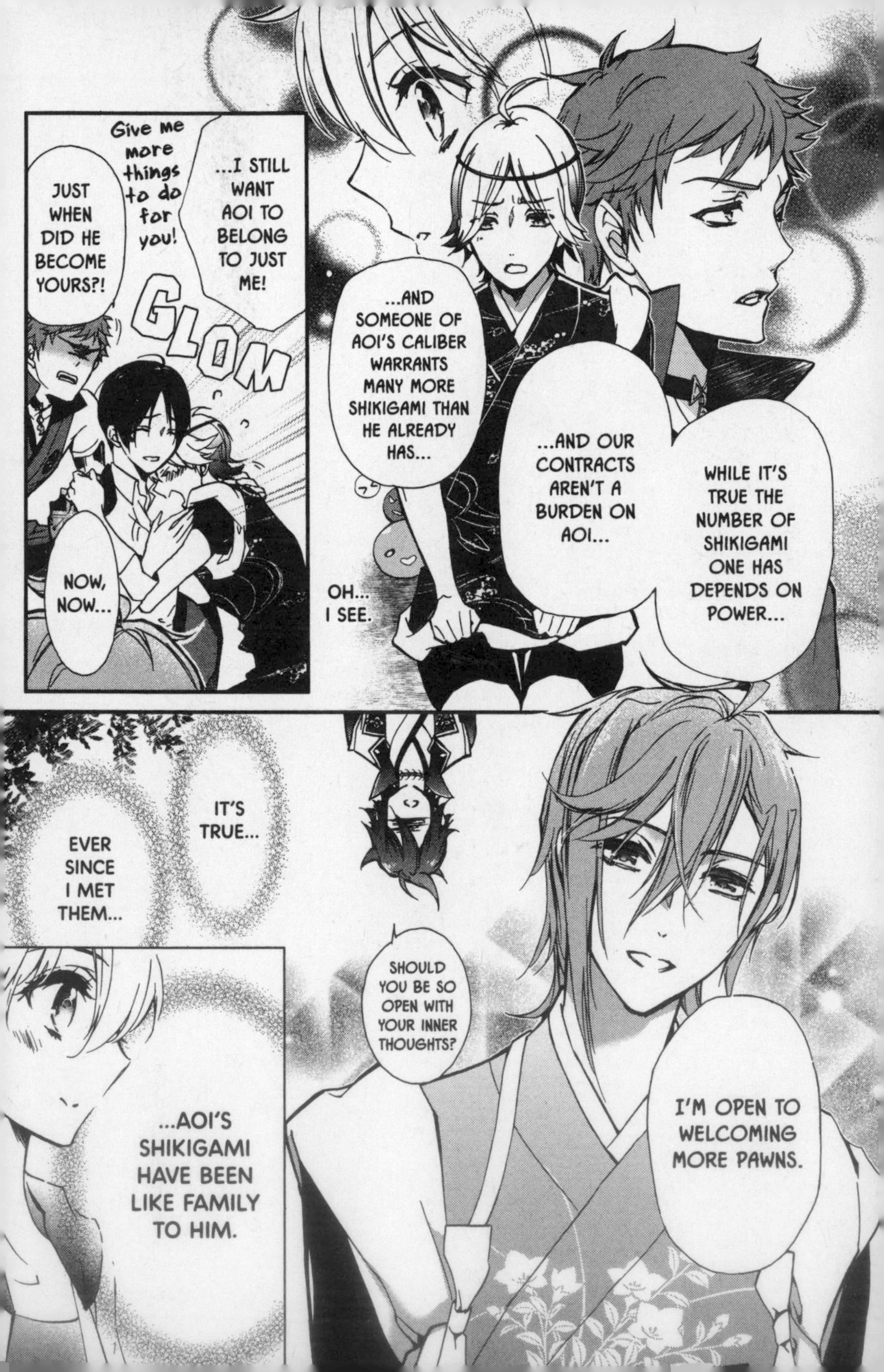
WHILE IT'S TRUE THE NUMBER OF SHIKIGAMI ONE HAS DEPENDS ON POWER...
...AND OUR CONTRACTS AREN'T A BURDEN ON AOI...
...AND SOMEONE OF AOI'S CALIBER WARRANTS MANY MORE SHIKIGAMI THAN HE ALREADY HAS...
OH... I SEE.
...I STILL WANT AOI TO BELONG TO JUST ME!
Give me more things to do for you!
JUST WHEN DID HE BECOME YOURS?!
GLOM
NOW, NOW...
I'M OPEN TO WELCOMING MORE PAWNS.
SHOULD YOU BE SO OPEN WITH YOUR INNER THOUGHTS?
IT'S TRUE...
EVER SINCE I MET THEM...
...AOI'S SHIKIGAMI HAVE BEEN LIKE FAMILY TO HIM.

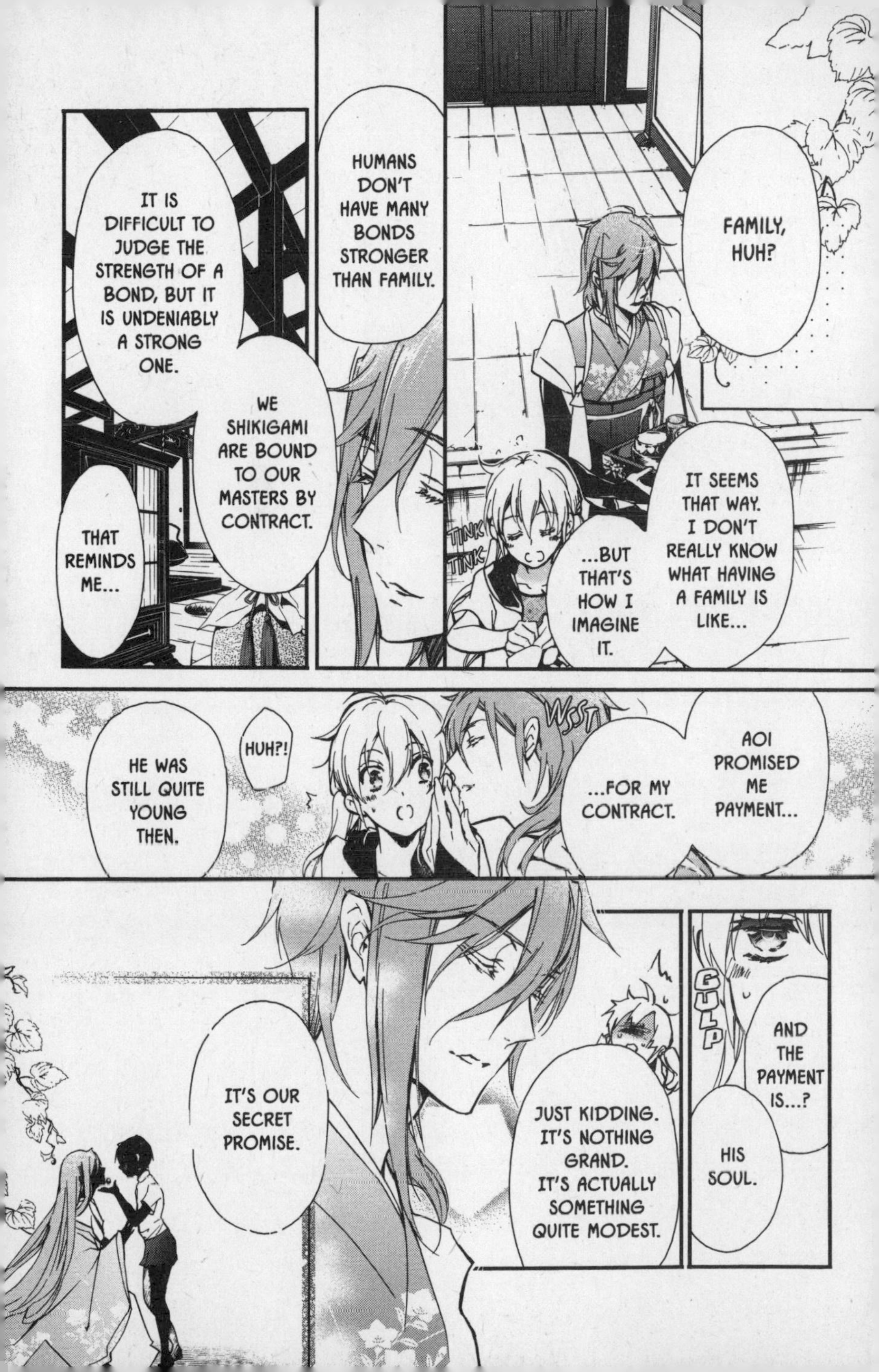
FAMILY, HUH?
IT SEEMS THAT WAY. I DON'T REALLY KNOW WHAT HAVING A FAMILY IS LIKE...
...BUT THAT'S HOW I IMAGINE IT.
TINK TINK
HUMANS DON'T HAVE MANY BONDS STRONGER THAN FAMILY.
WE SHIKIGAMI ARE BOUND TO OUR MASTERS BY CONTRACT.
IT IS DIFFICULT TO JUDGE THE STRENGTH OF A BOND, BUT IT IS UNDENIABLY A STRONG ONE.
THAT REMINDS ME...
AOI PROMISED ME PAYMENT...
...FOR MY CONTRACT.
WSST
HUH?!
HE WAS STILL QUITE YOUNG THEN.
AND THE PAYMENT IS...?
HIS SOUL.
GULP
JUST KIDDING. IT'S NOTHING GRAND. IT'S ACTUALLY SOMETHING QUITE MODEST.
IT'S OUR SECRET PROMISE.

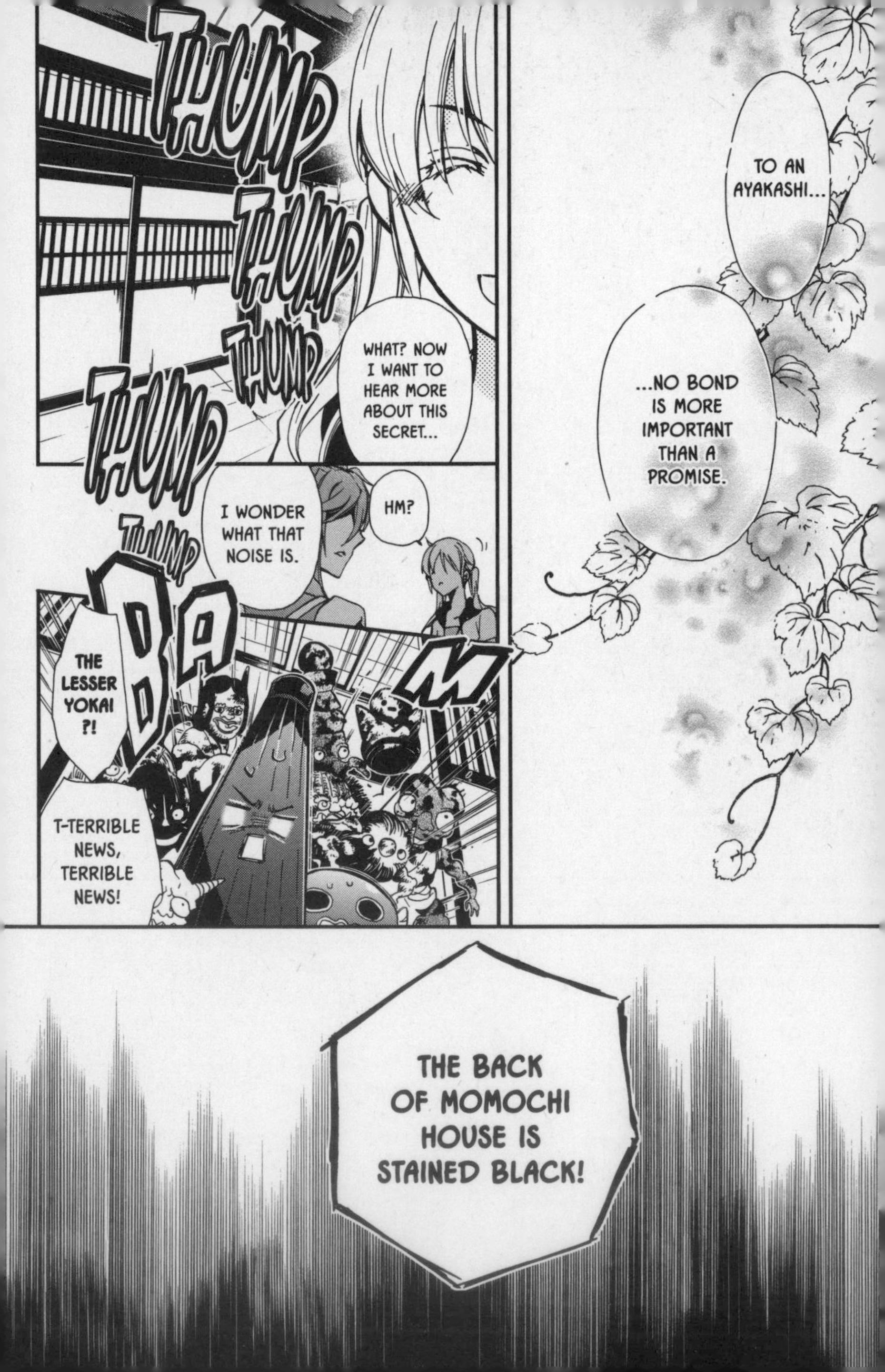
TO AN AYAKASHI...
...NO BOND IS MORE IMPORTANT THAN A PROMISE.
WHAT? NOW I WANT TO HEAR MORE ABOUT THIS SECRET...
THUMP
THUMP
THUMP
THUMP
HM?
I WONDER WHAT THAT NOISE IS.
THUMP
BAM
THE LESSER YOKAI ?!
T-TERRIBLE NEWS, TERRIBLE NEWS!
THE BACK OF MOMOCHI HOUSE IS STAINED BLACK!

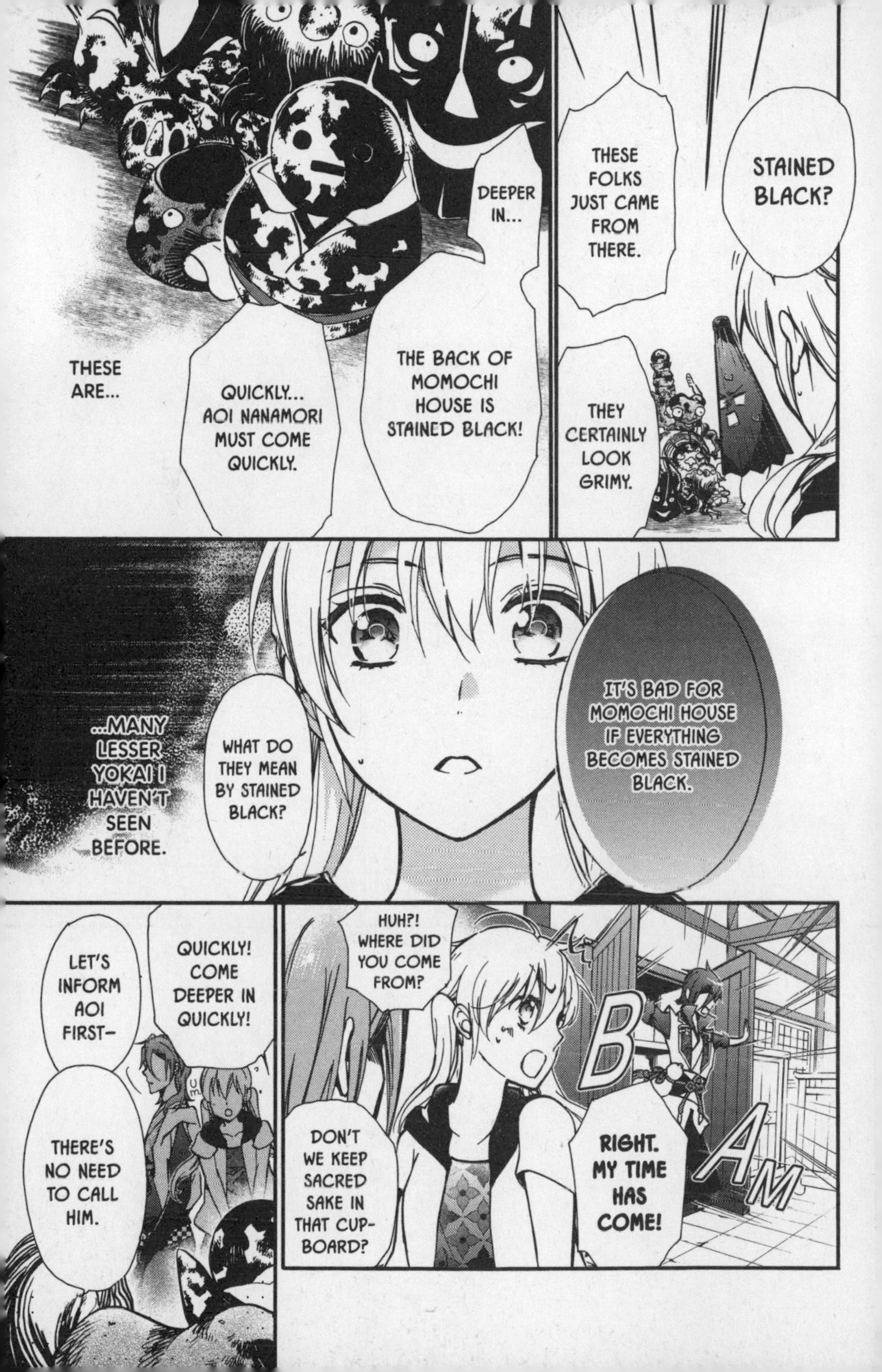
STAINED BLACK?
THESE FOLKS JUST CAME FROM THERE.
THEY CERTAINLY LOOK GRIMY.
DEEPER IN...
THE BACK OF MOMOCHI HOUSE IS STAINED BLACK!
QUICKLY... AOI NANAMORI MUST COME QUICKLY.
THESE ARE...
IT'S BAD FOR MOMOCHI HOUSE IF EVERYTHING BECOMES STAINED BLACK.
WHAT DO THEY MEAN BY STAINED BLACK?
...MANY LESSER YOKAI I HAVEN'T SEEN BEFORE.
BAM
RIGHT. MY TIME HAS COME!
HUH?! WHERE DID YOU COME FROM?
DON'T WE KEEP SACRED SAKE IN THAT CUP-BOARD?
QUICKLY! COME DEEPER IN QUICKLY!
LET'S INFORM AOI FIRST–
UM
THERE'S NO NEED TO CALL HIM.

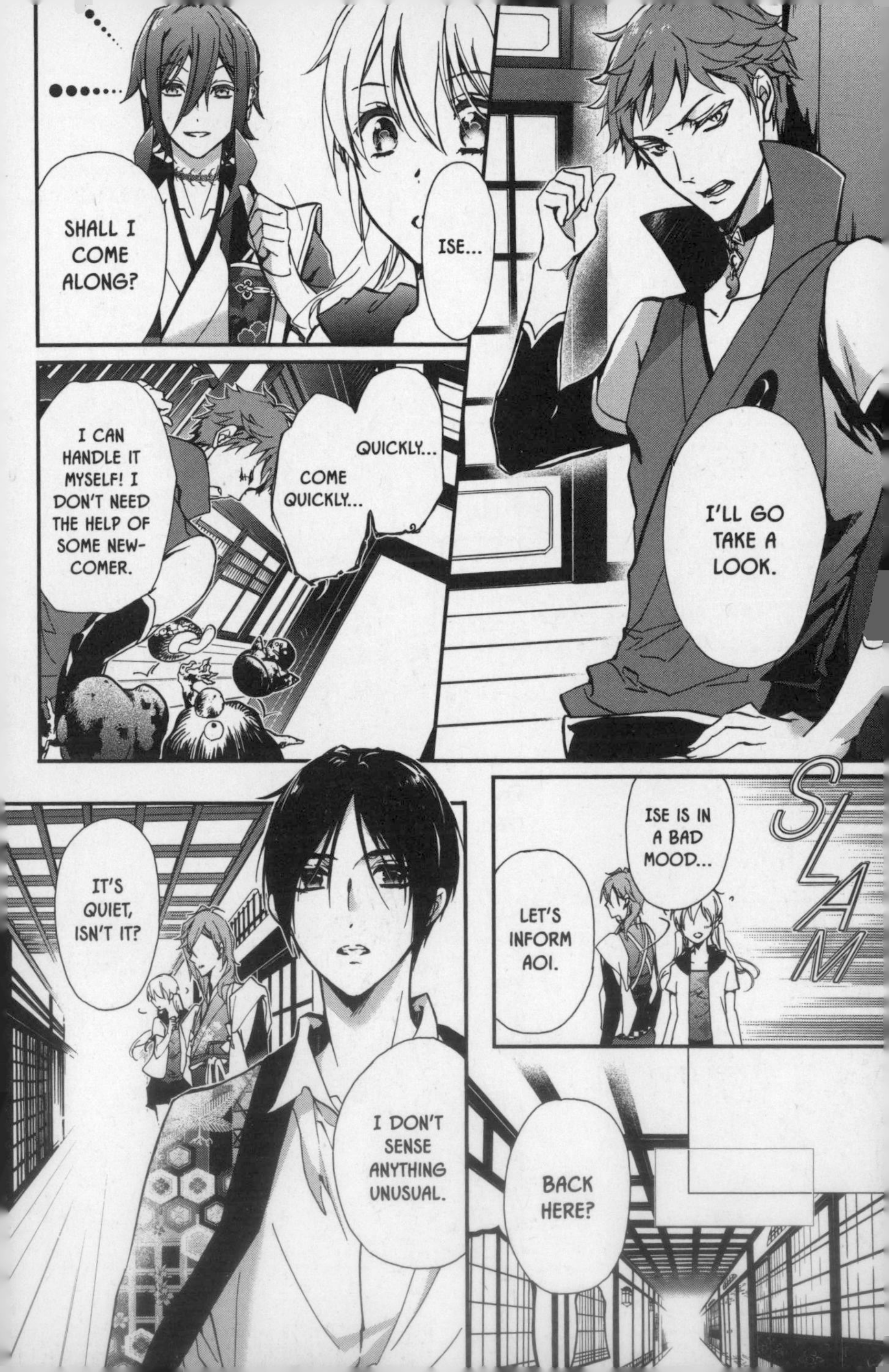
I'LL GO TAKE A LOOK.
ISE...
●●●●......
SHALL I COME ALONG?
QUICKLY...
COME QUICKLY...
I CAN HANDLE IT MYSELF! I DON'T NEED THE HELP OF SOME NEW-COMER.
SLAM
ISE IS IN A BAD MOOD...
LET'S INFORM AOI.
IT'S QUIET, ISN'T IT?
I DON'T SENSE ANYTHING UNUSUAL.
BACK HERE?

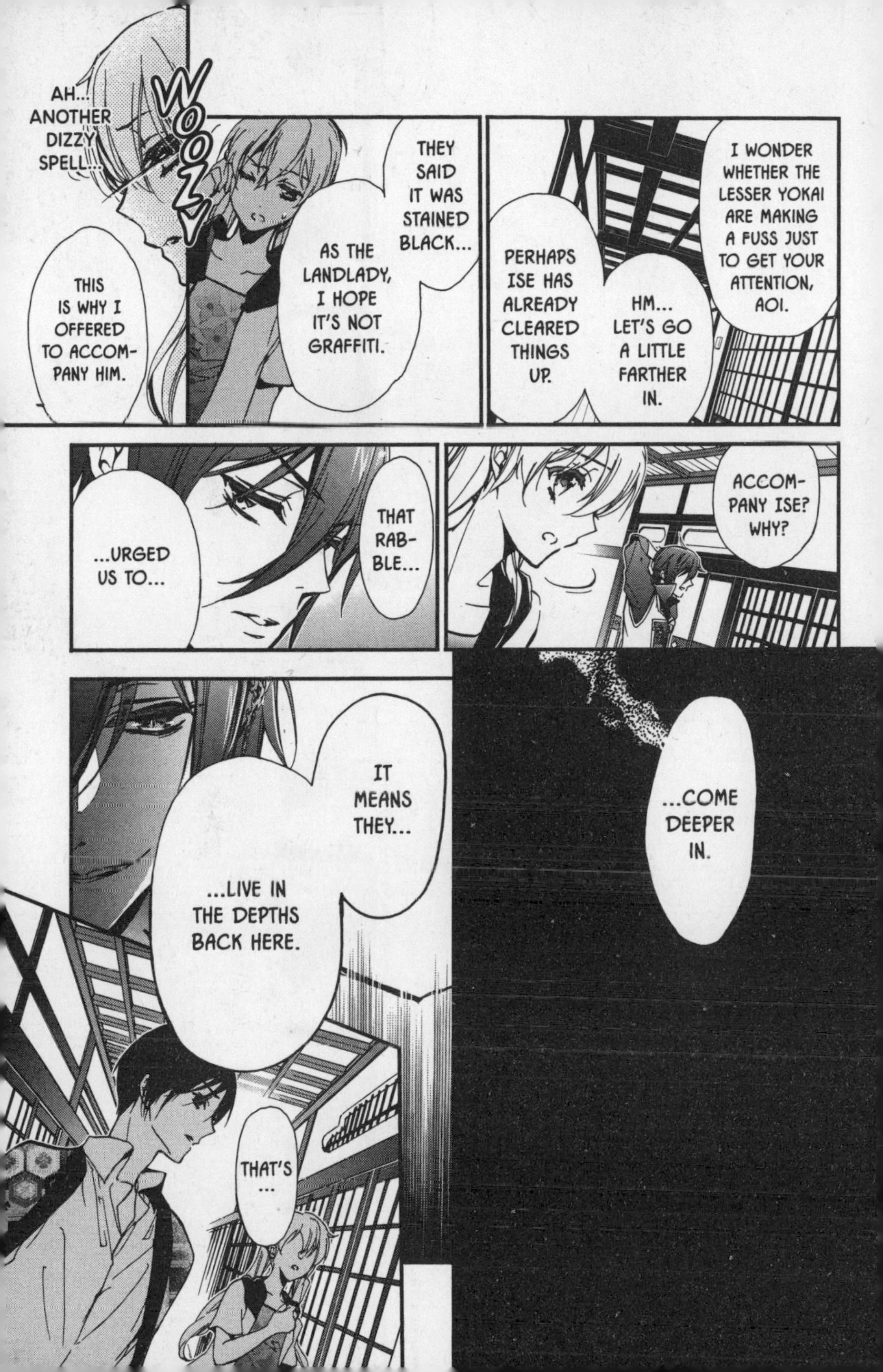
I WONDER WHETHER THE LESSER YOKAI ARE MAKING A FUSS JUST TO GET YOUR ATTENTION, AOI.
HM... LET'S GO A LITTLE FARTHER IN.
PERHAPS ISE HAS ALREADY CLEARED THINGS UP.
THEY SAID IT WAS STAINED BLACK...
AS THE LANDLADY, I HOPE IT'S NOT GRAFFITI.
WOOZY
AH... ANOTHER DIZZY SPELL...
THIS IS WHY I OFFERED TO ACCOMPANY HIM.
ACCOMPANY ISE? WHY?
THAT RABBLE...
...URGED US TO...
...COME DEEPER IN.
IT MEANS THEY...
...LIVE IN THE DEPTHS BACK HERE.
THAT'S ...

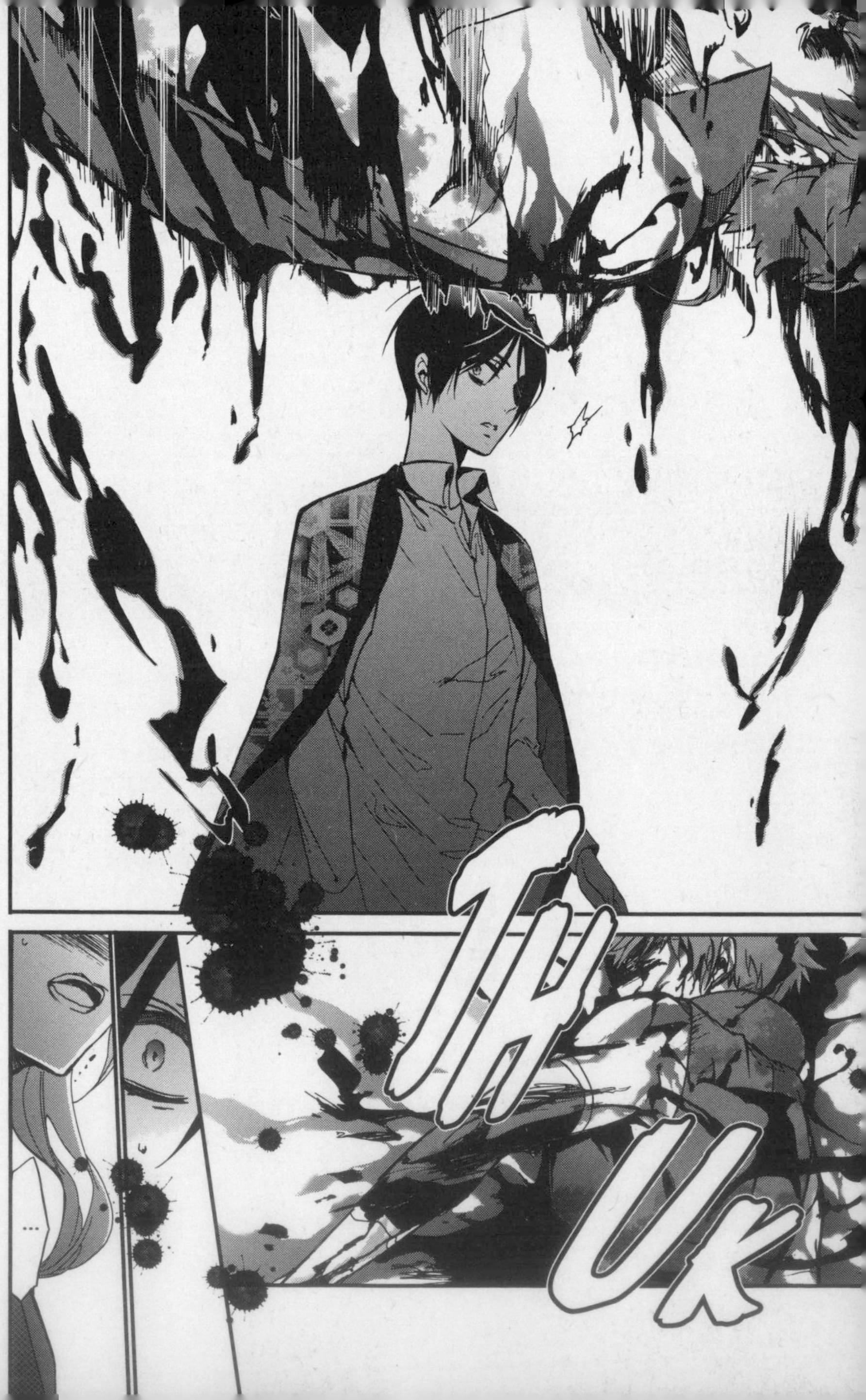
THUK
...

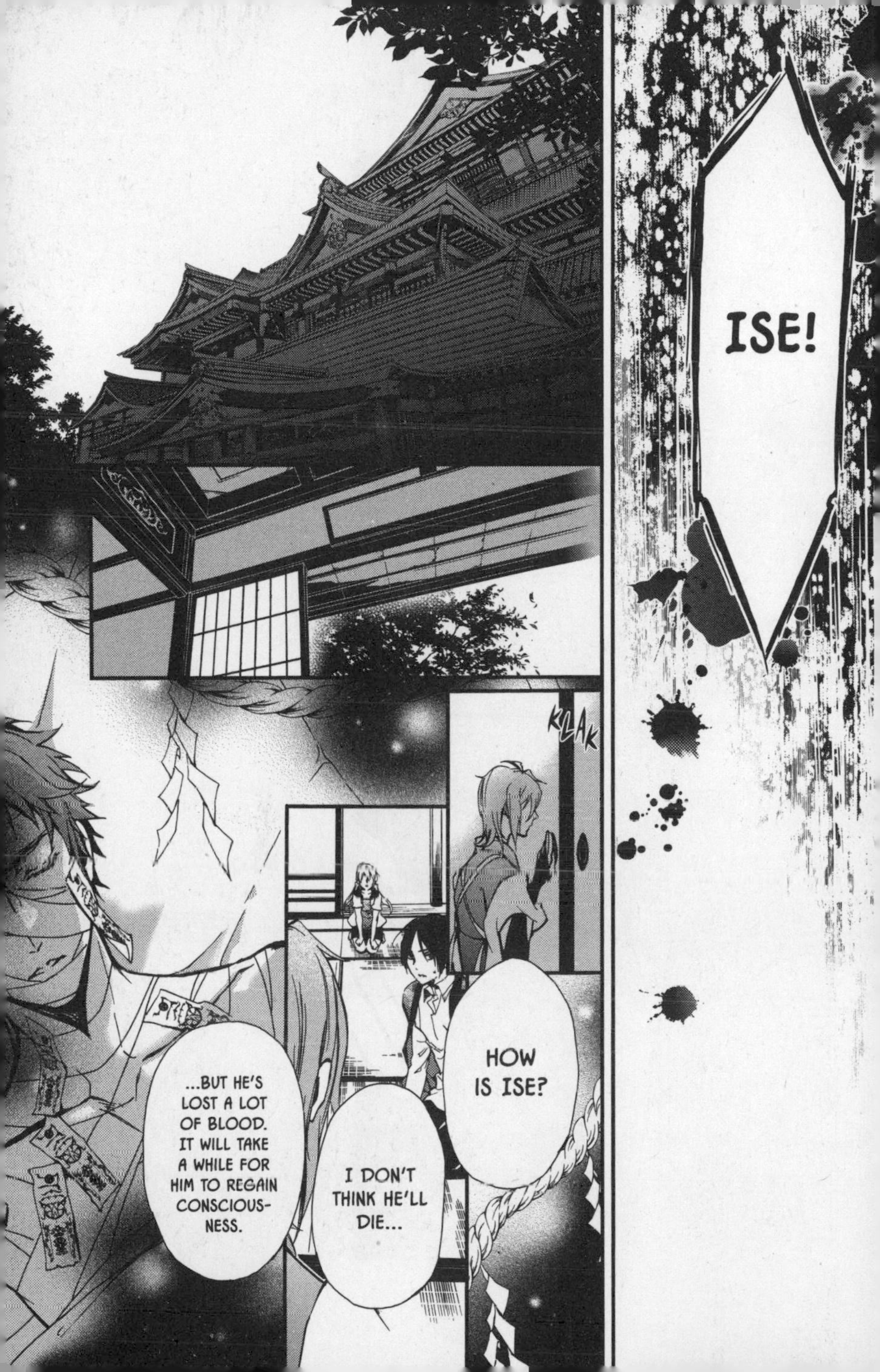
ISE!
KLAK
HOW IS ISE?
I DON'T THINK HE'LL DIE...
...BUT HE'S LOST A LOT OF BLOOD. IT WILL TAKE A WHILE FOR HIM TO REGAIN CONSCIOUS-NESS.

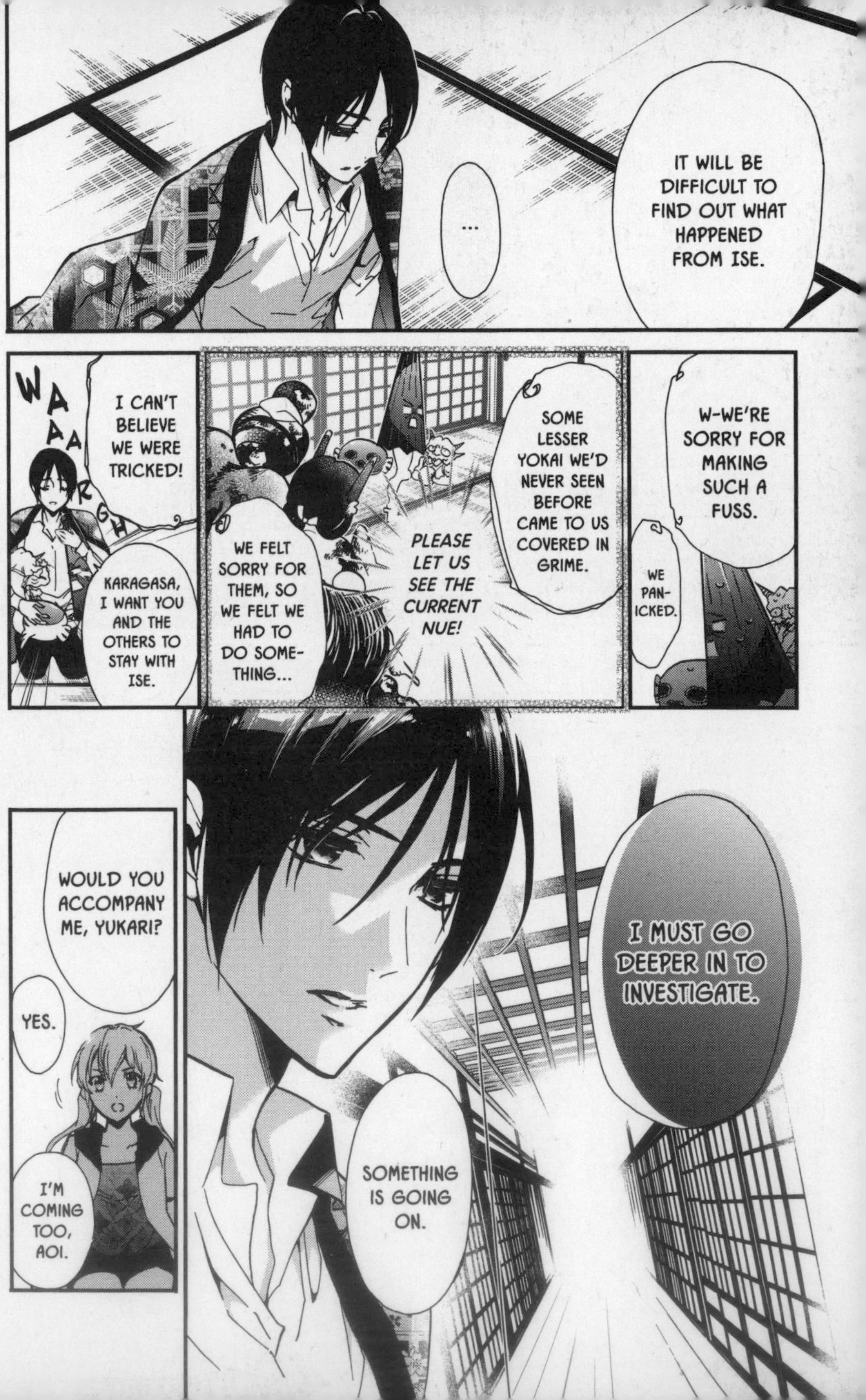
IT WILL BE DIFFICULT TO FIND OUT WHAT HAPPENED FROM ISE.
...
W-WE'RE SORRY FOR MAKING SUCH A FUSS.
WE PAN-ICKED.
SOME LESSER YOKAI WE'D NEVER SEEN BEFORE CAME TO US COVERED IN GRIME.
PLEASE LET US SEE THE CURRENT NUE!
WE FELT SORRY FOR THEM, SO WE FELT WE HAD TO DO SOME-THING...
I CAN'T BELIEVE WE WERE TRICKED!
WAAARGH
KARAGASA, I WANT YOU AND THE OTHERS TO STAY WITH ISE.
I MUST GO DEEPER IN TO INVESTIGATE.
SOMETHING IS GOING ON.
WOULD YOU ACCOMPANY ME, YUKARI?
YES.
I'M COMING TOO, AOI.

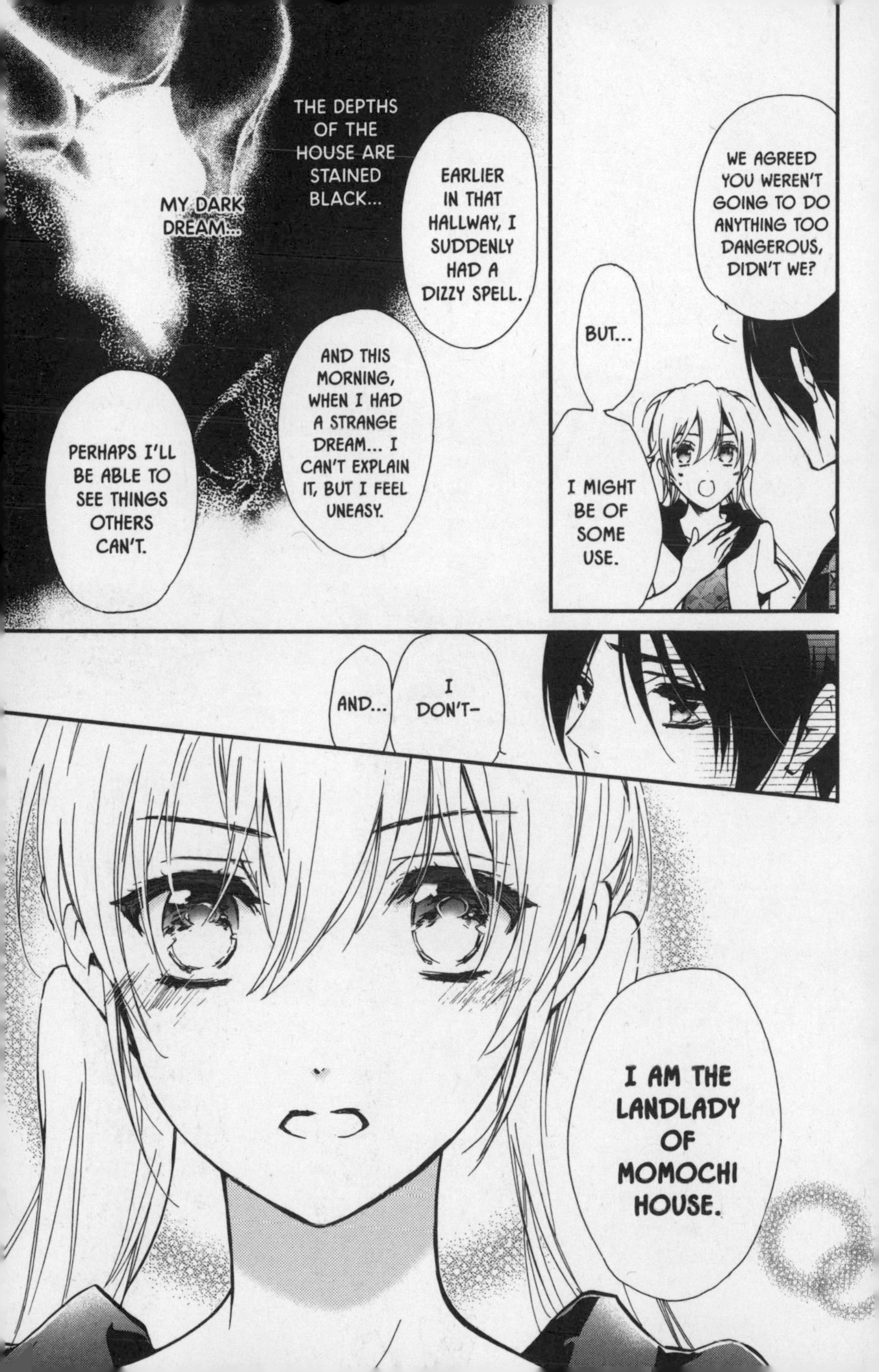
WE AGREED YOU WEREN'T GOING TO DO ANYTHING TOO DANGEROUS, DIDN'T WE?
BUT...
I MIGHT BE OF SOME USE.
EARLIER IN THAT HALLWAY, I SUDDENLY HAD A DIZZY SPELL.
THE DEPTHS OF THE HOUSE ARE STAINED BLACK...
MY DARK DREAM...
AND THIS MORNING, WHEN I HAD A STRANGE DREAM... I CAN'T EXPLAIN IT, BUT I FEEL UNEASY.
PERHAPS I'LL BE ABLE TO SEE THINGS OTHERS CAN'T.
I DON'T-
AND...
I AM THE LANDLADY OF MOMOCHI HOUSE.

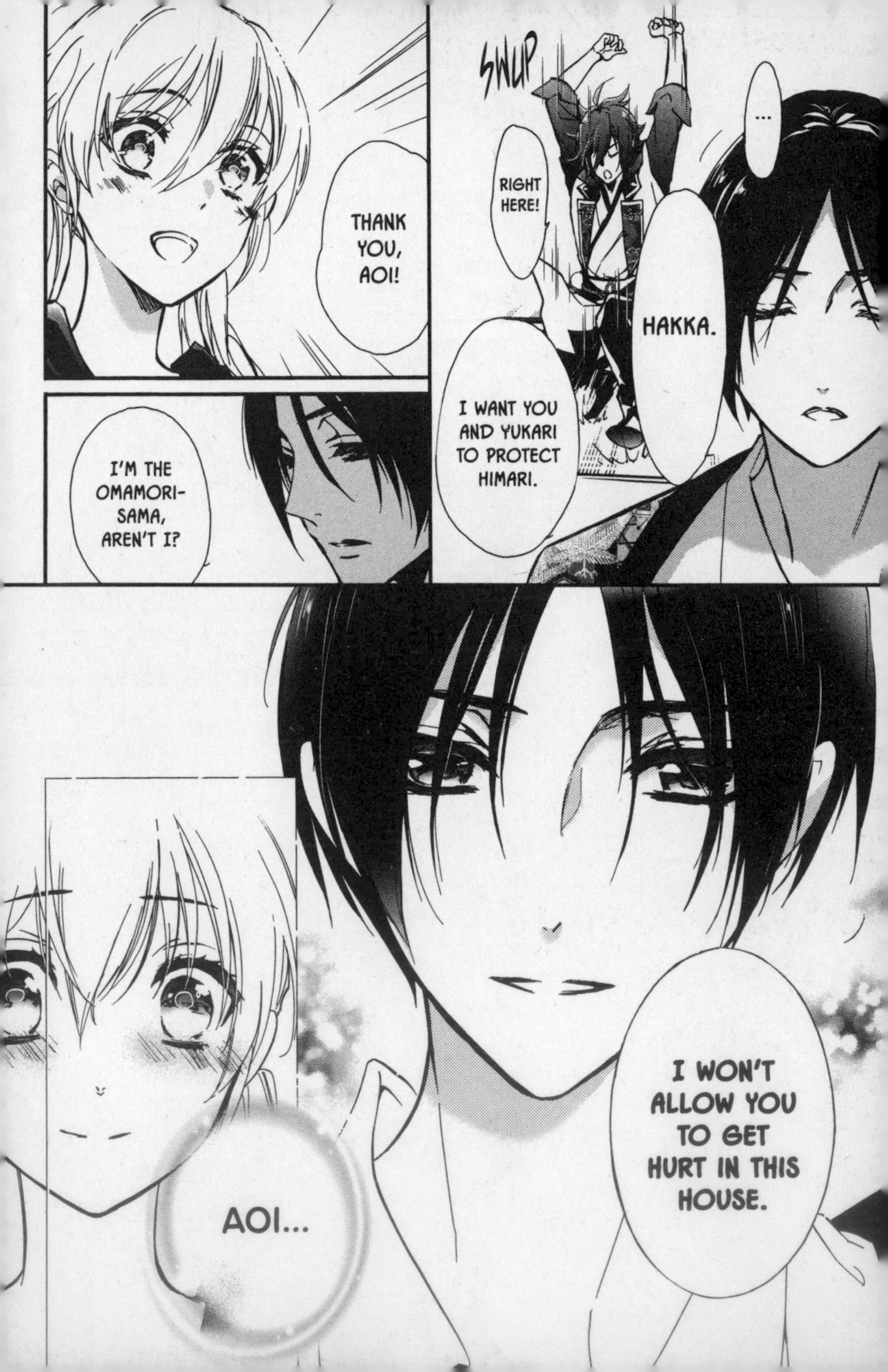
...
HAKKA.
SWUP
RIGHT HERE!
I WANT YOU AND YUKARI TO PROTECT HIMARI.
THANK YOU, AOI!
I'M THE OMAMORI-SAMA, AREN'T I?
I WON'T ALLOW YOU TO GET HURT IN THIS HOUSE.
AOI...

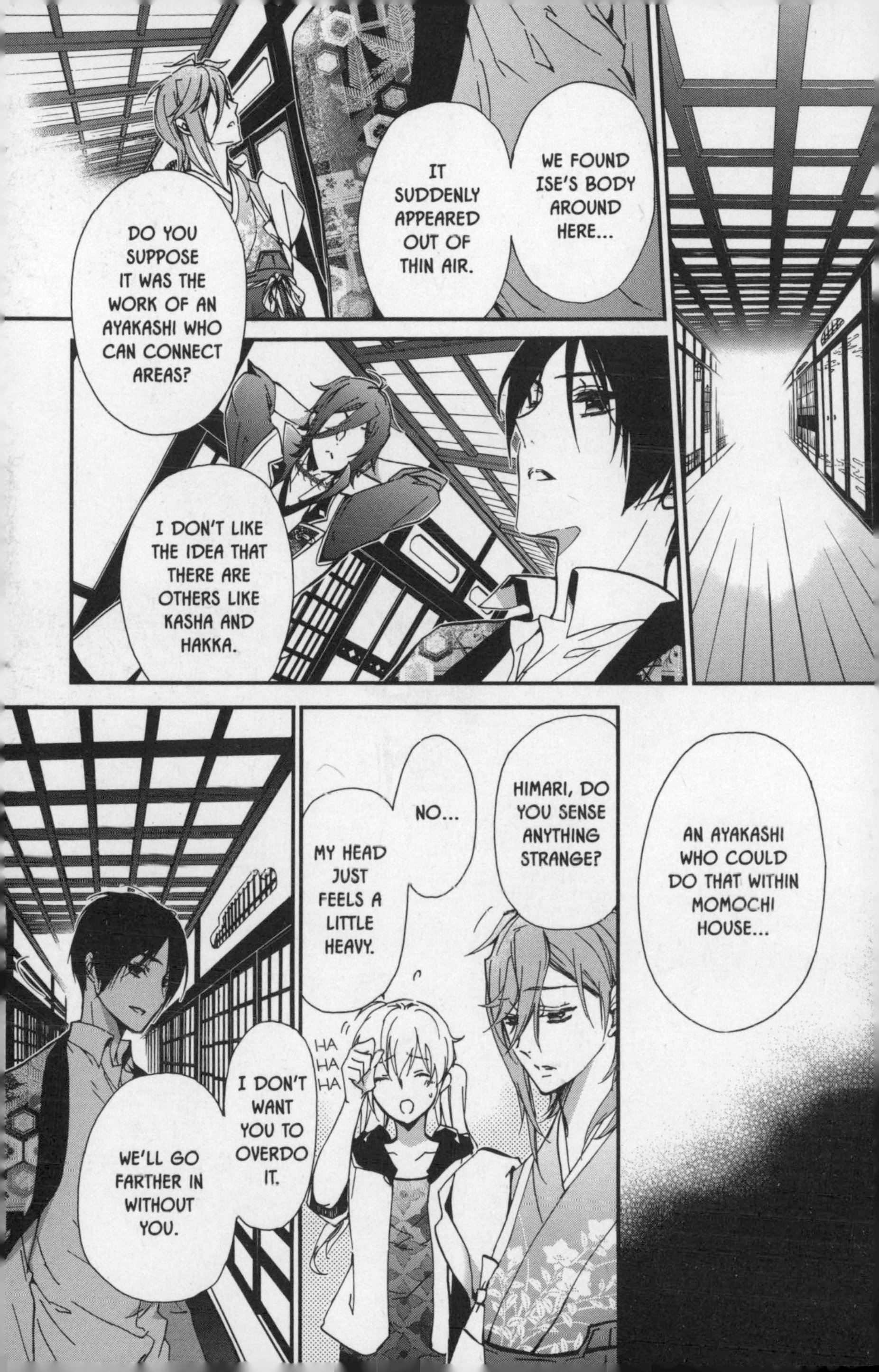
WE FOUND ISE'S BODY AROUND HERE...
IT SUDDENLY APPEARED OUT OF THIN AIR.
DO YOU SUPPOSE IT WAS THE WORK OF AN AYAKASHI WHO CAN CONNECT AREAS?
I DON'T LIKE THE IDEA THAT THERE ARE OTHERS LIKE KASHA AND HAKKA.
AN AYAKASHI WHO COULD DO THAT WITHIN MOMOCHI HOUSE...
HIMARI, DO YOU SENSE ANYTHING STRANGE?
NO...
MY HEAD JUST FEELS A LITTLE HEAVY.
HA HA HA
I DON'T WANT YOU TO OVERDO IT.
WE'LL GO FARTHER IN WITHOUT YOU.

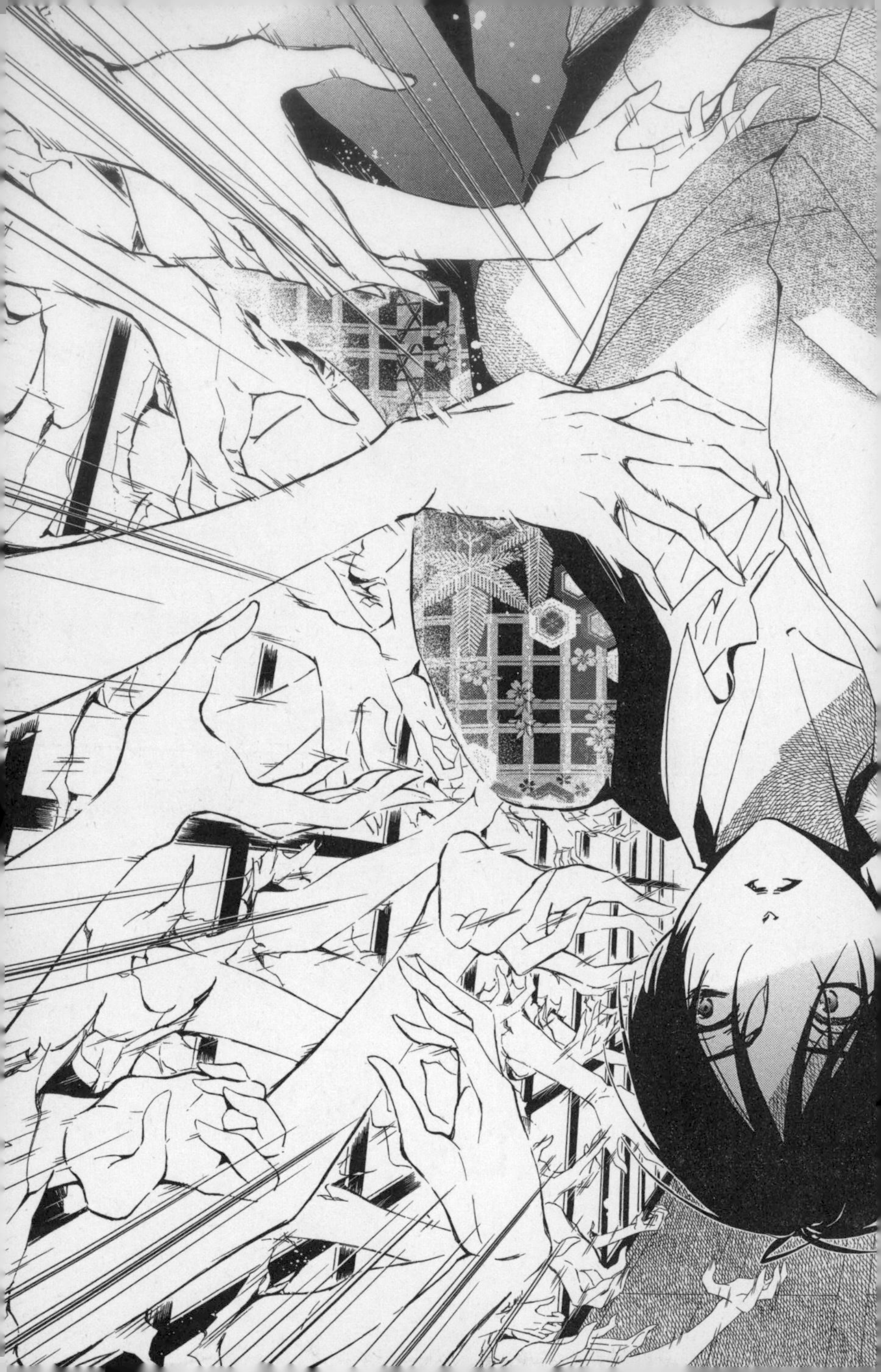

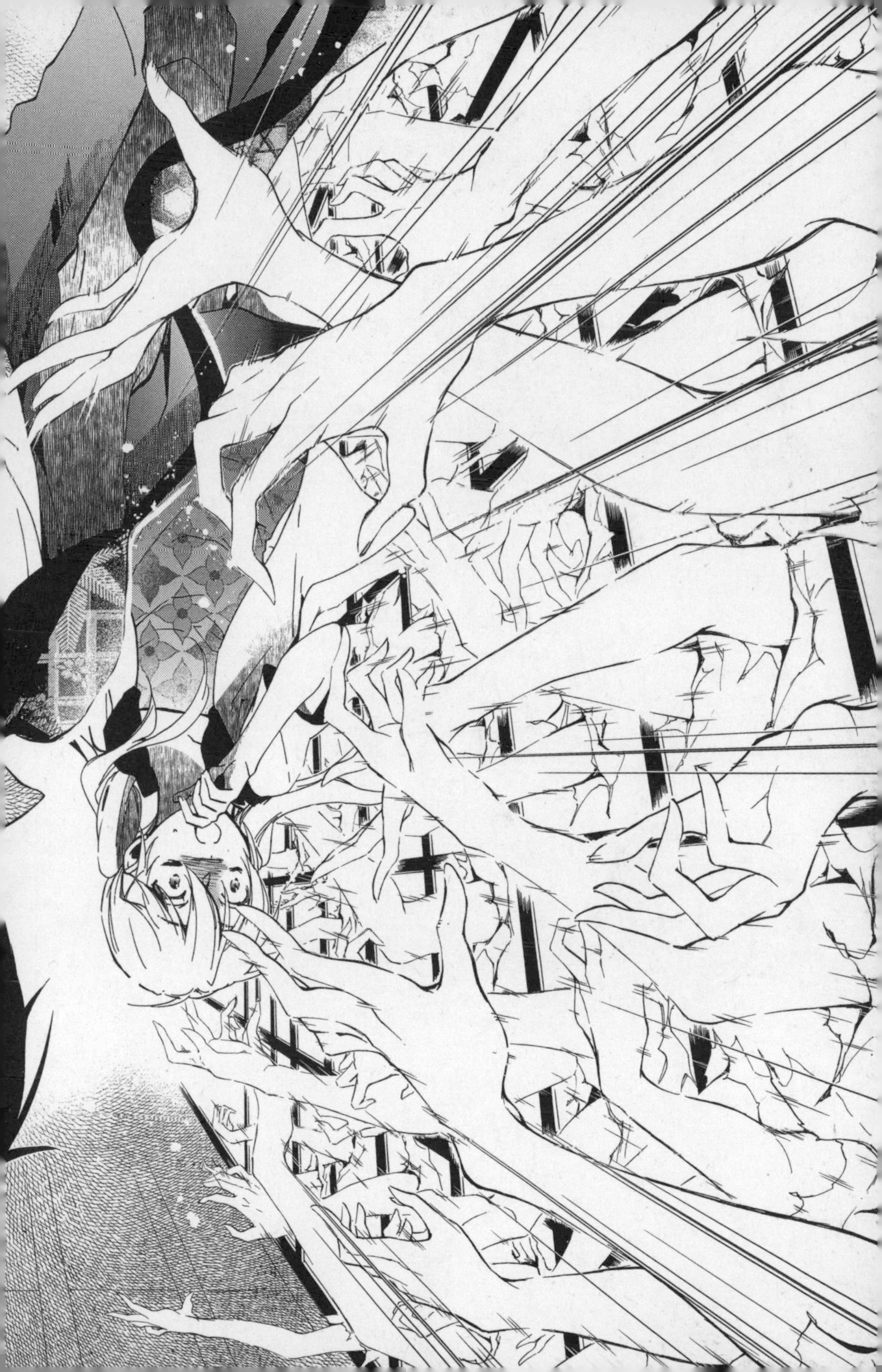

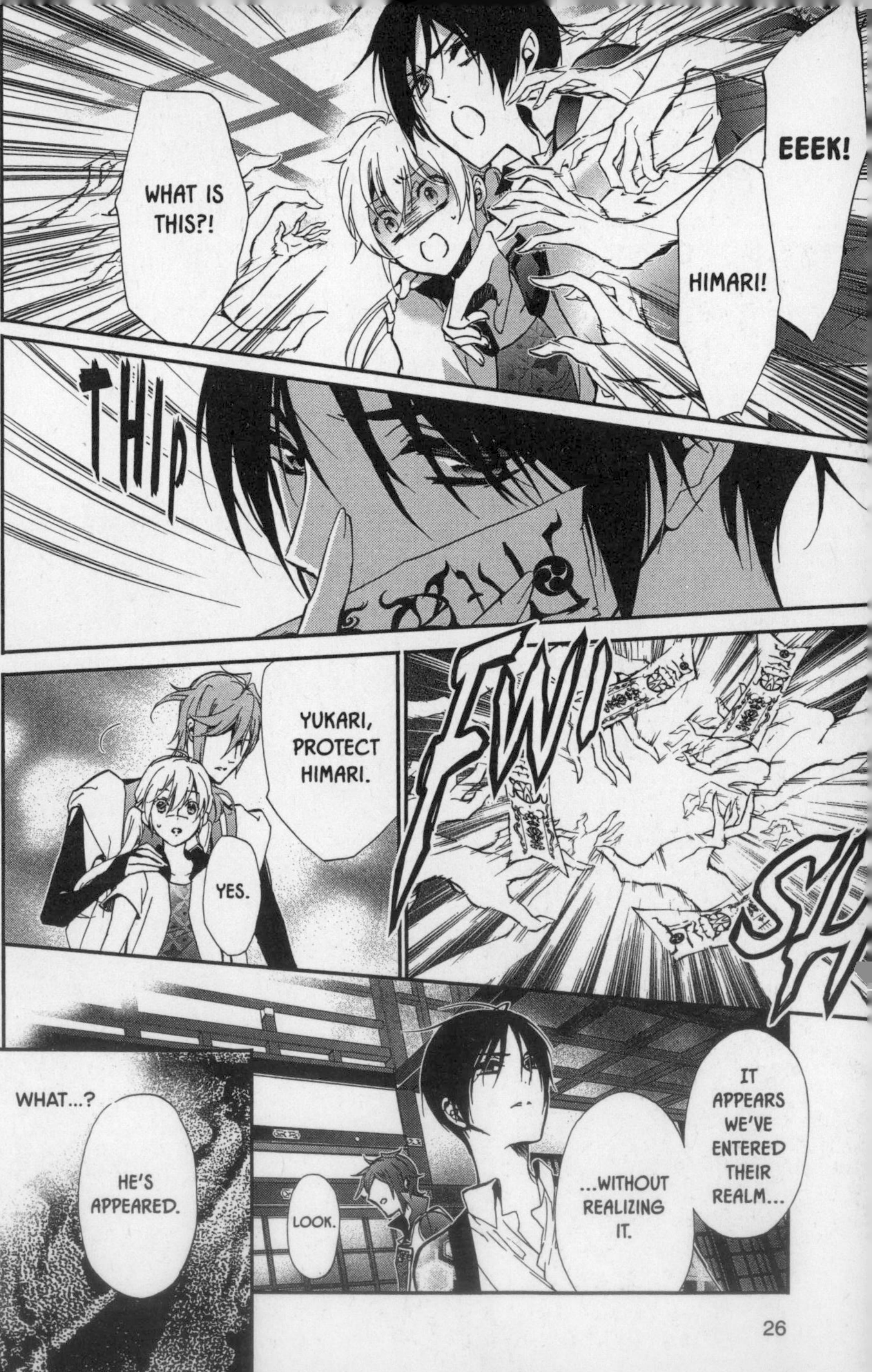
EEEK!
HIMARI!
WHAT IS THIS?!
THIP
FWI
SH
YUKARI, PROTECT HIMARI.
YES.
IT APPEARS WE'VE ENTERED THEIR REALM...
...WITHOUT REALIZING IT.
LOOK.
WHAT...?
HE'S APPEARED.

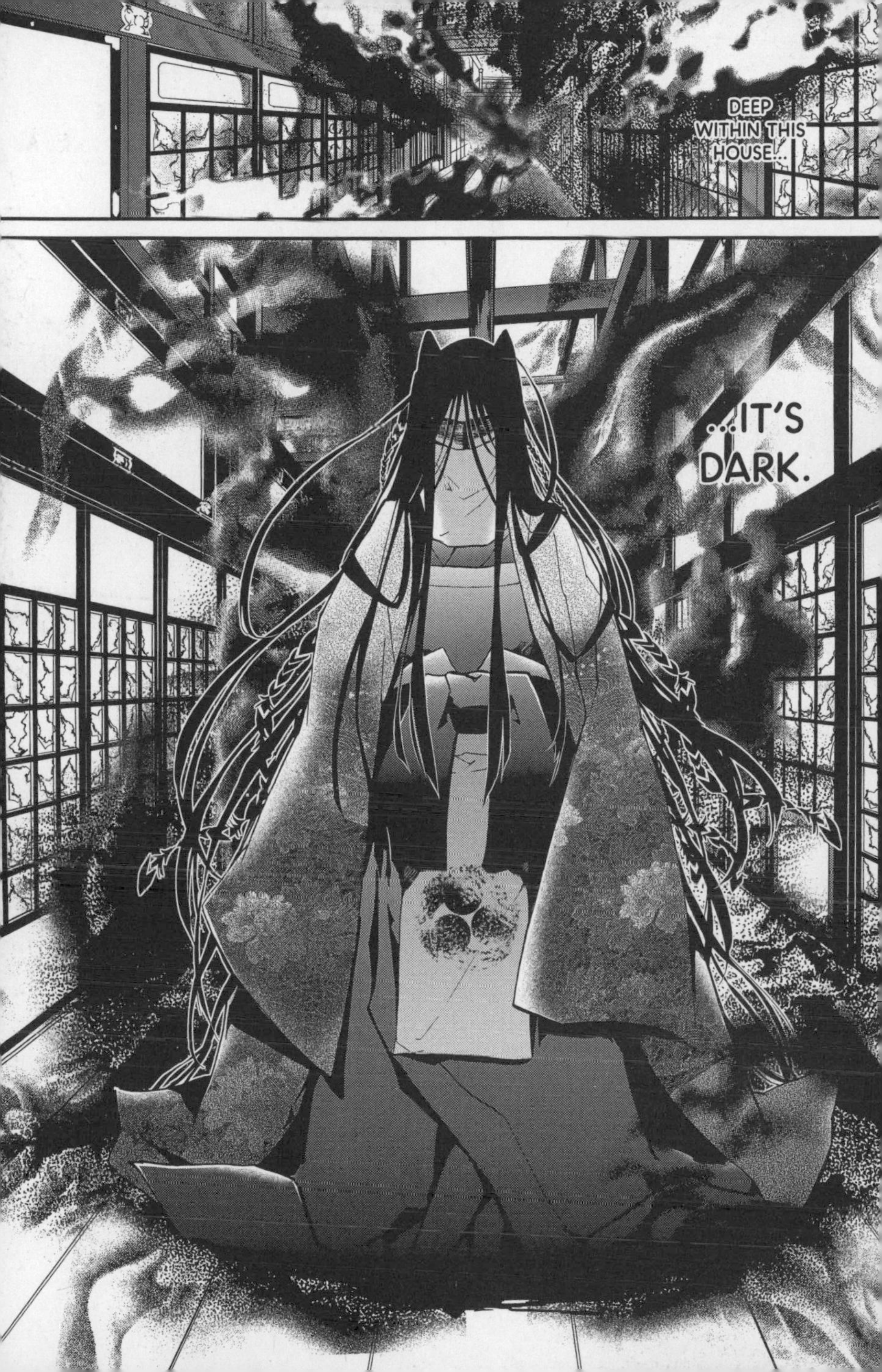
DEEP WITHIN THIS HOUSE...
...IT'S DARK.

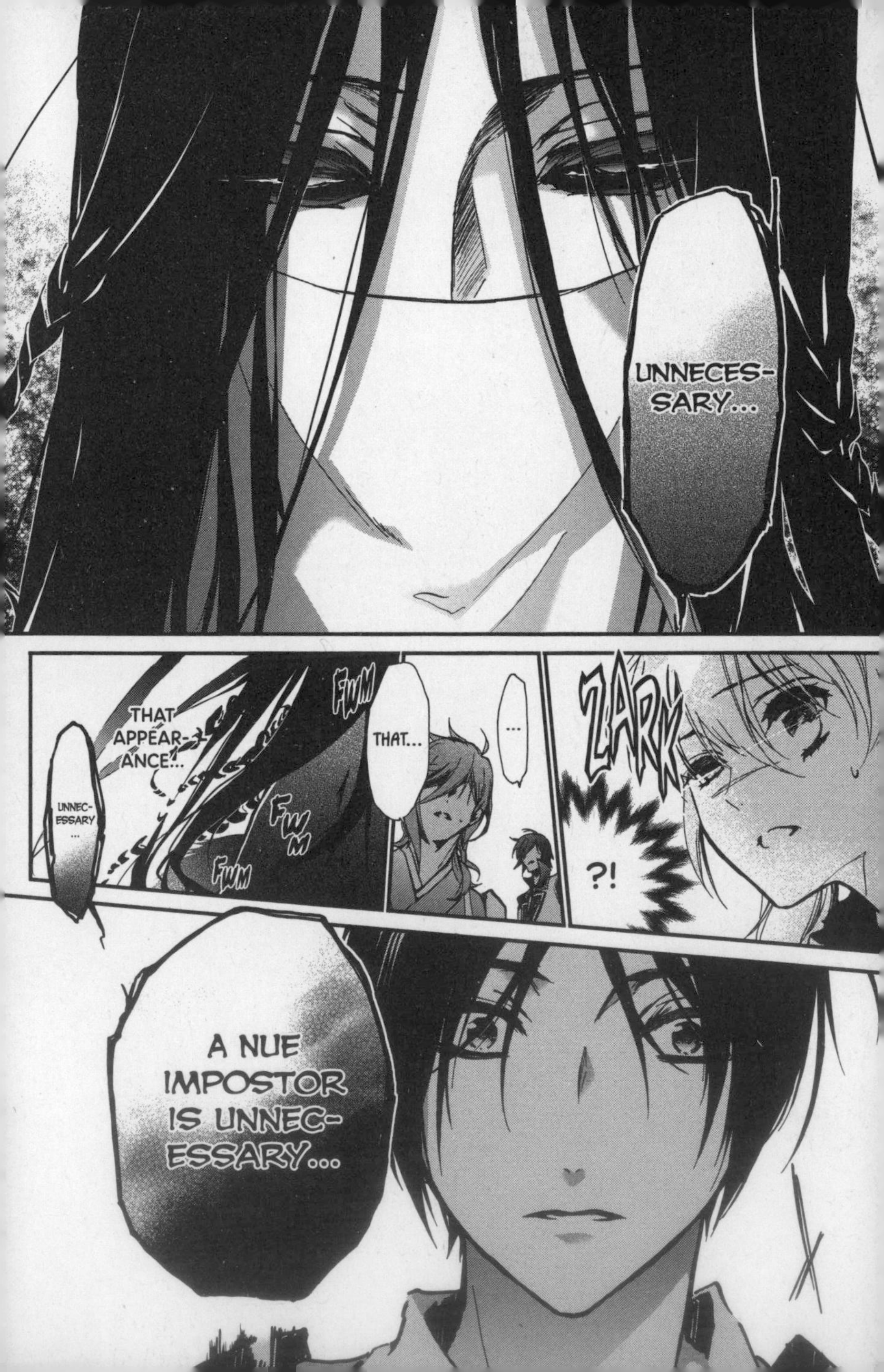
UNNECES-SARY...
ZARK
?!
...
THAT...
FWM
FWM
FWM
THAT APPEAR-ANCE...
UNNEC-ESSARY...
A NUE IMPOSTOR IS UNNEC-ESSARY...

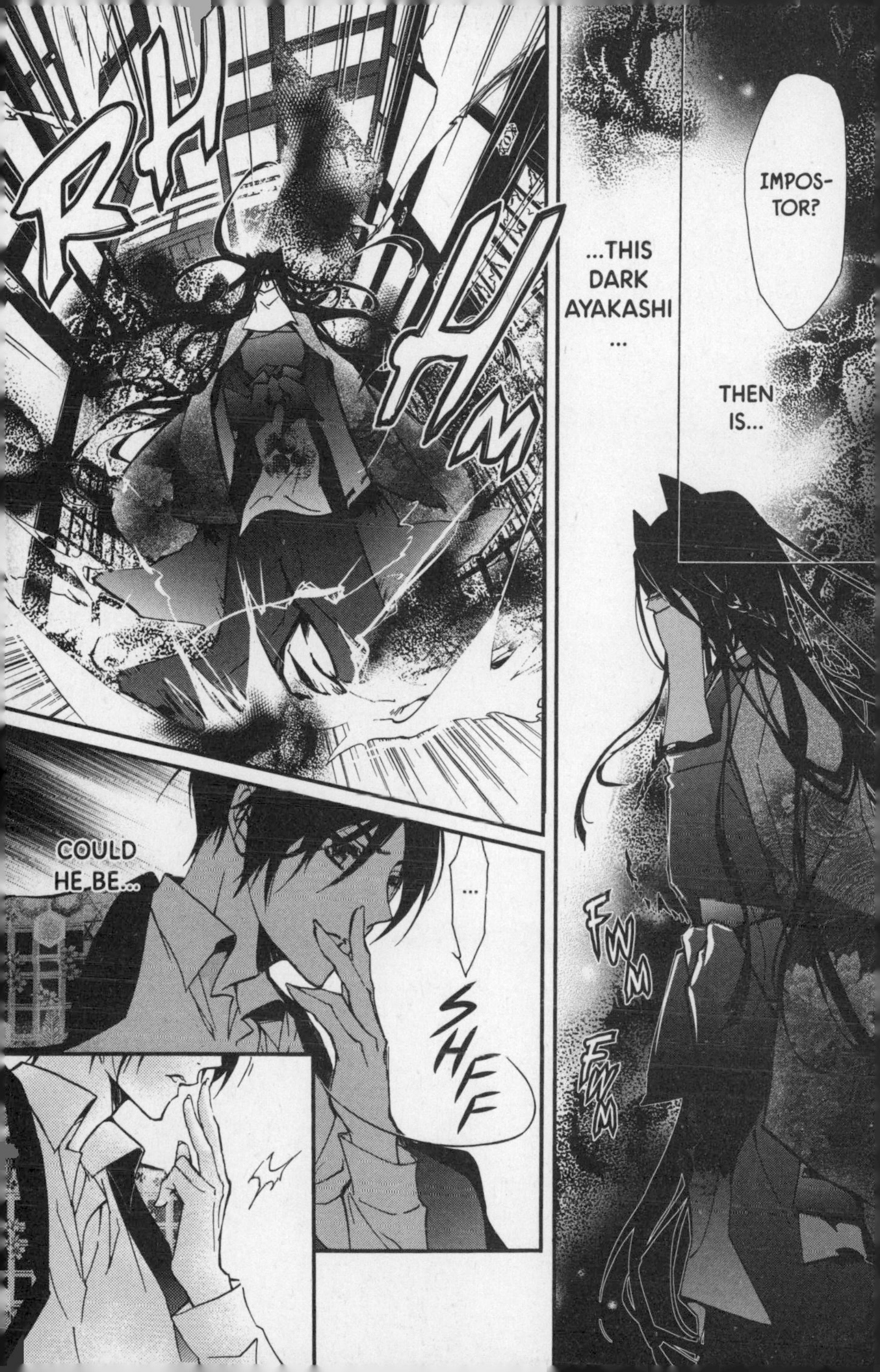
IMPOSTOR?
THEN IS...
...THIS DARK AYAKASHI ...
FWM
FWM
RHHM
COULD HE BE...
...
SHFF

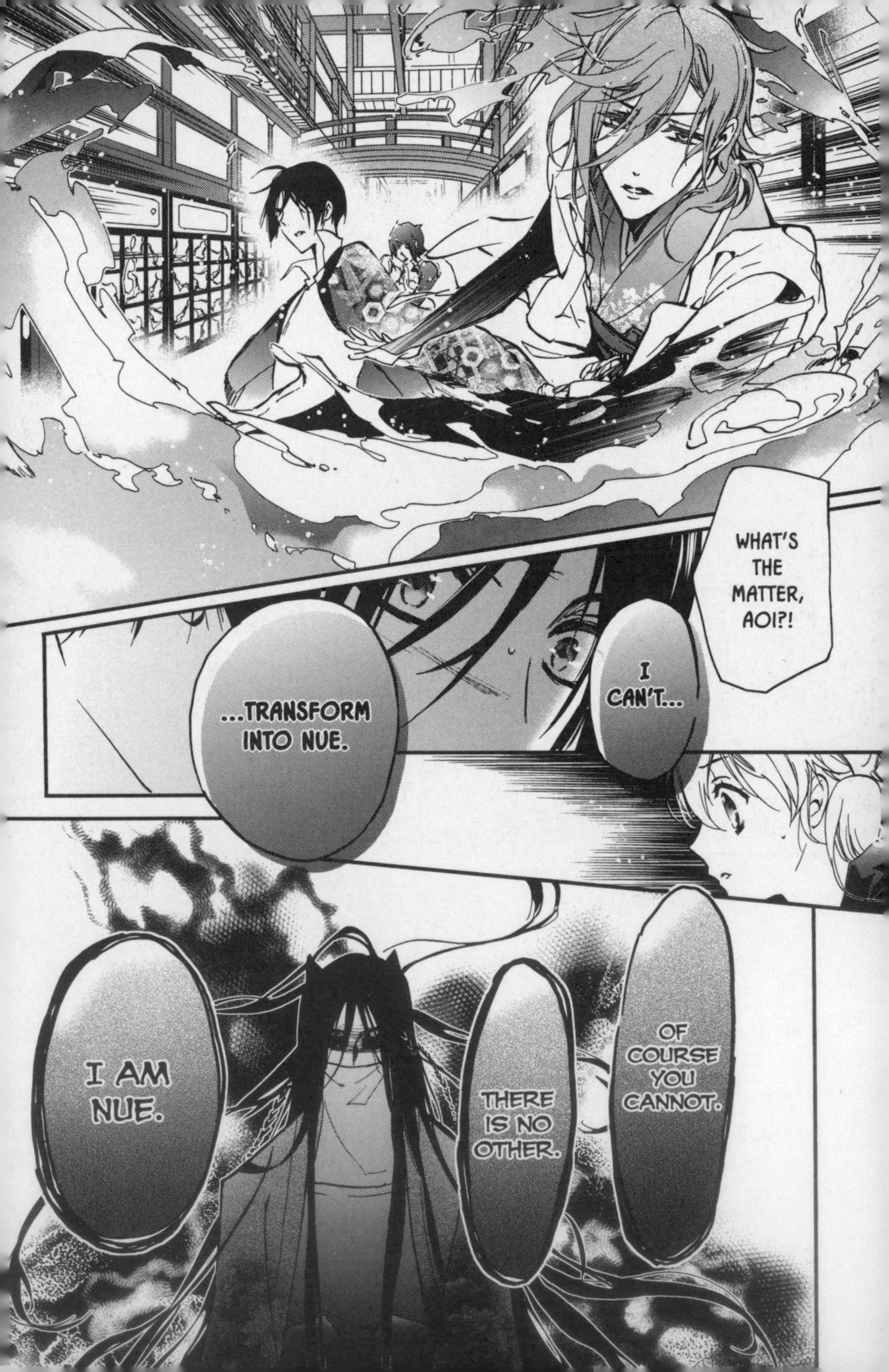
WHAT'S THE MATTER, AOI?!
I CAN'T...
...TRANSFORM INTO NUE.
OF COURSE YOU CANNOT.
THERE IS NO OTHER.
I AM NUE.

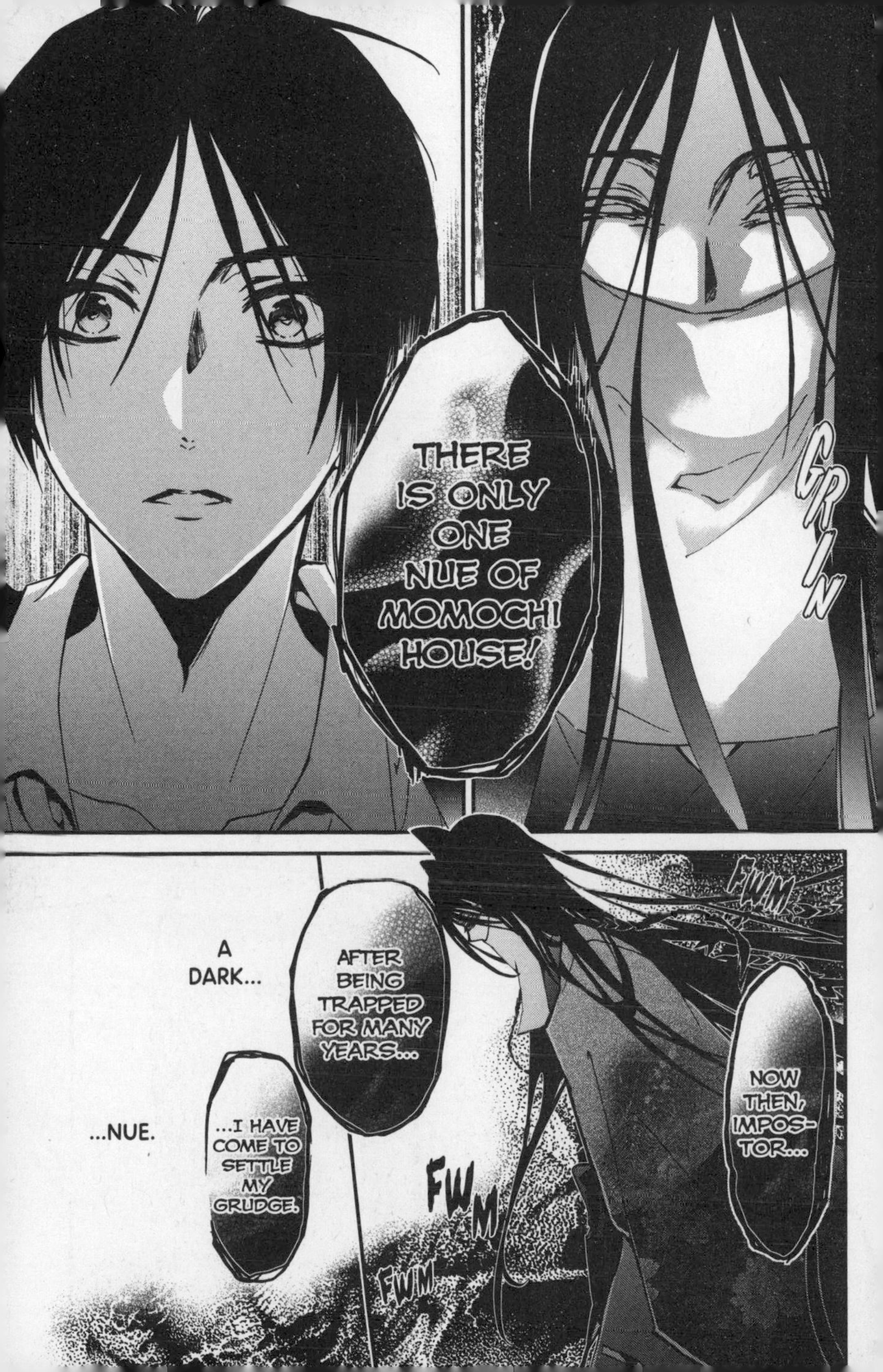
GRIN
THERE IS ONLY ONE NUE OF MOMOCHI HOUSE!
FWM
NOW THEN, IMPOS-TOR...
AFTER BEING TRAPPED FOR MANY YEARS...
A DARK...
FWM
FWM
...I HAVE COME TO SETTLE MY GRUDGE.
...NUE.

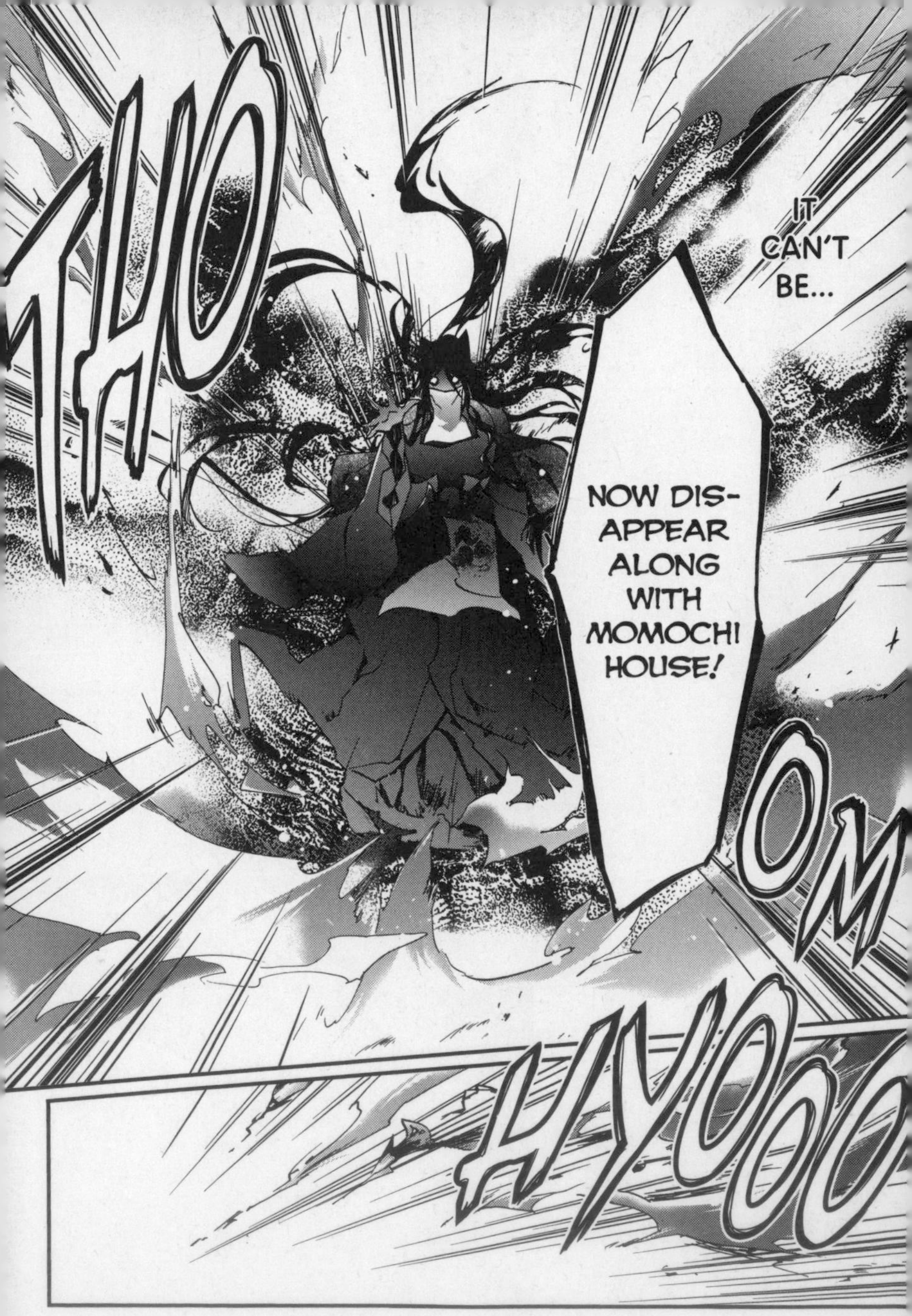
IT CAN'T BE...
NOW DIS-APPEAR ALONG WITH MOMOCHI HOUSE!
OHHHH
OM
HYOOOO

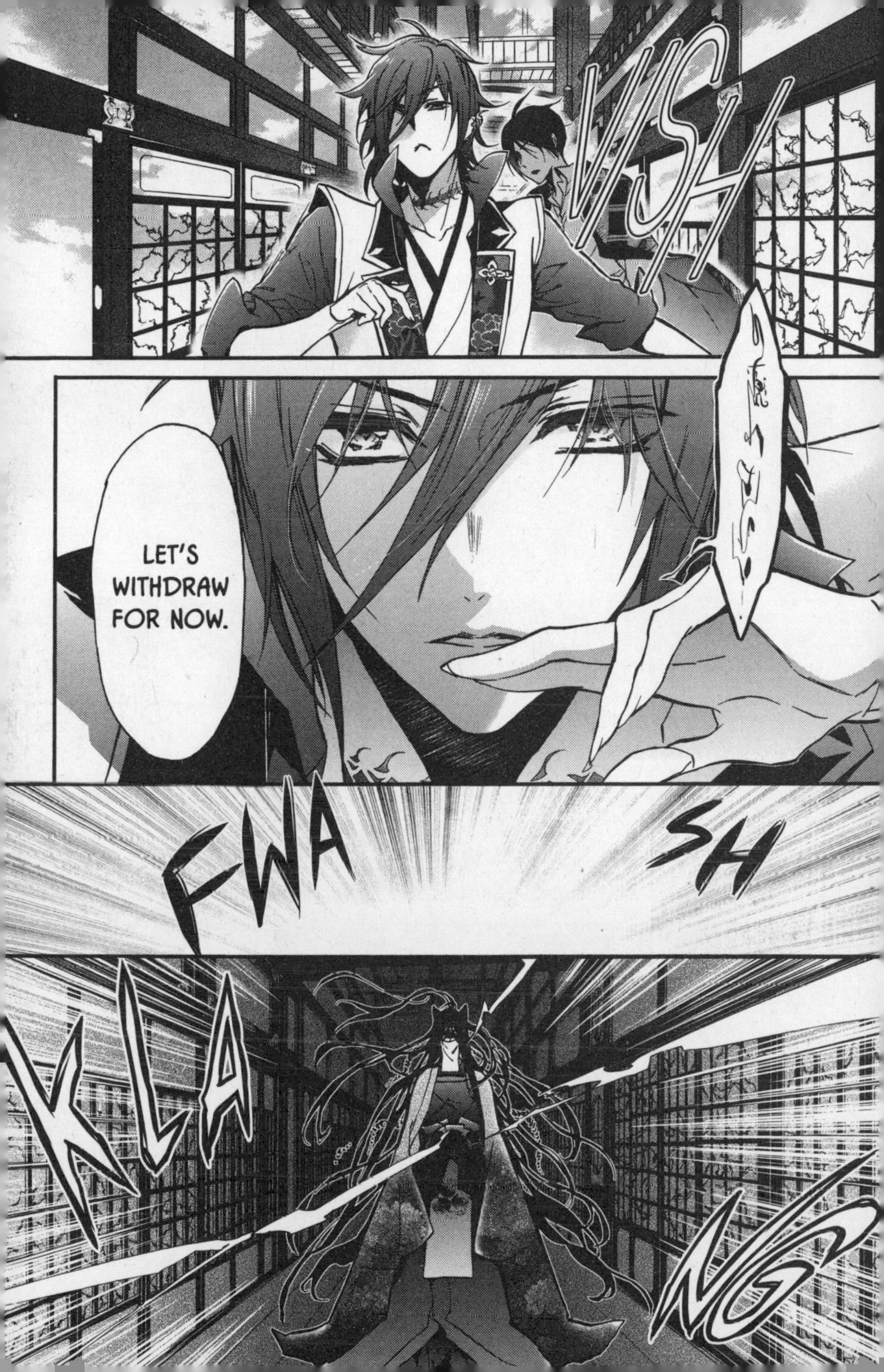
VISH
LET'S WITHDRAW FOR NOW.
FWA
SH
KLA
NG

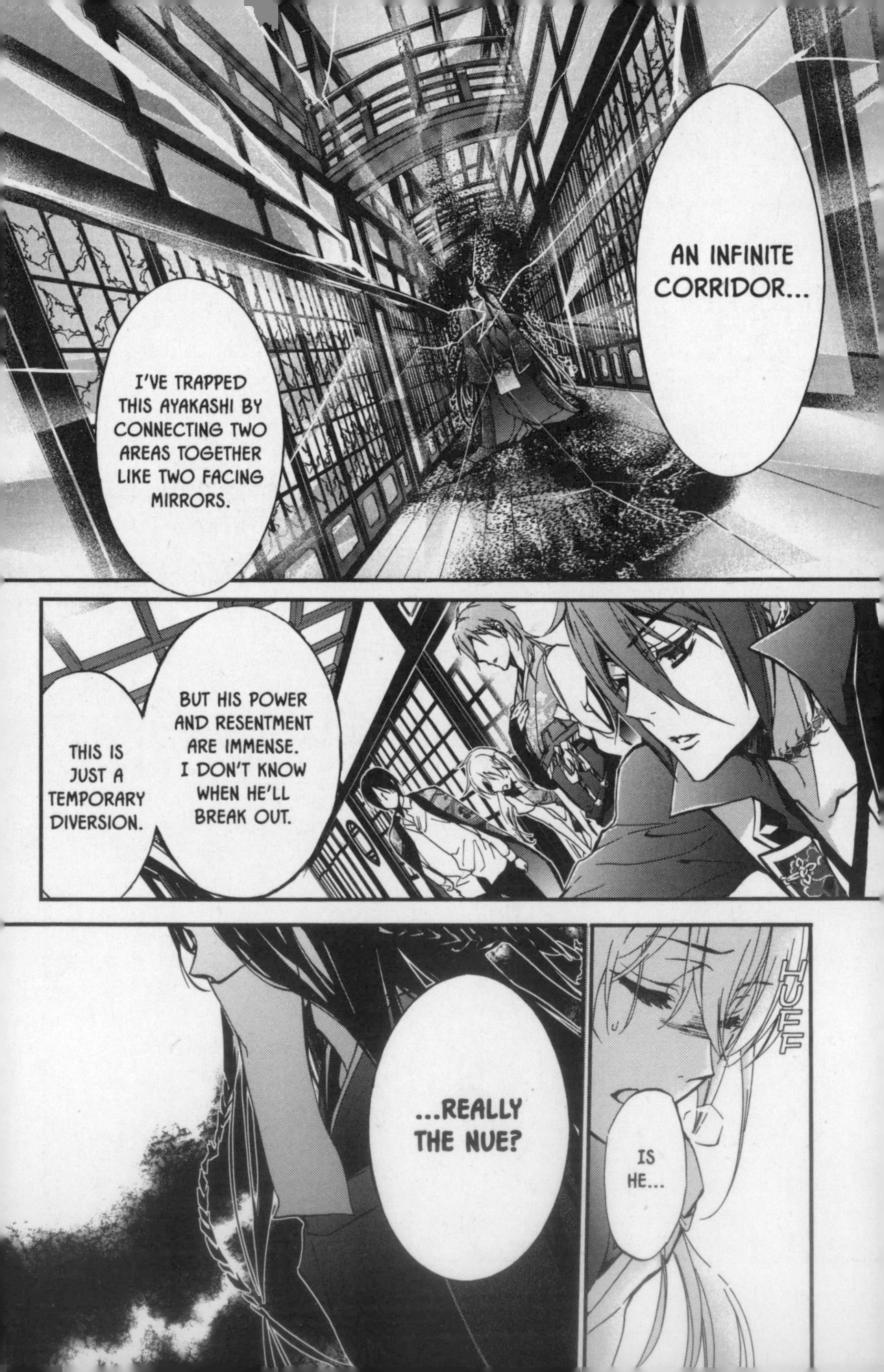
AN INFINITE CORRIDOR...
I'VE TRAPPED THIS AYAKASHI BY CONNECTING TWO AREAS TOGETHER LIKE TWO FACING MIRRORS.
BUT HIS POWER AND RESENTMENT ARE IMMENSE. I DON'T KNOW WHEN HE'LL BREAK OUT.
THIS IS JUST A TEMPORARY DIVERSION.
HUFF
IS HE...
...REALLY THE NUE?

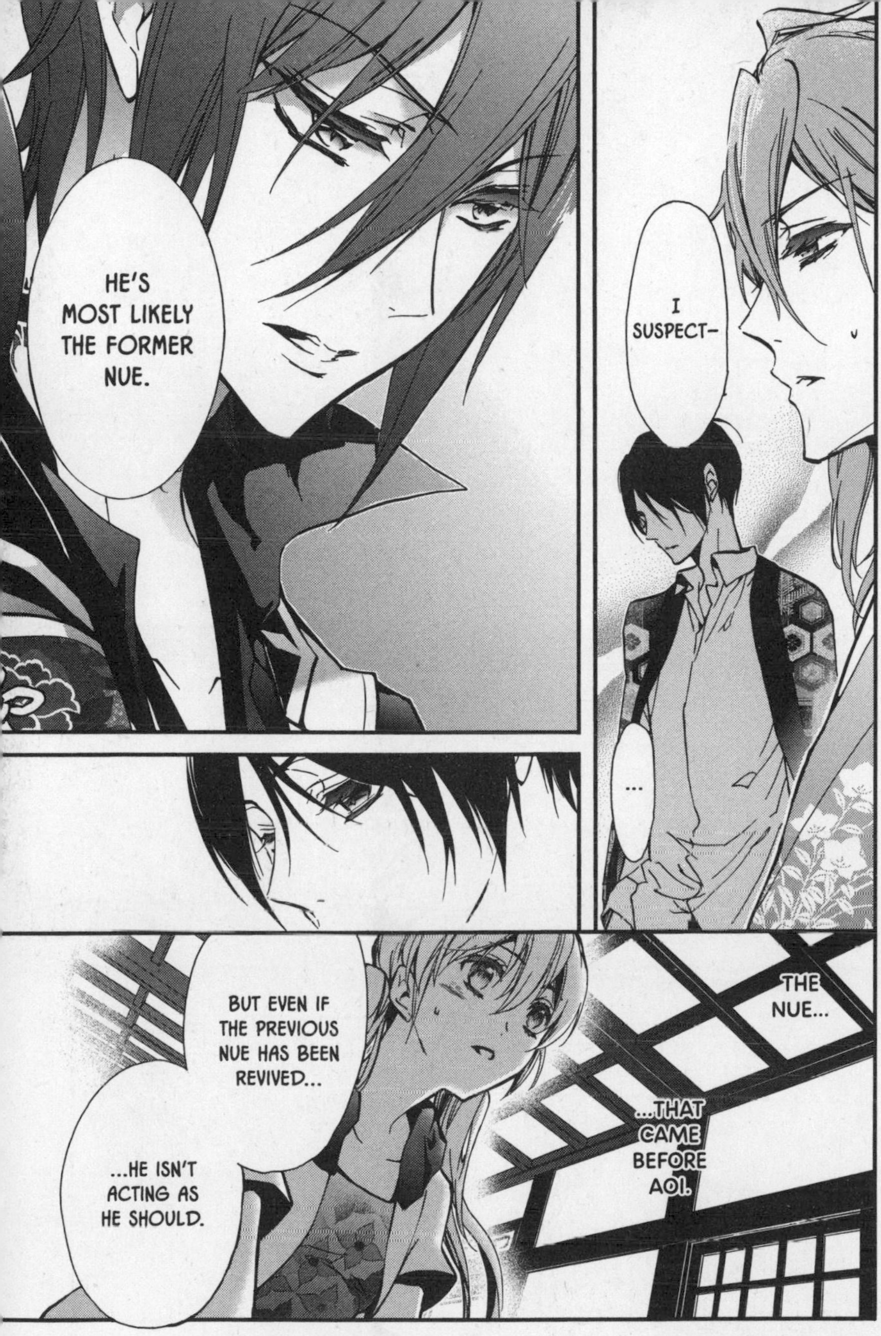
I SUSPECT—
...
HE'S MOST LIKELY THE FORMER NUE.
THE NUE...
...THAT CAME BEFORE AOI.
BUT EVEN IF THE PREVIOUS NUE HAS BEEN REVIVED...
...HE ISN'T ACTING AS HE SHOULD.

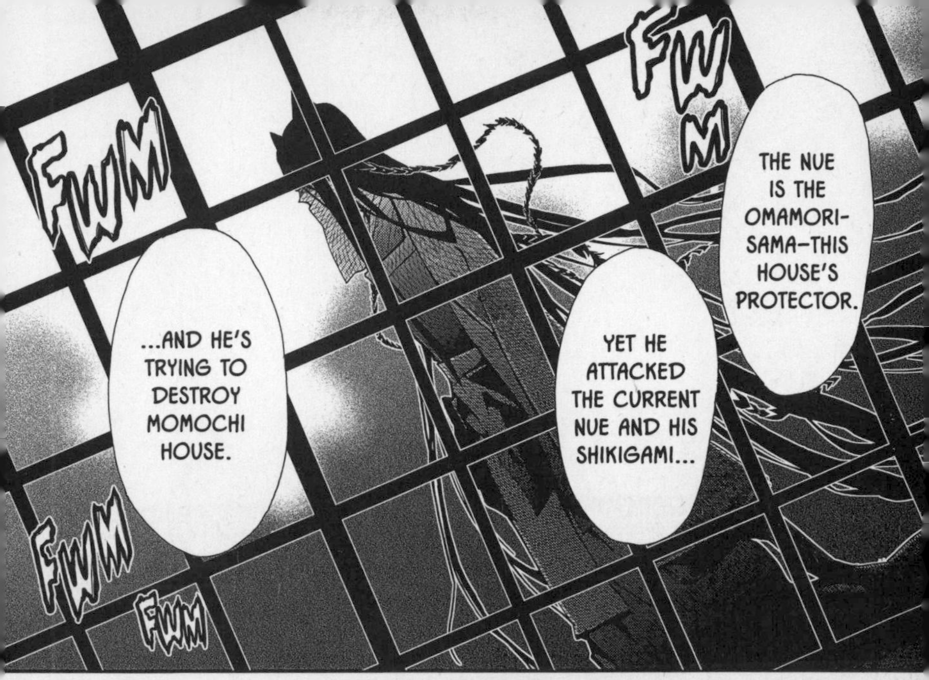
FWM
THE NUE IS THE OMAMORI-SAMA—THIS HOUSE'S PROTECTOR.
YET HE ATTACKED THE CURRENT NUE AND HIS SHIKIGAMI...
...AND HE'S TRYING TO DESTROY MOMOCHI HOUSE.
FWM
FWM
FWM

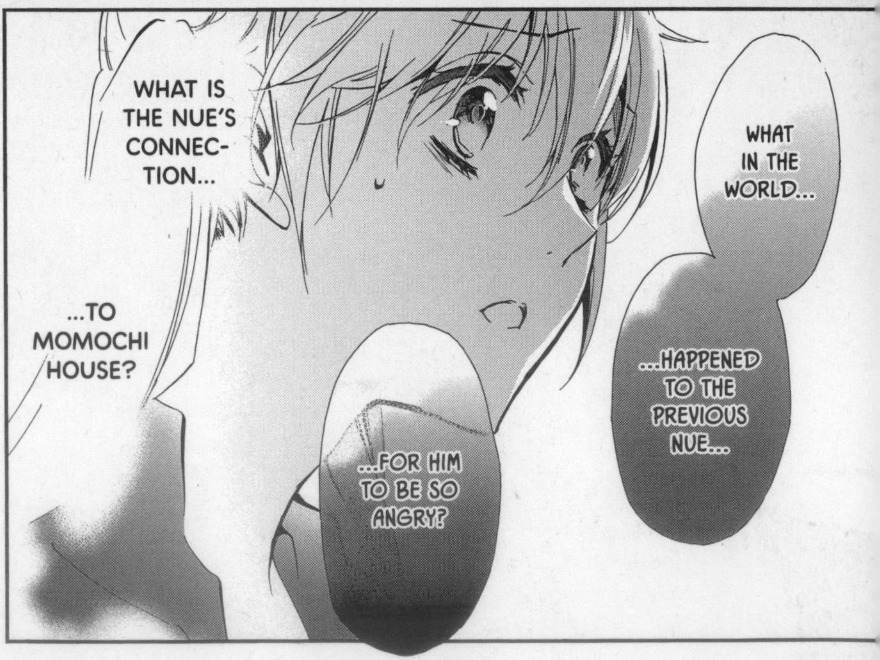
WHAT IN THE WORLD...
...HAPPENED TO THE PREVIOUS NUE...
...FOR HIM TO BE SO ANGRY?
WHAT IS THE NUE'S CONNECTION...
...TO MOMOCHI HOUSE?

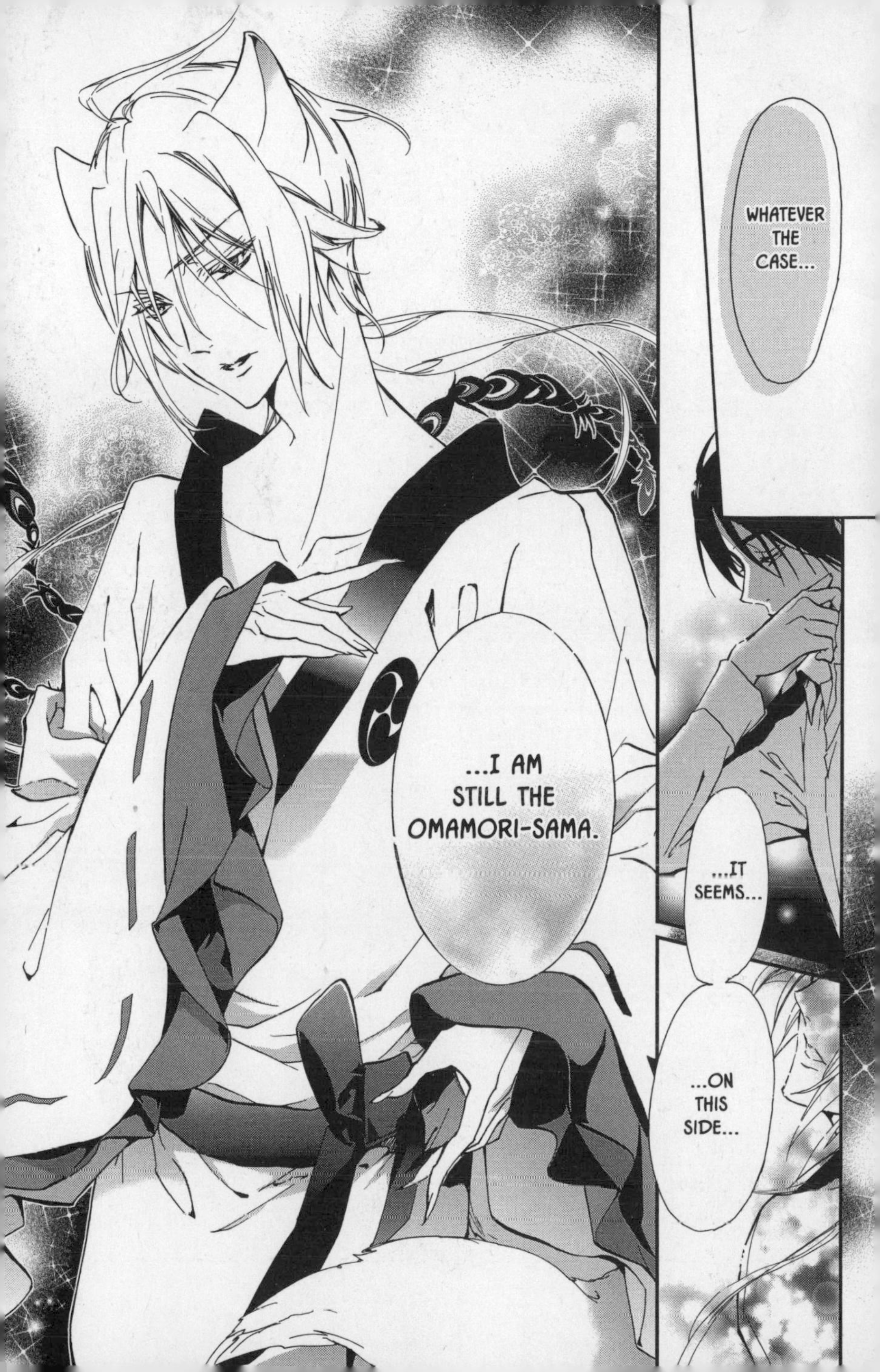
WHATEVER THE CASE...
...IT SEEMS...
...ON THIS SIDE...
...I AM STILL THE OMAMORI-SAMA.

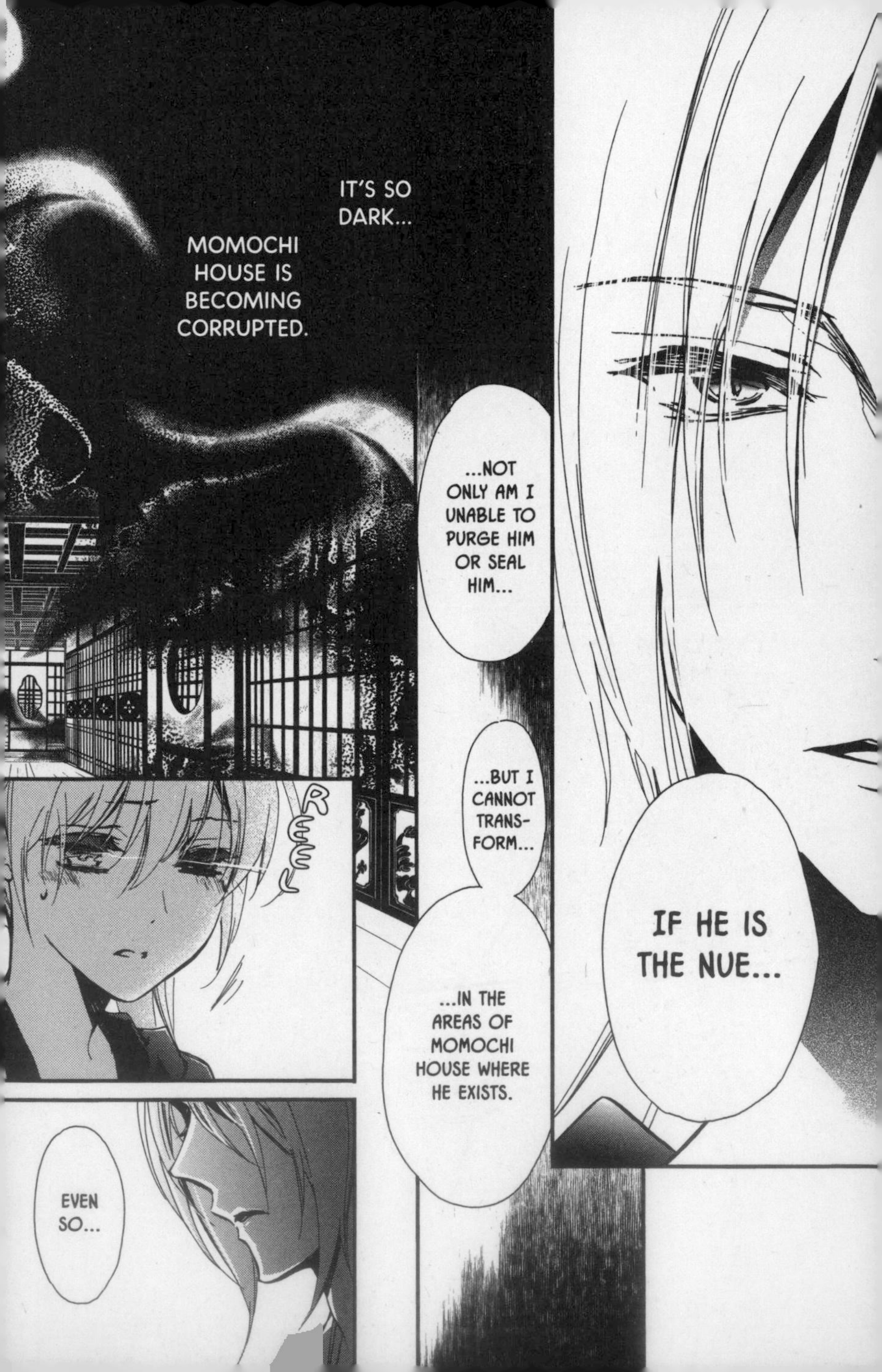
IF HE IS THE NUE...
...NOT ONLY AM I UNABLE TO PURGE HIM OR SEAL HIM...
...BUT I CANNOT TRANS-FORM...
...IN THE AREAS OF MOMOCHI HOUSE WHERE HE EXISTS.
IT'S SO DARK...
MOMOCHI HOUSE IS BECOMING CORRUPTED.
REEL
EVEN SO...

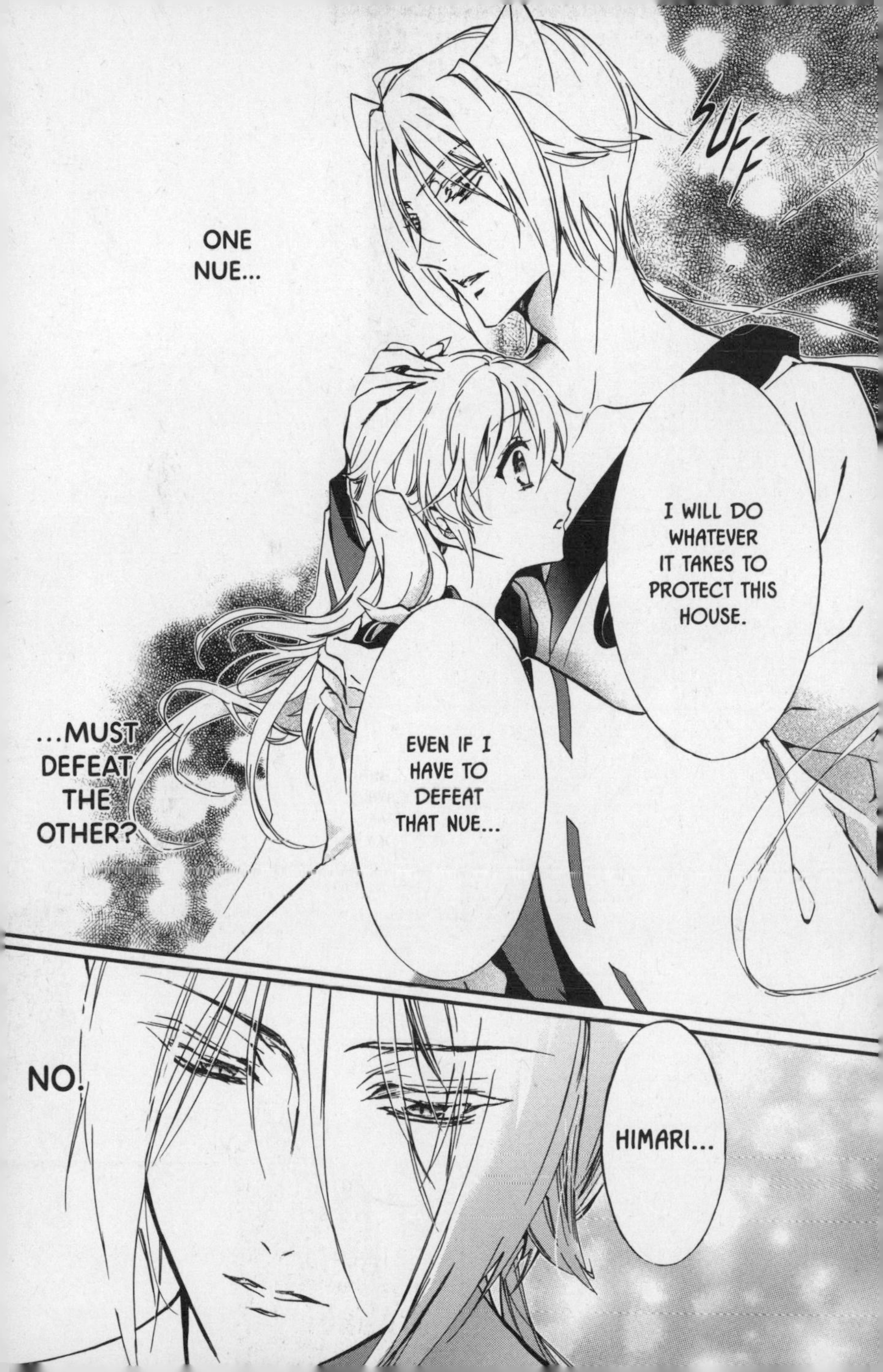
SUFF
I WILL DO WHATEVER IT TAKES TO PROTECT THIS HOUSE.
EVEN IF I HAVE TO DEFEAT THAT NUE...
ONE NUE...
...MUST DEFEAT THE OTHER?
HIMARI...
NO.

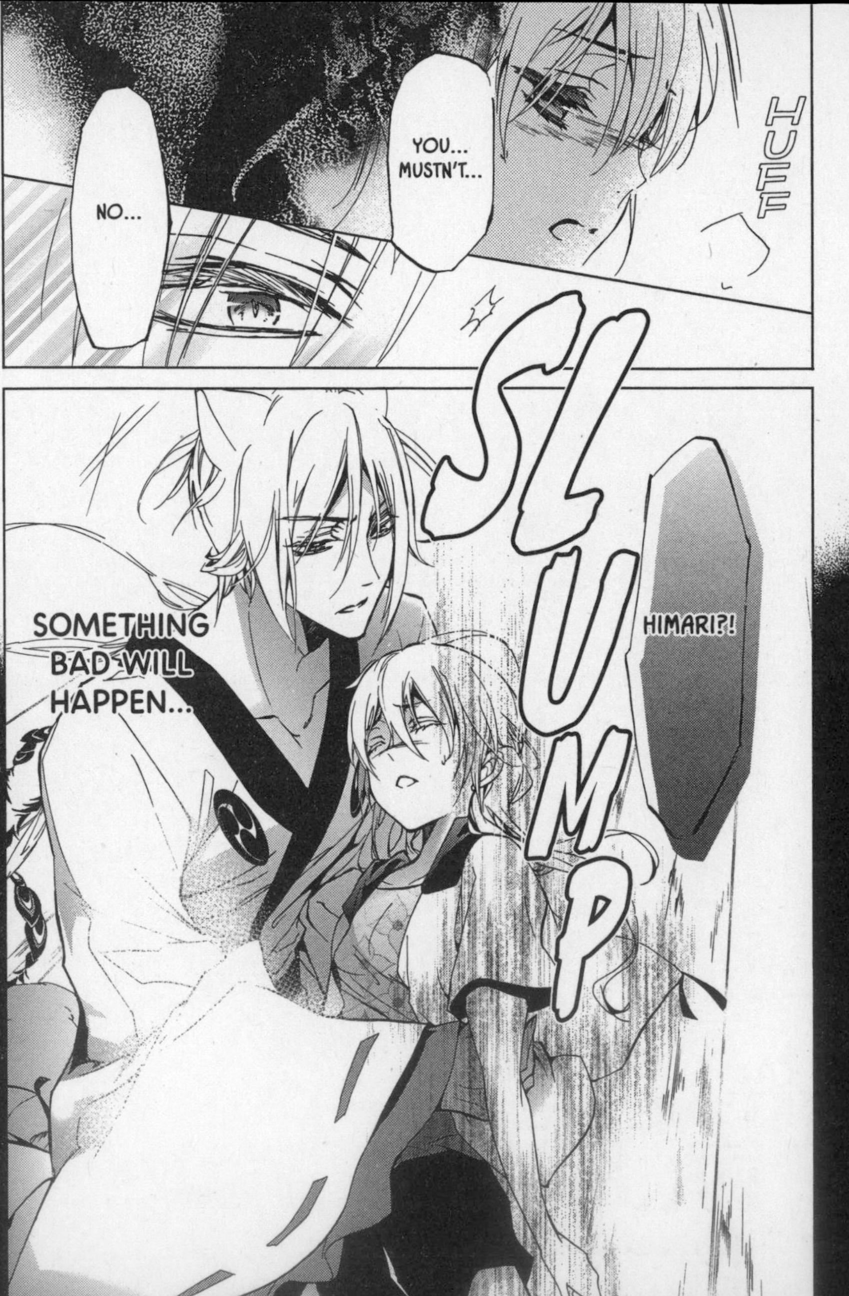
HUFF
YOU... MUSTN'T...
NO...
SLUMP
HIMARI?!
SOMETHING BAD WILL HAPPEN...

Chapter 39/End

The
DEMON
PRINCE
of MOMOCHI
HOUSE

The
DEMON
PRINCE
of MOMOCHI
HOUSE

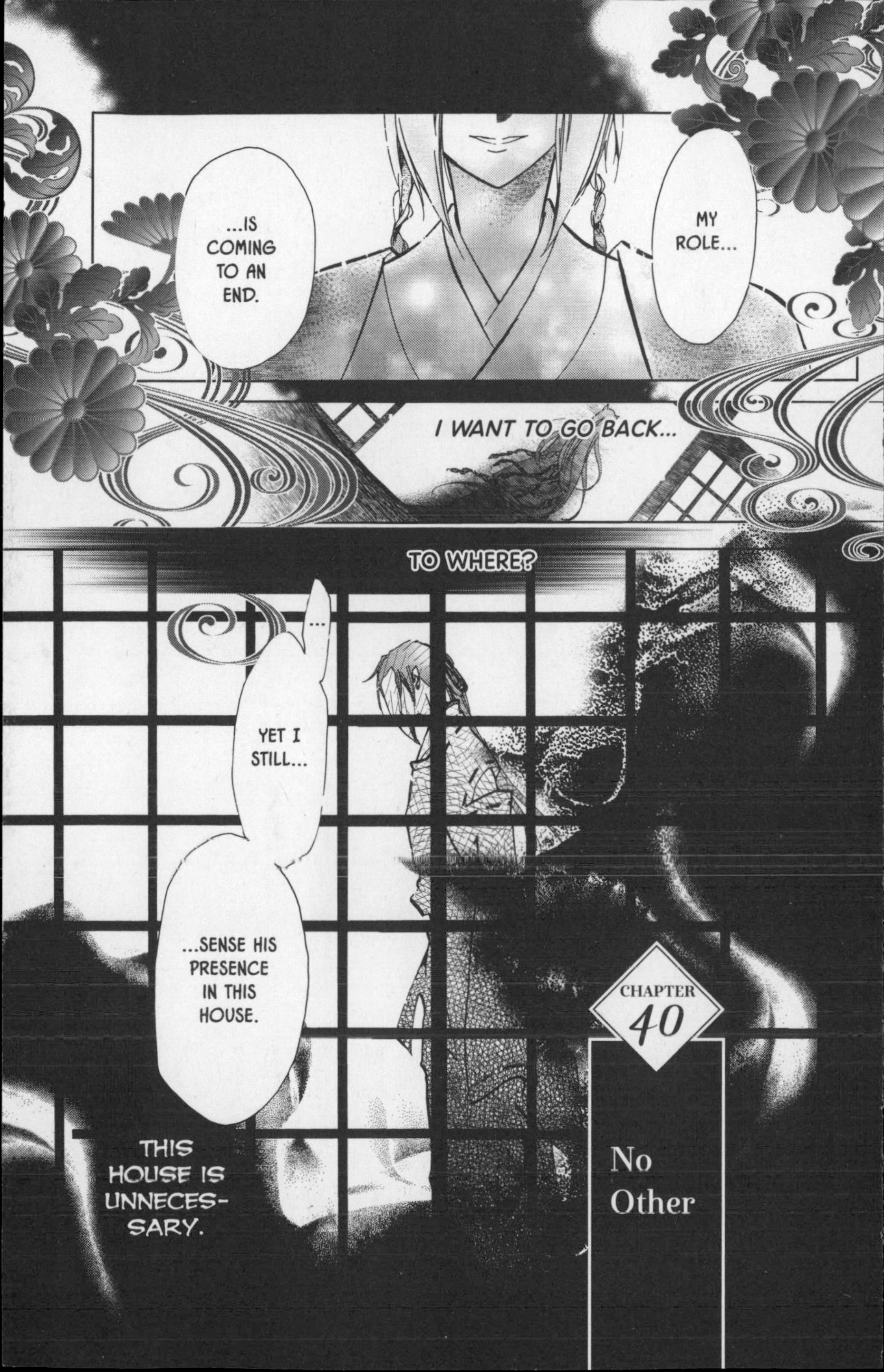
MY ROLE...
...IS COMING TO AN END.
I WANT TO GO BACK...
TO WHERE?
...
YET I STILL...
...SENSE HIS PRESENCE IN THIS HOUSE.
CHAPTER 40
No Other
THIS HOUSE IS UNNECES-SARY.

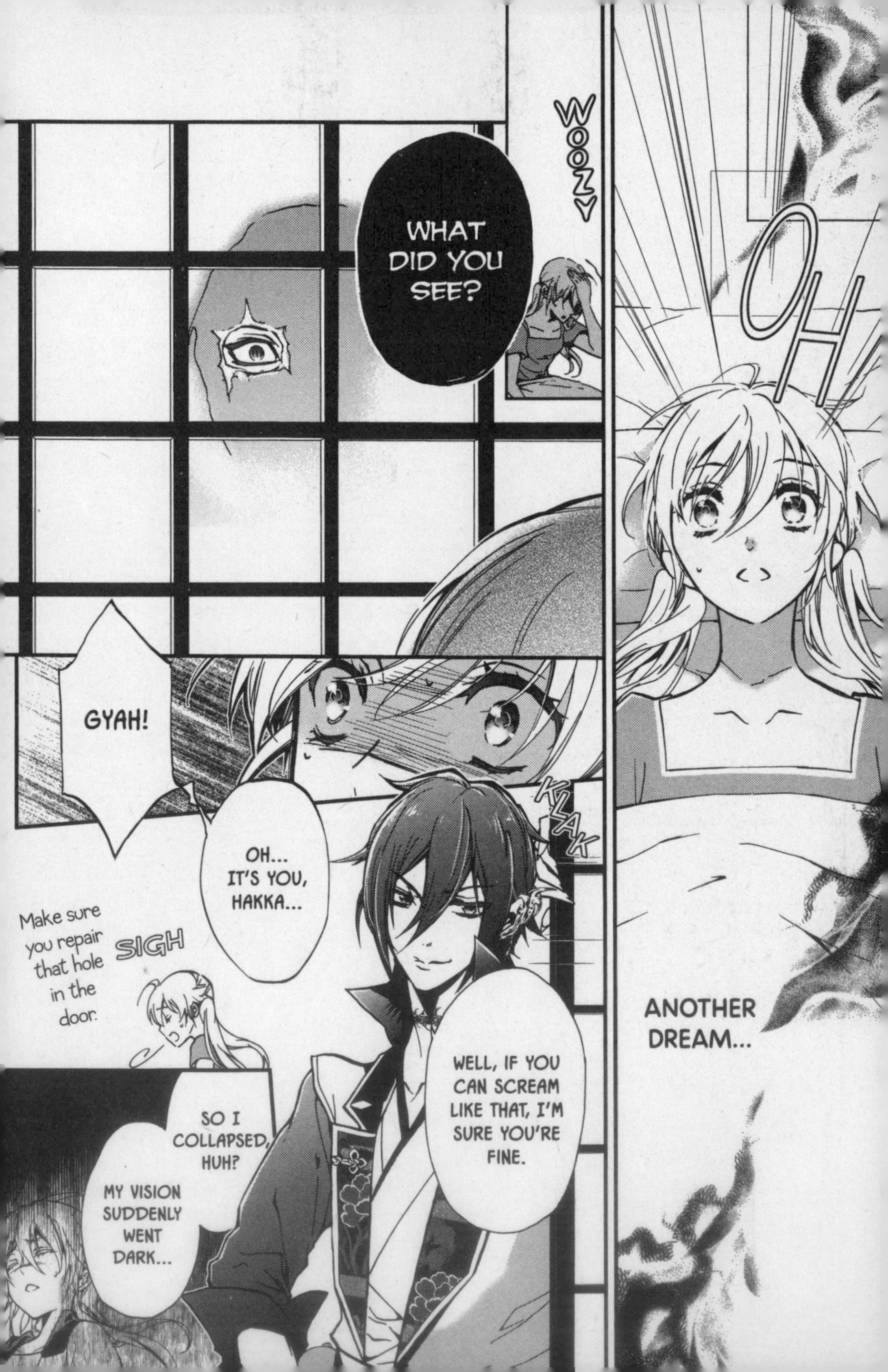
OH
ANOTHER DREAM...
WOOZY
WHAT DID YOU SEE?
GYAH!
KLAK
OH... IT'S YOU, HAKKA...
WELL, IF YOU CAN SCREAM LIKE THAT, I'M SURE YOU'RE FINE.
SIGH
Make sure you repair that hole in the door.
SO I COLLAPSED, HUH?
MY VISION SUDDENLY WENT DARK...

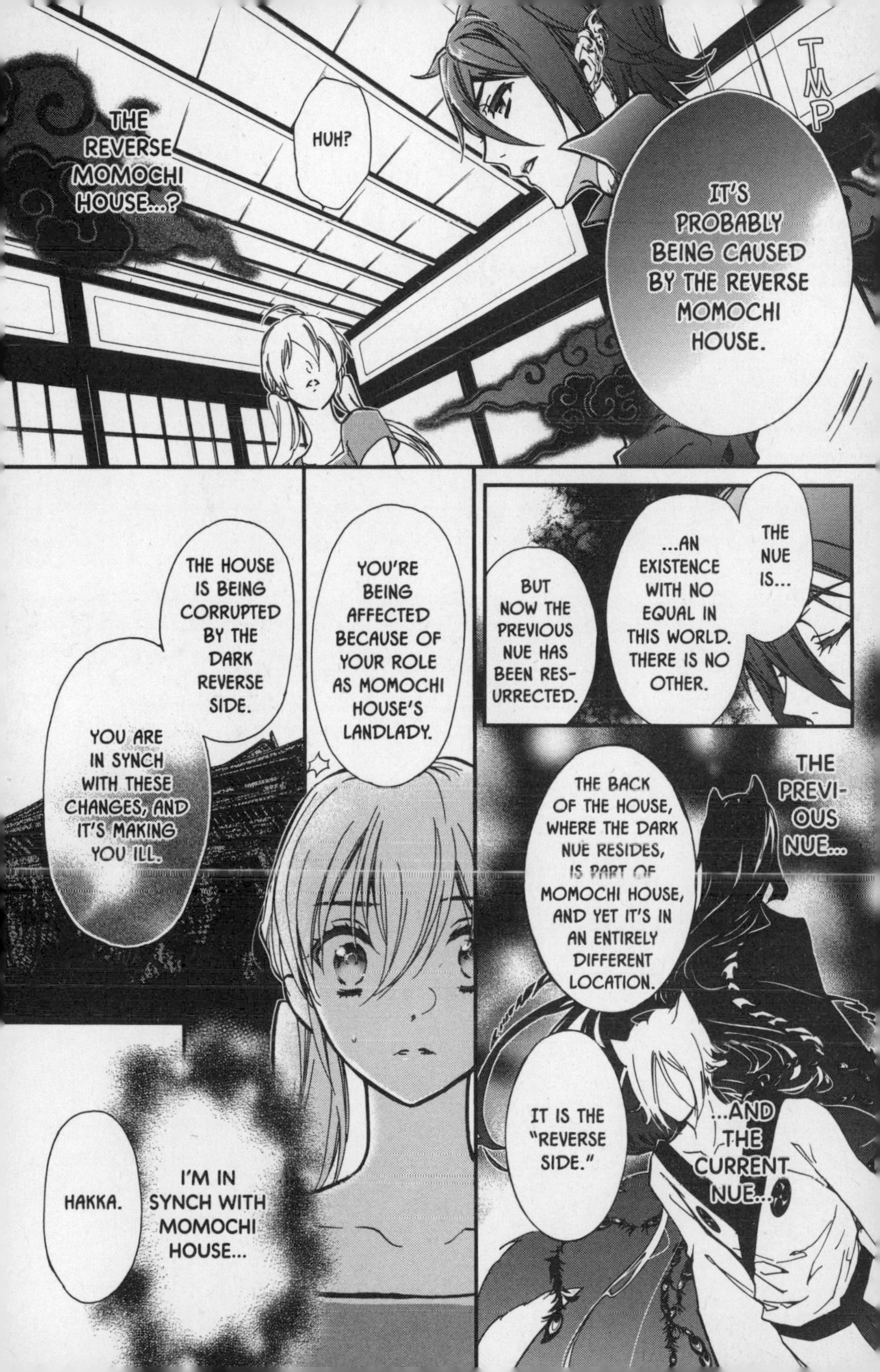
TMP
IT'S PROBABLY BEING CAUSED BY THE REVERSE MOMOCHI HOUSE.
HUH?
THE REVERSE MOMOCHI HOUSE...?
THE NUE IS...
...AN EXISTENCE WITH NO EQUAL IN THIS WORLD. THERE IS NO OTHER.
BUT NOW THE PREVIOUS NUE HAS BEEN RES-URRECTED.
THE PREVI-OUS NUE...
THE BACK OF THE HOUSE, WHERE THE DARK NUE RESIDES, IS PART OF MOMOCHI HOUSE, AND YET IT'S IN AN ENTIRELY DIFFERENT LOCATION.
...AND THE CURRENT NUE...
IT IS THE "REVERSE SIDE."
YOU'RE BEING AFFECTED BECAUSE OF YOUR ROLE AS MOMOCHI HOUSE'S LANDLADY.
THE HOUSE IS BEING CORRUPTED BY THE DARK REVERSE SIDE.
YOU ARE IN SYNCH WITH THESE CHANGES, AND IT'S MAKING YOU ILL.
I'M IN SYNCH WITH MOMOCHI HOUSE...
HAKKA.

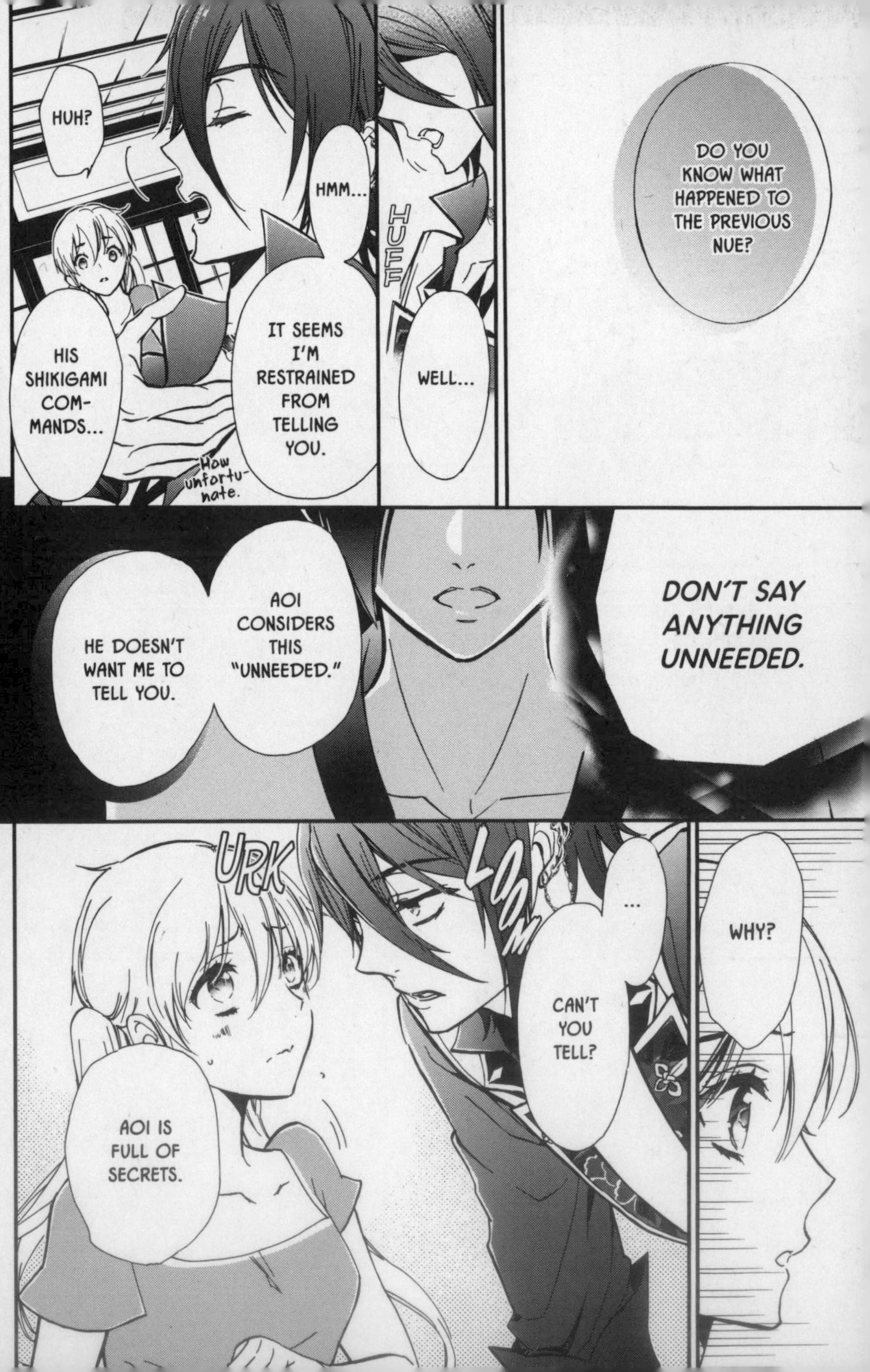
DO YOU KNOW WHAT HAPPENED TO THE PREVIOUS NUE?
WELL...
HUFF
HMM...
IT SEEMS I'M RESTRAINED FROM TELLING YOU.
How unfortunate.
HUH?
HIS SHIKIGAMI COM-MANDS...
DON'T SAY ANYTHING UNNEEDED.
AOI CONSIDERS THIS "UNNEEDED."
HE DOESN'T WANT ME TO TELL YOU.
WHY?
...
CAN'T YOU TELL?
LOOM
URK
AOI IS FULL OF SECRETS.

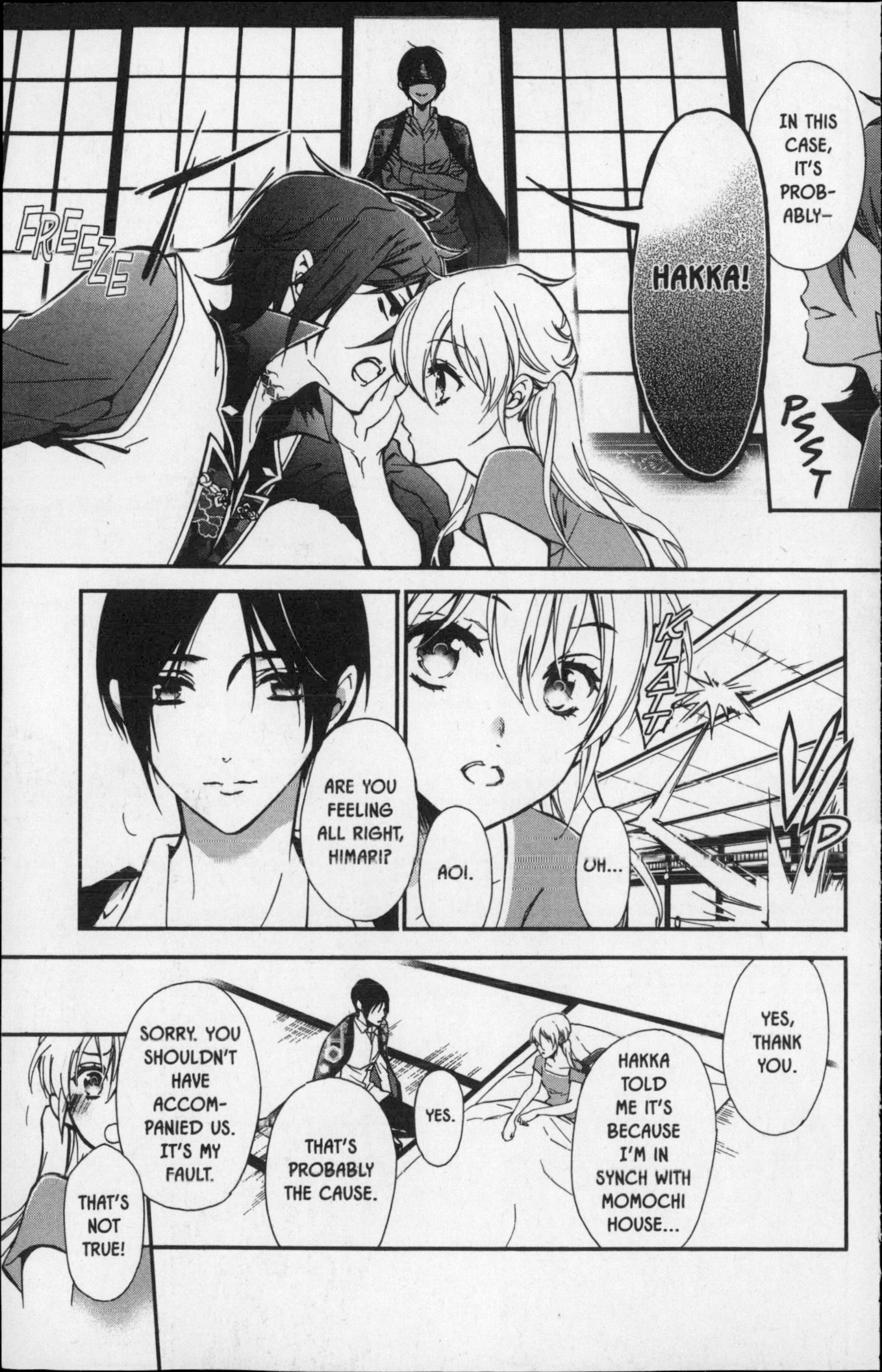
IN THIS CASE, IT'S PROB-ABLY—
PSST
HAKKA!
FREEZE
KLATT
VIP
UH...
AOI.
ARE YOU FEELING ALL RIGHT, HIMARI?
YES, THANK YOU.
HAKKA TOLD ME IT'S BECAUSE I'M IN SYNCH WITH MOMOCHI HOUSE...
YES.
THAT'S PROBABLY THE CAUSE.
SORRY. YOU SHOULDN'T HAVE ACCOM-PANIED US. IT'S MY FAULT.
THAT'S NOT TRUE!

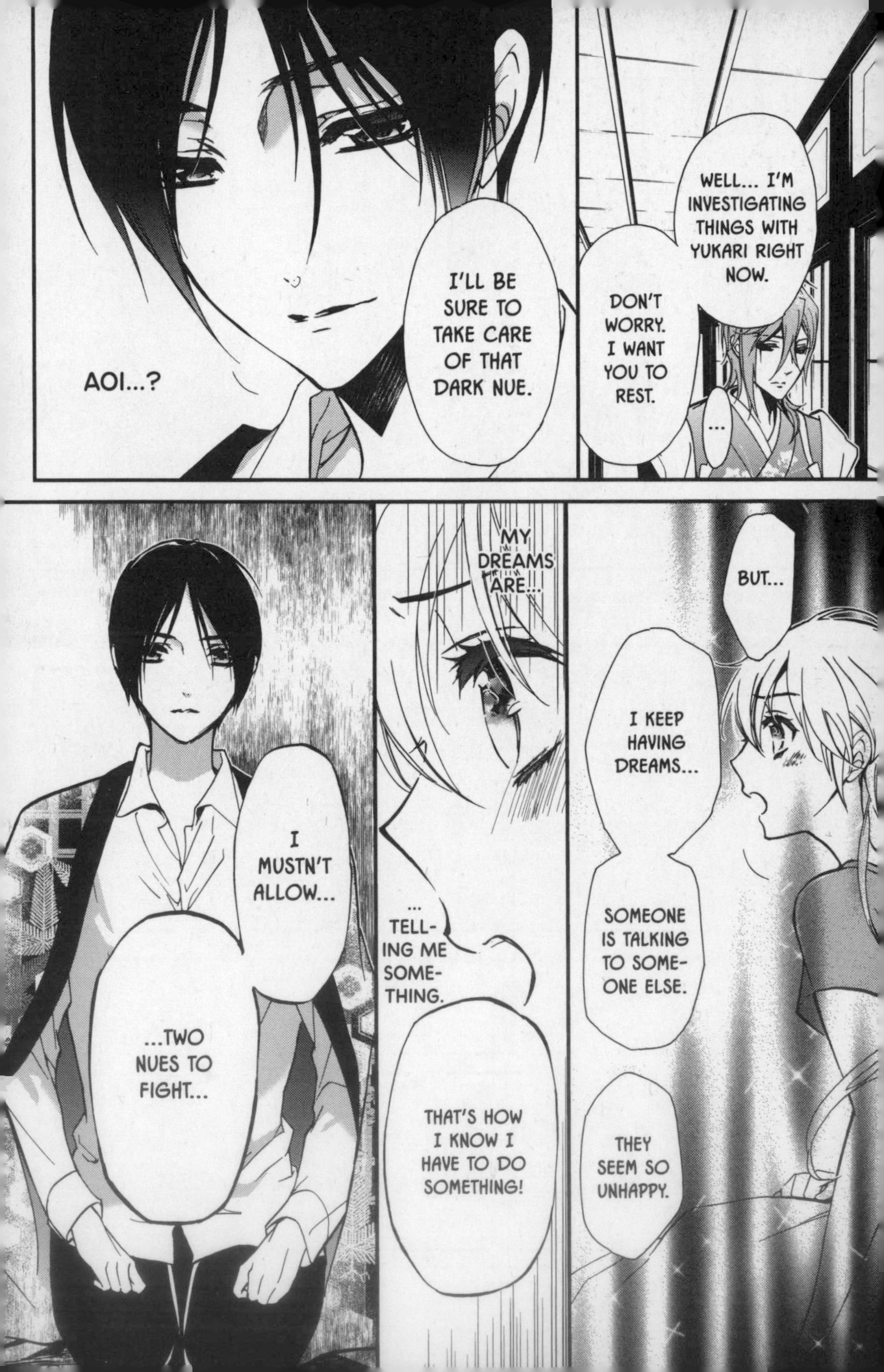
WELL... I'M INVESTIGATING THINGS WITH YUKARI RIGHT NOW.
DON'T WORRY. I WANT YOU TO REST.
...
I'LL BE SURE TO TAKE CARE OF THAT DARK NUE.
AOI...?
BUT...
I KEEP HAVING DREAMS...
SOMEONE IS TALKING TO SOMEONE ELSE.
THEY SEEM SO UNHAPPY.
MY DREAMS ARE...
...TELLING ME SOMETHING.
THAT'S HOW I KNOW I HAVE TO DO SOMETHING!
I MUSTN'T ALLOW...
...TWO NUES TO FIGHT...

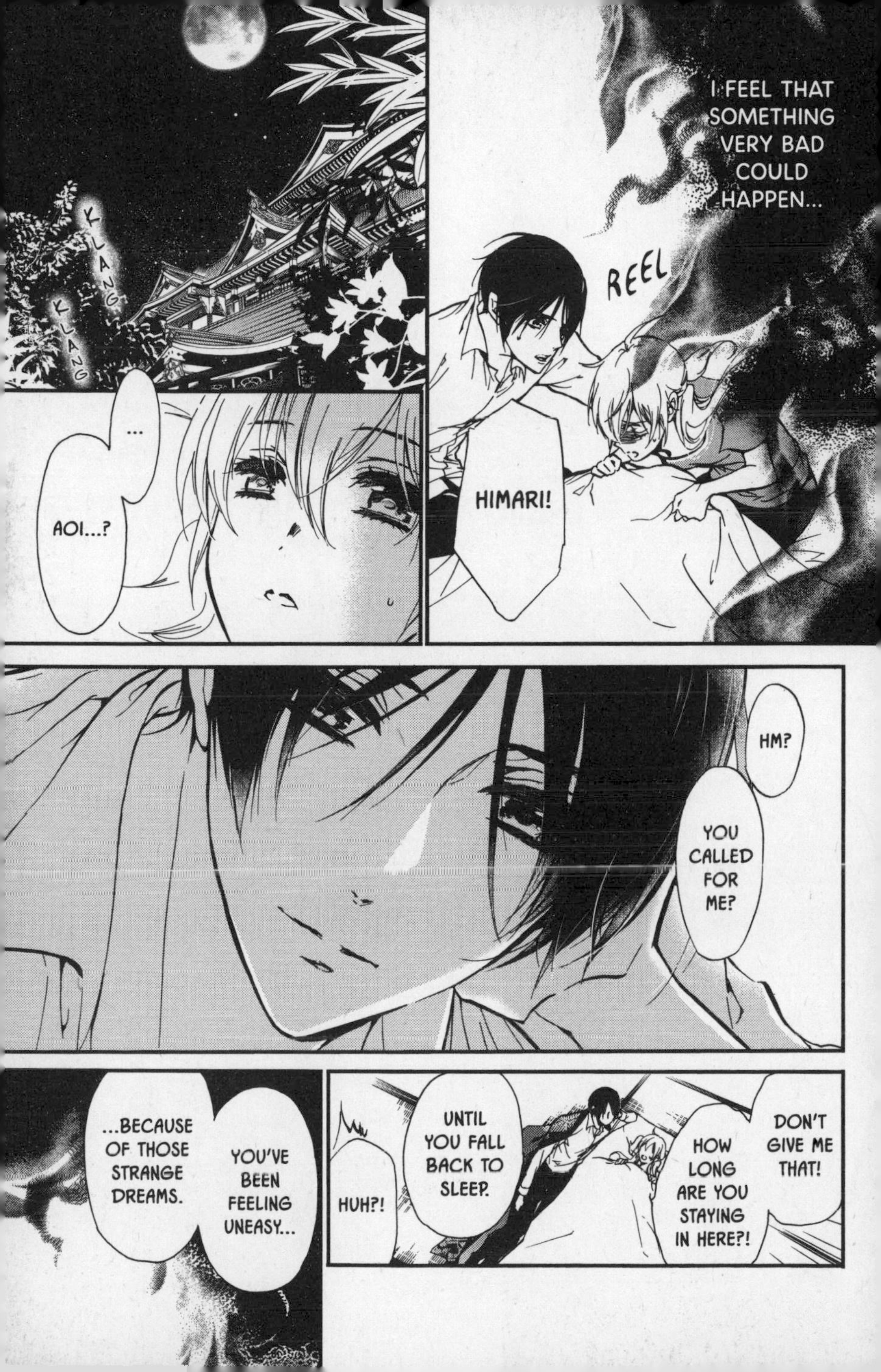
I FEEL THAT SOMETHING VERY BAD COULD HAPPEN...
REEL
HIMARI!
KLANG
KLANG
...
AOI...?
HM?
YOU CALLED FOR ME?
DON'T GIVE ME THAT!
HOW LONG ARE YOU STAYING IN HERE?!
UNTIL YOU FALL BACK TO SLEEP.
HUH?!
YOU'VE BEEN FEELING UNEASY...
...BECAUSE OF THOSE STRANGE DREAMS.

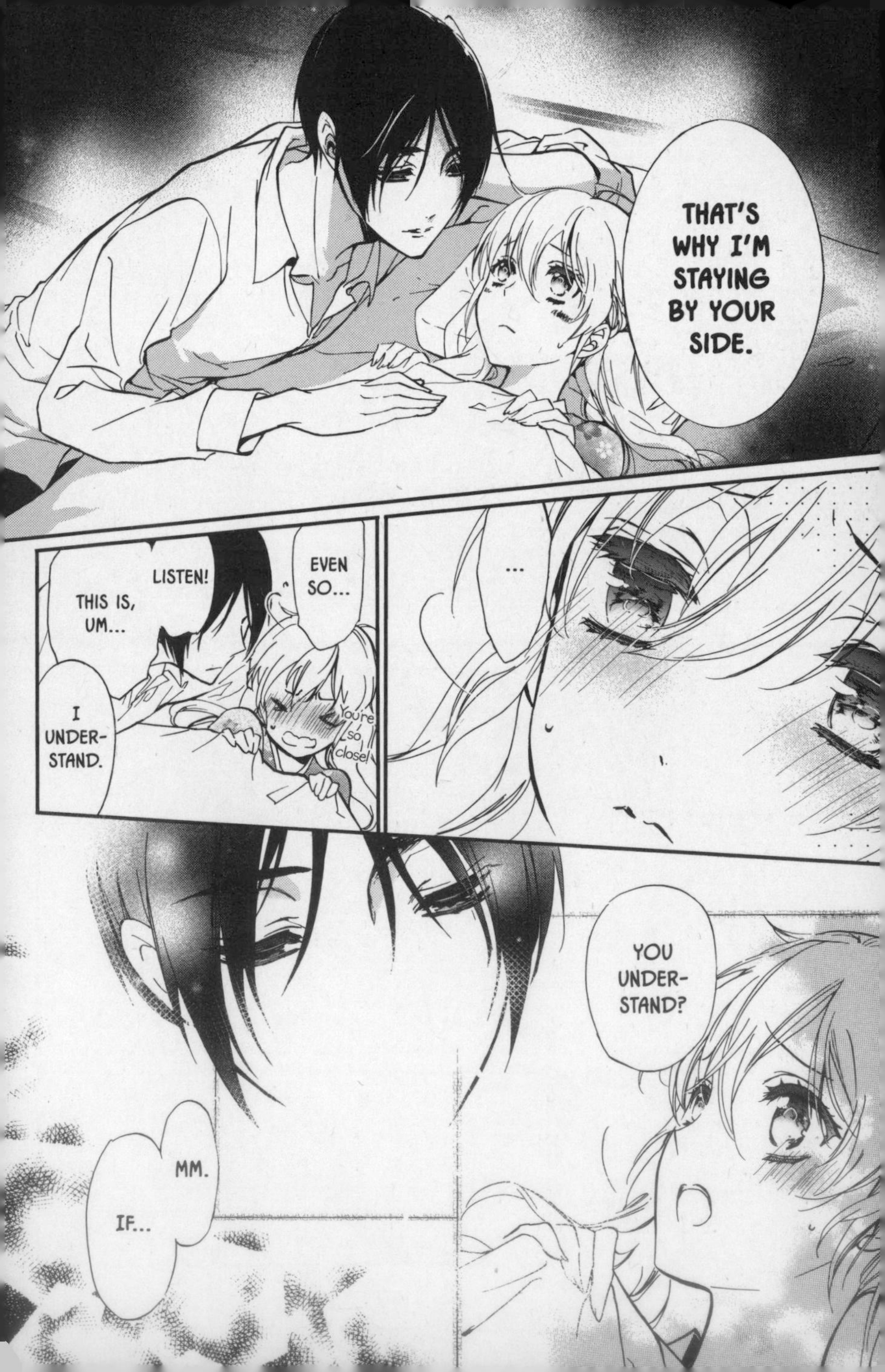
THAT'S WHY I'M STAYING BY YOUR SIDE.
...
EVEN SO...
LISTEN!
THIS IS, UM...
You're so close!
I UNDER-STAND.
YOU UNDER-STAND?
MM.
IF...

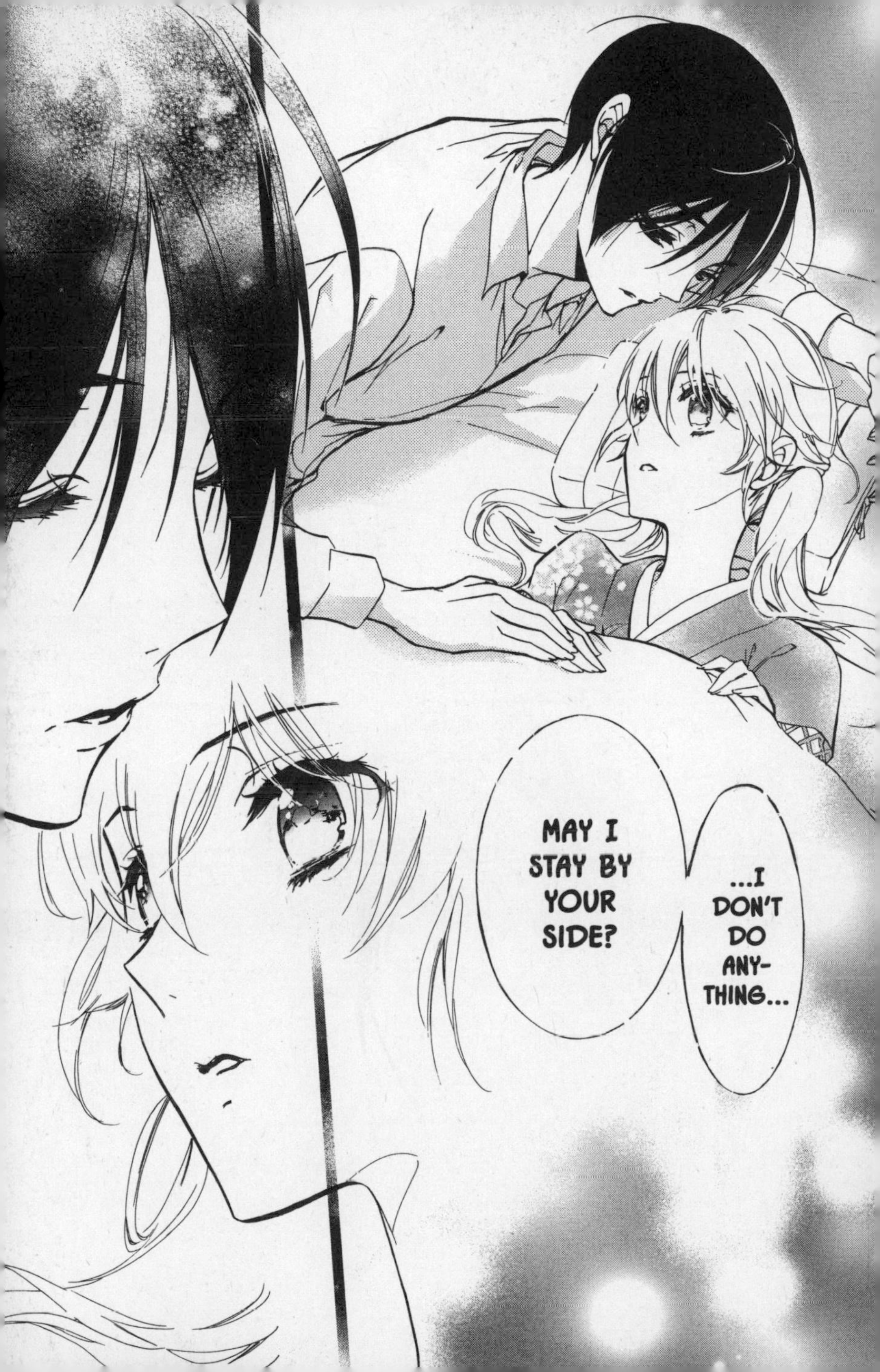
...I DON'T DO ANY-THING...
MAY I STAY BY YOUR SIDE?

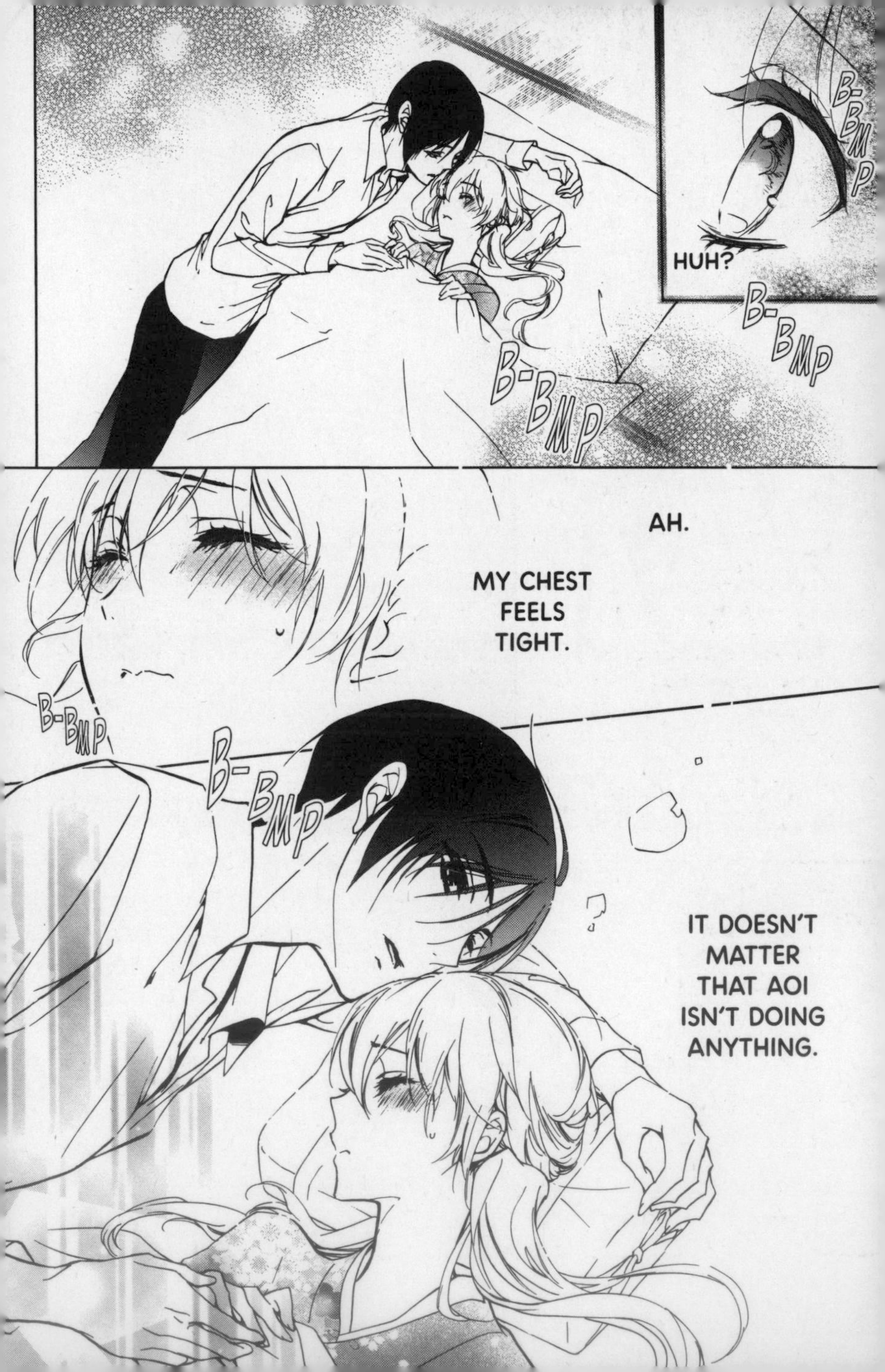
B-BMP
HUH?
B-BMP
B-BMP
AH.
MY CHEST FEELS TIGHT.
B-BMP
B-BMP
IT DOESN'T MATTER THAT AOI ISN'T DOING ANYTHING.

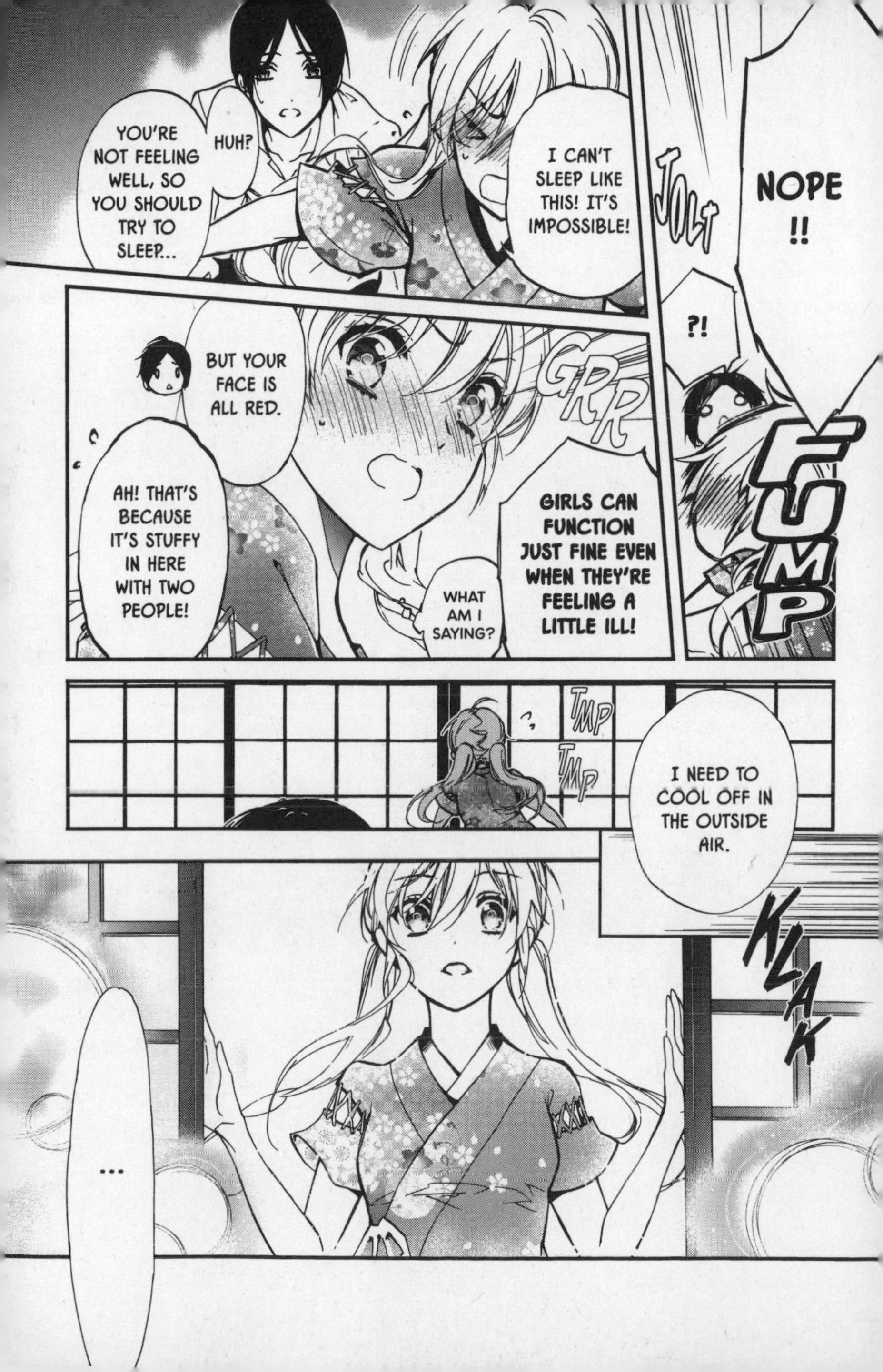
NOPE !!
JOLT
?!
FUMP
I CAN'T SLEEP LIKE THIS! IT'S IMPOSSIBLE!
HUH?
YOU'RE NOT FEELING WELL, SO YOU SHOULD TRY TO SLEEP...
GRR
BUT YOUR FACE IS ALL RED.
AH! THAT'S BECAUSE IT'S STUFFY IN HERE WITH TWO PEOPLE!
GIRLS CAN FUNCTION JUST FINE EVEN WHEN THEY'RE FEELING A LITTLE ILL!
WHAT AM I SAYING?
I NEED TO COOL OFF IN THE OUTSIDE AIR.
TMP
TMP
KLAK
...

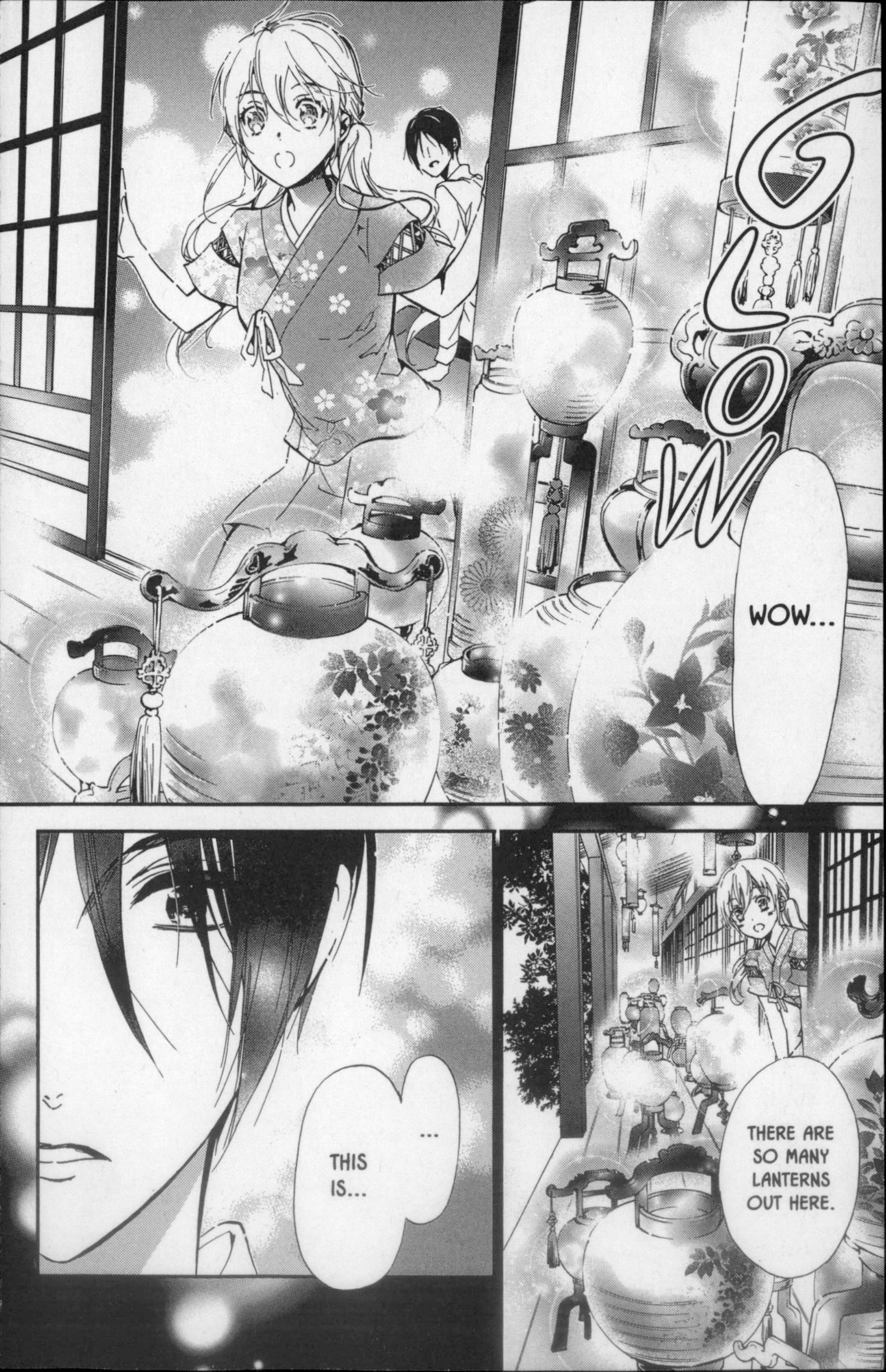
GLOW
WOW...
THERE ARE SO MANY LANTERNS OUT HERE.
...
THIS IS...

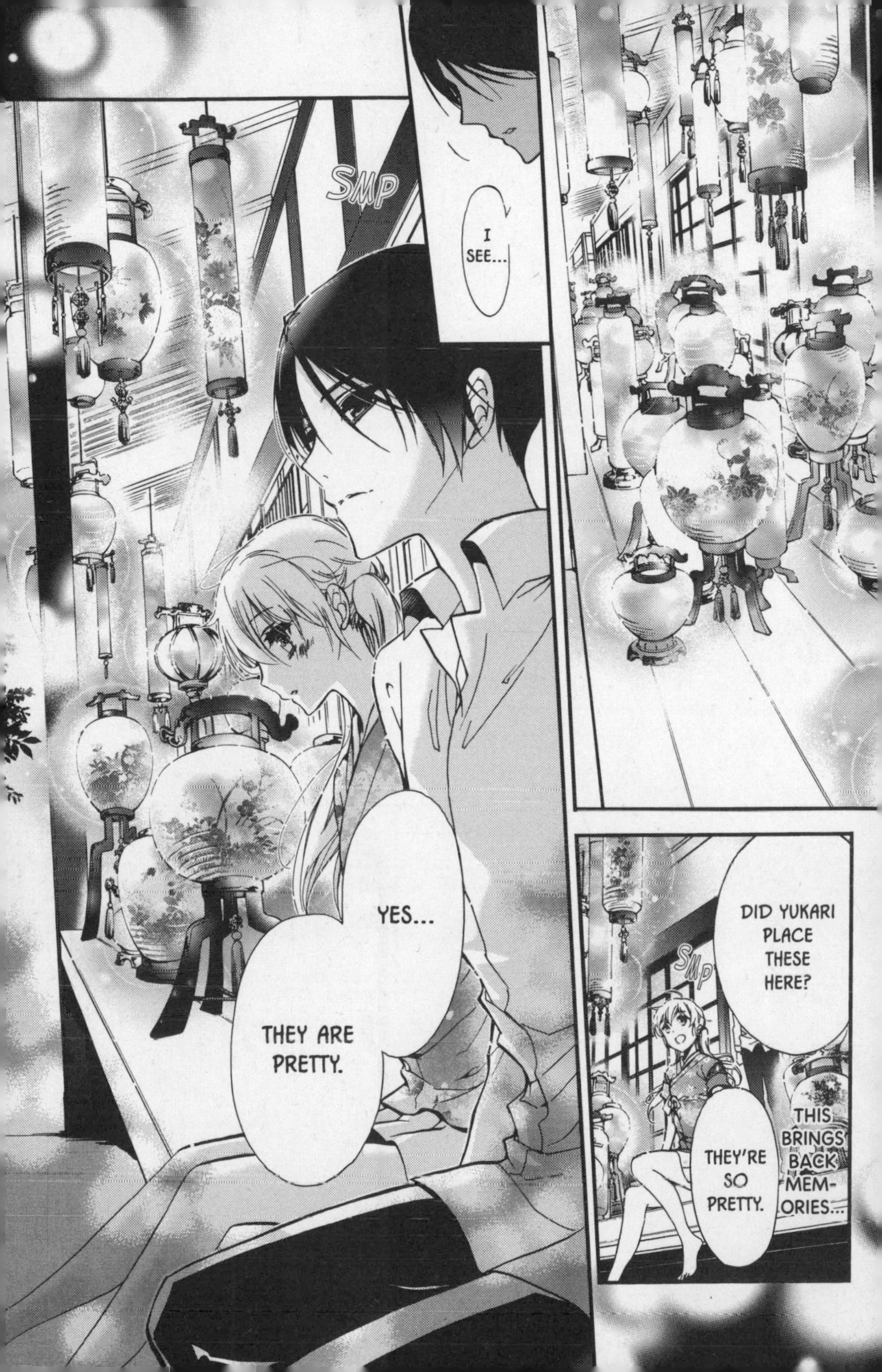
DID YUKARI PLACE THESE HERE?
SMP
THIS BRINGS BACK MEM- ORIES...
THEY'RE SO PRETTY.
SMP
I SEE...
YES...
THEY ARE PRETTY.

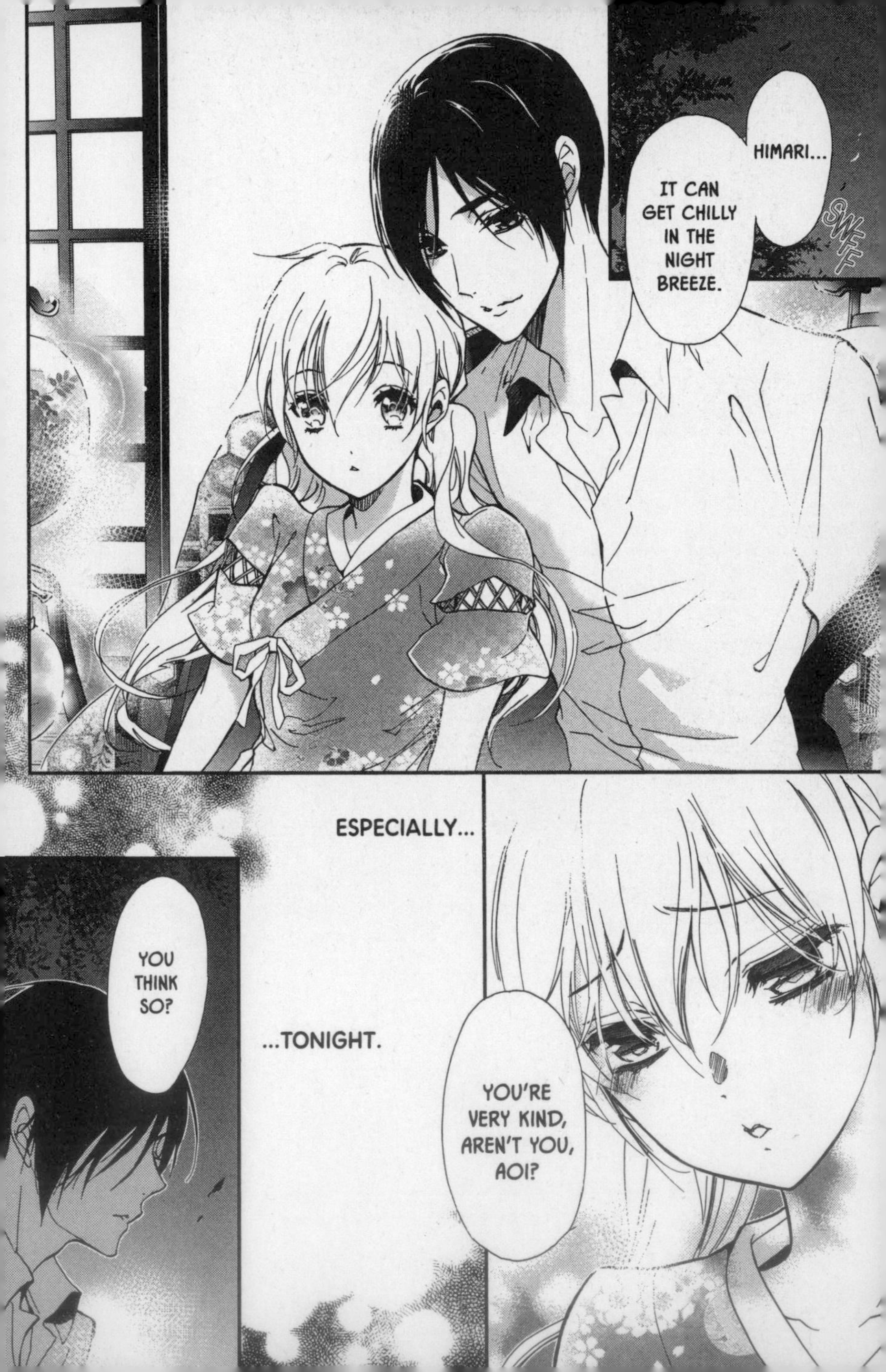
HIMARI...
SWFF
IT CAN GET CHILLY IN THE NIGHT BREEZE.
ESPECIALLY...
YOU'RE VERY KIND, AREN'T YOU, AOI?
...TONIGHT.
YOU THINK SO?

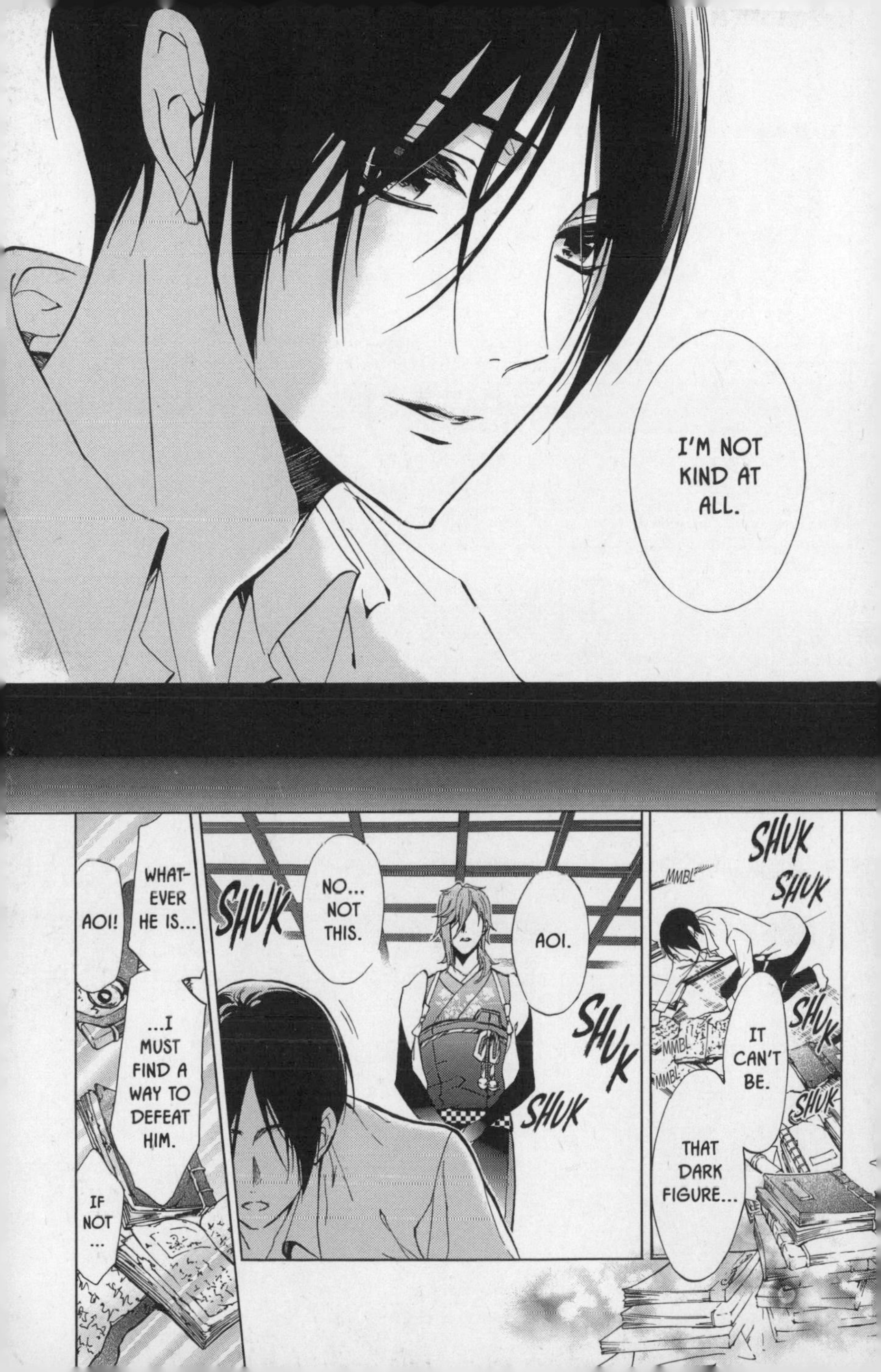
I'M NOT KIND AT ALL.
SHUK
MMBL
SHUK
IT CAN'T BE.
THAT DARK FIGURE...
MMBL
MMBL
SHUK
SHUK
AOI.
SHUK
SHUK
NO... NOT THIS.
SHUK
WHATEVER HE IS...
...I MUST FIND A WAY TO DEFEAT HIM.
AOI!
IF NOT ...

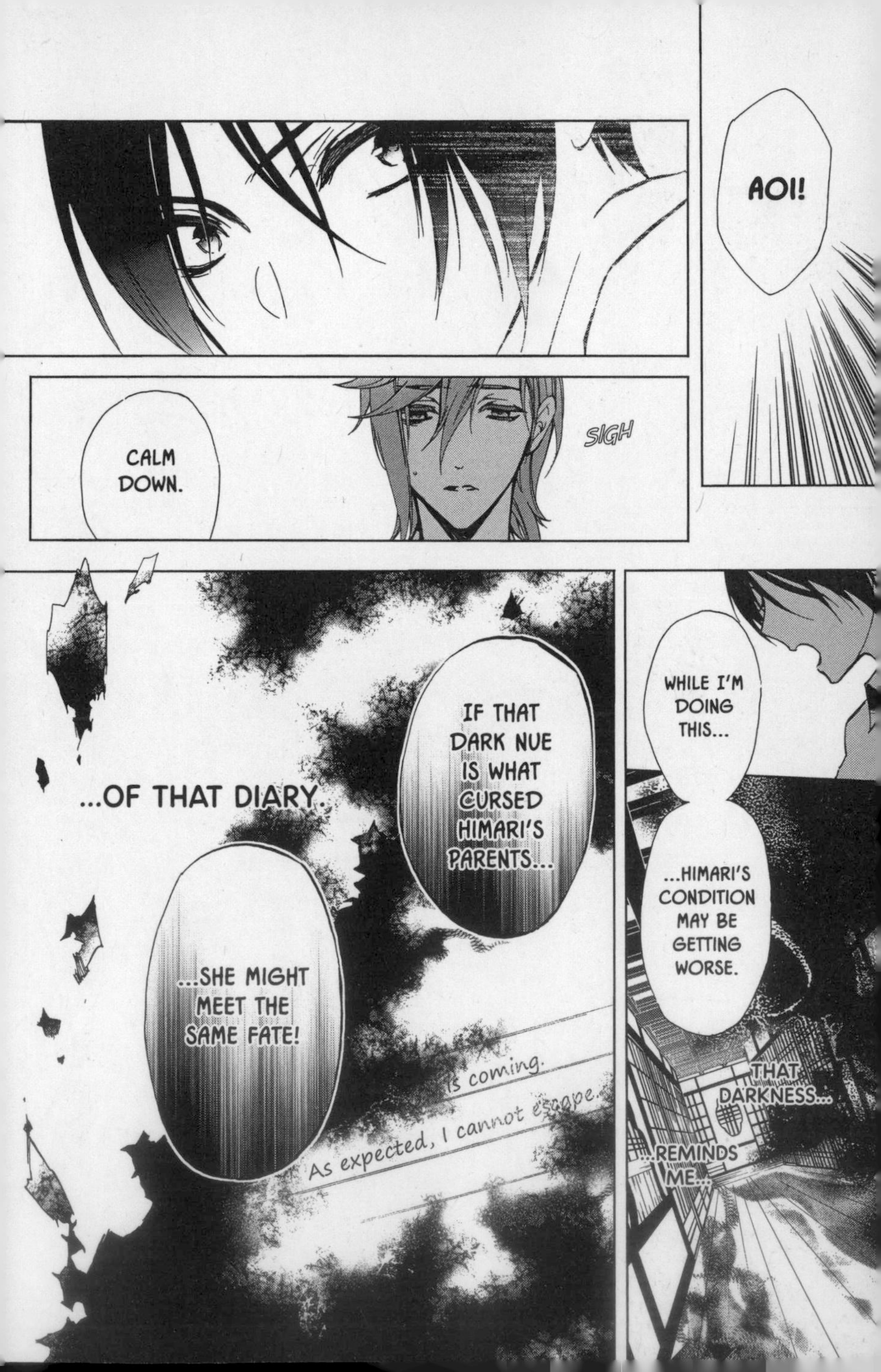
AOI!
SIGH
CALM DOWN.
WHILE I'M DOING THIS...
...HIMARI'S CONDITION MAY BE GETTING WORSE.
THAT DARKNESS...
...REMINDS ME...
...OF THAT DIARY.
IF THAT DARK NUE IS WHAT CURSED HIMARI'S PARENTS...
...SHE MIGHT MEET THE SAME FATE!
As expected, I cannot escape.
is coming.

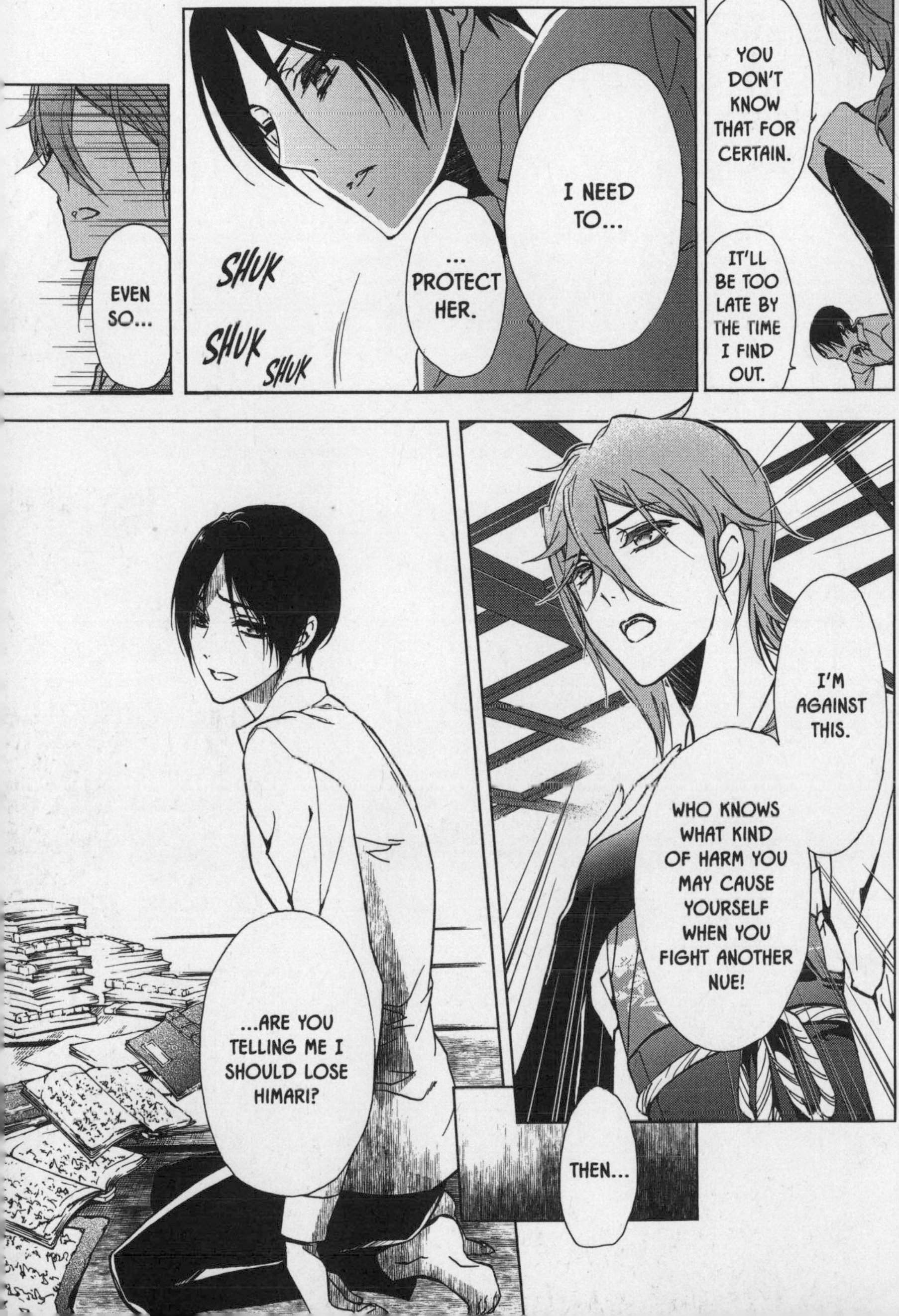
YOU DON'T KNOW THAT FOR CERTAIN.
IT'LL BE TOO LATE BY THE TIME I FIND OUT.
I NEED TO...
... PROTECT HER.
SHUK
SHUK
SHUK
EVEN SO...
I'M AGAINST THIS.
WHO KNOWS WHAT KIND OF HARM YOU MAY CAUSE YOURSELF WHEN YOU FIGHT ANOTHER NUE!
THEN...
...ARE YOU TELLING ME I SHOULD LOSE HIMARI?

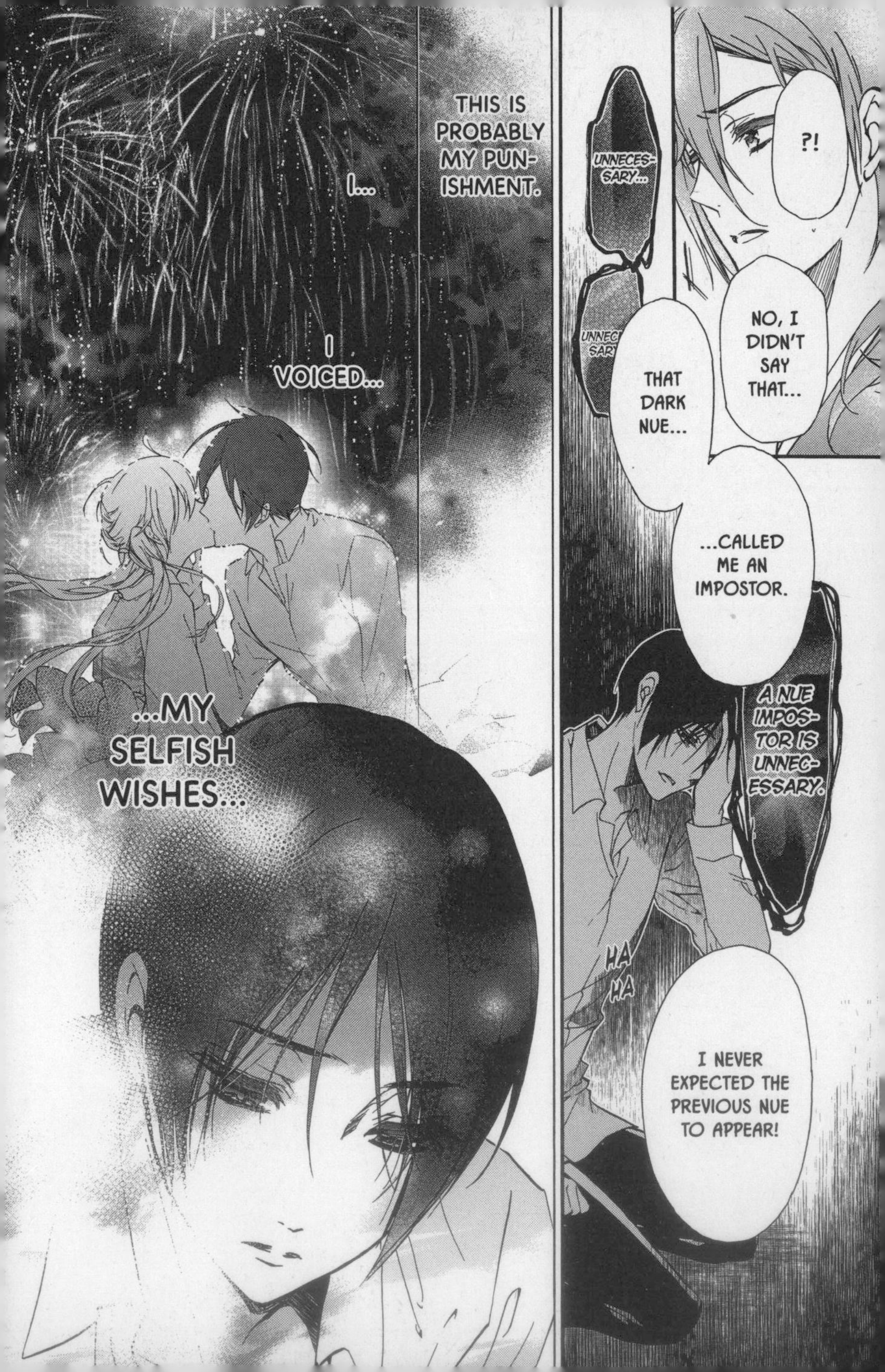
?!
UNNECES-SARY...
NO, I DIDN'T SAY THAT...
THAT DARK NUE...
...CALLED ME AN IMPOSTOR.
A NUE IMPOS-TOR IS UNNEC-ESSARY.
HA HA
I NEVER EXPECTED THE PREVIOUS NUE TO APPEAR!
THIS IS PROBABLY MY PUN-ISHMENT.
I...
I VOICED...
...MY SELFISH WISHES...

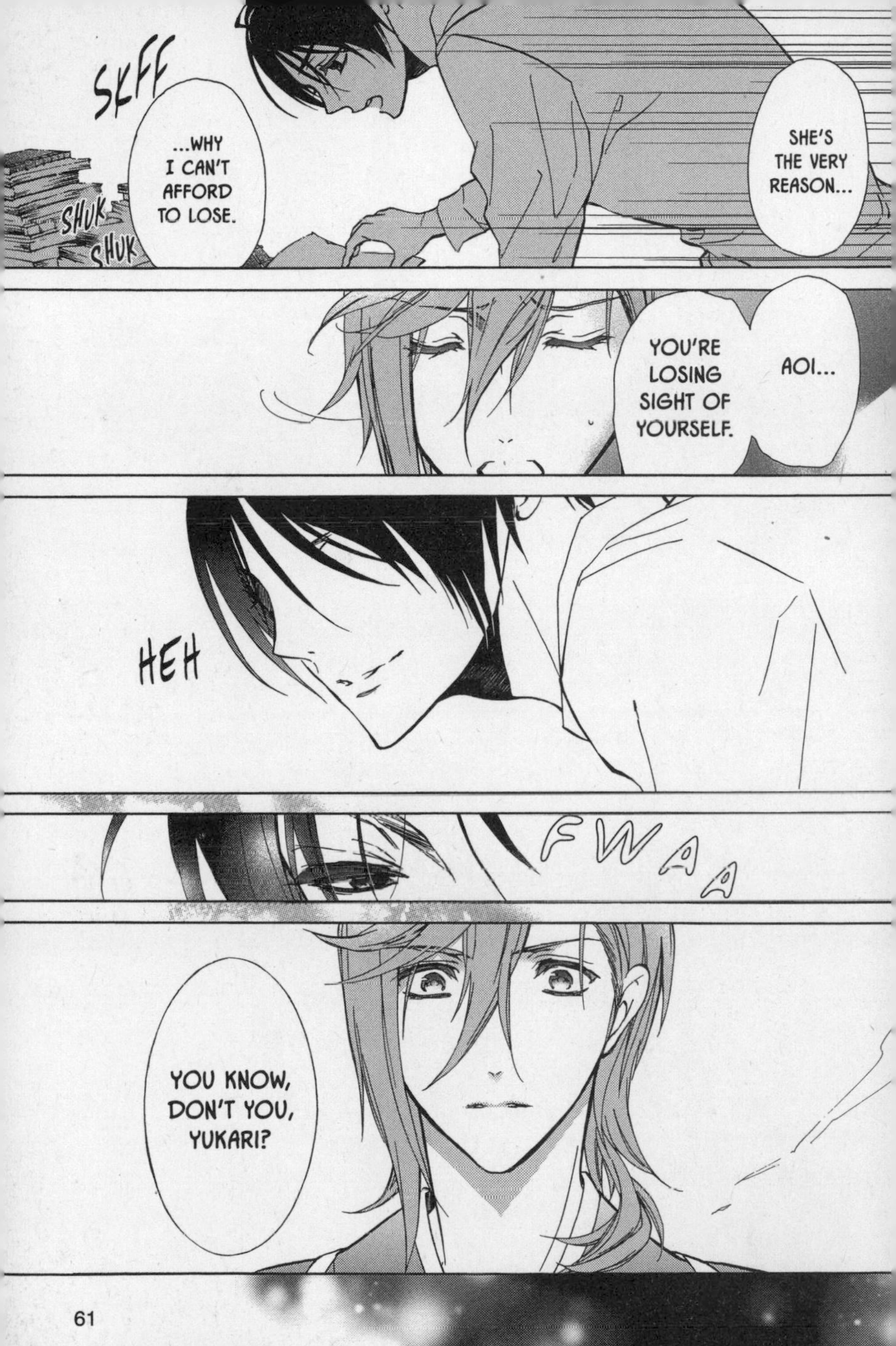
SHE'S THE VERY REASON...
...WHY I CAN'T AFFORD TO LOSE.
SKFF
SHUK SHUK
AOI...
YOU'RE LOSING SIGHT OF YOURSELF.
HEH
FWAA
YOU KNOW, DON'T YOU, YUKARI?

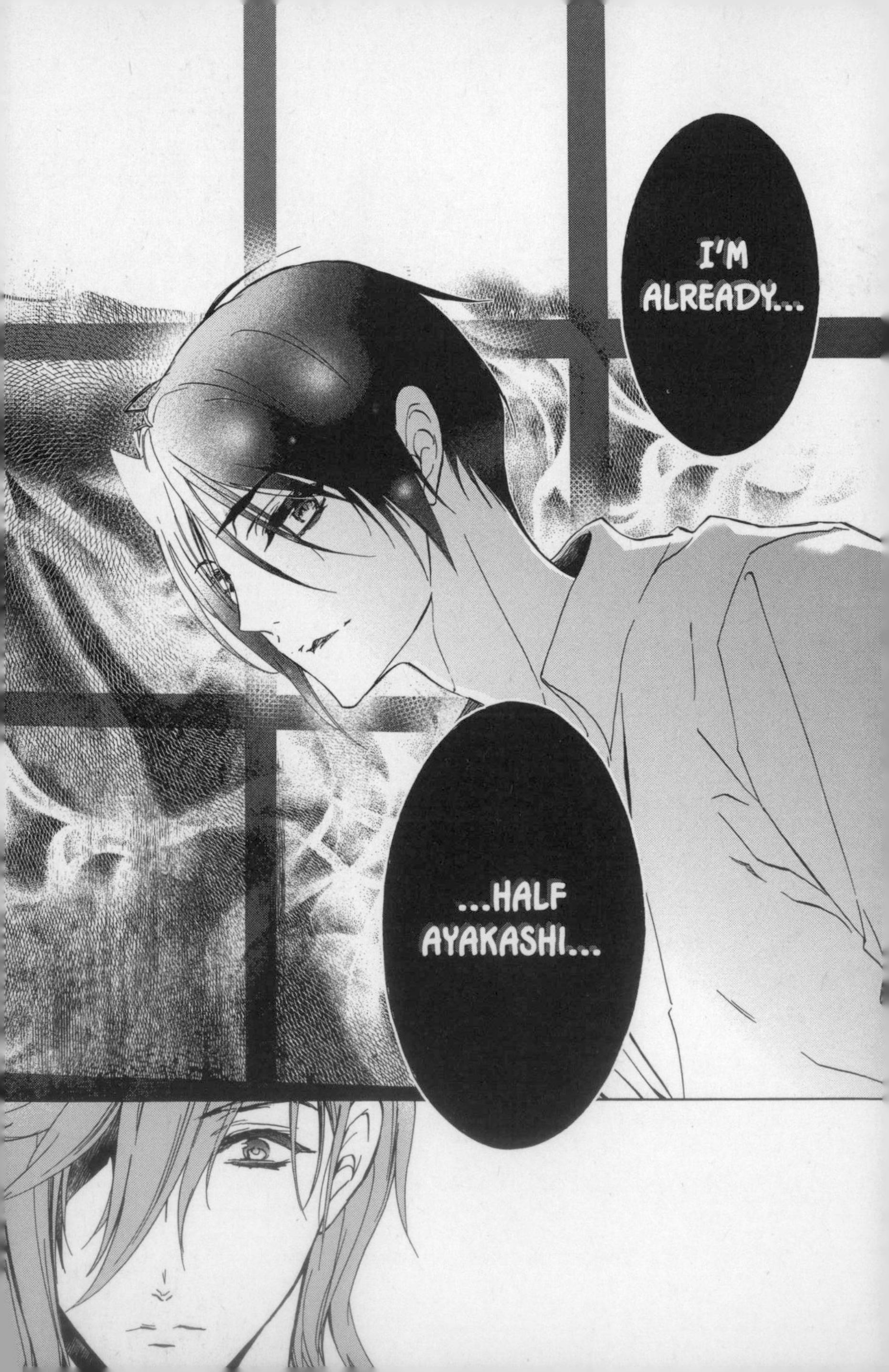
I'M ALREADY...
...HALF AYAKASHI...

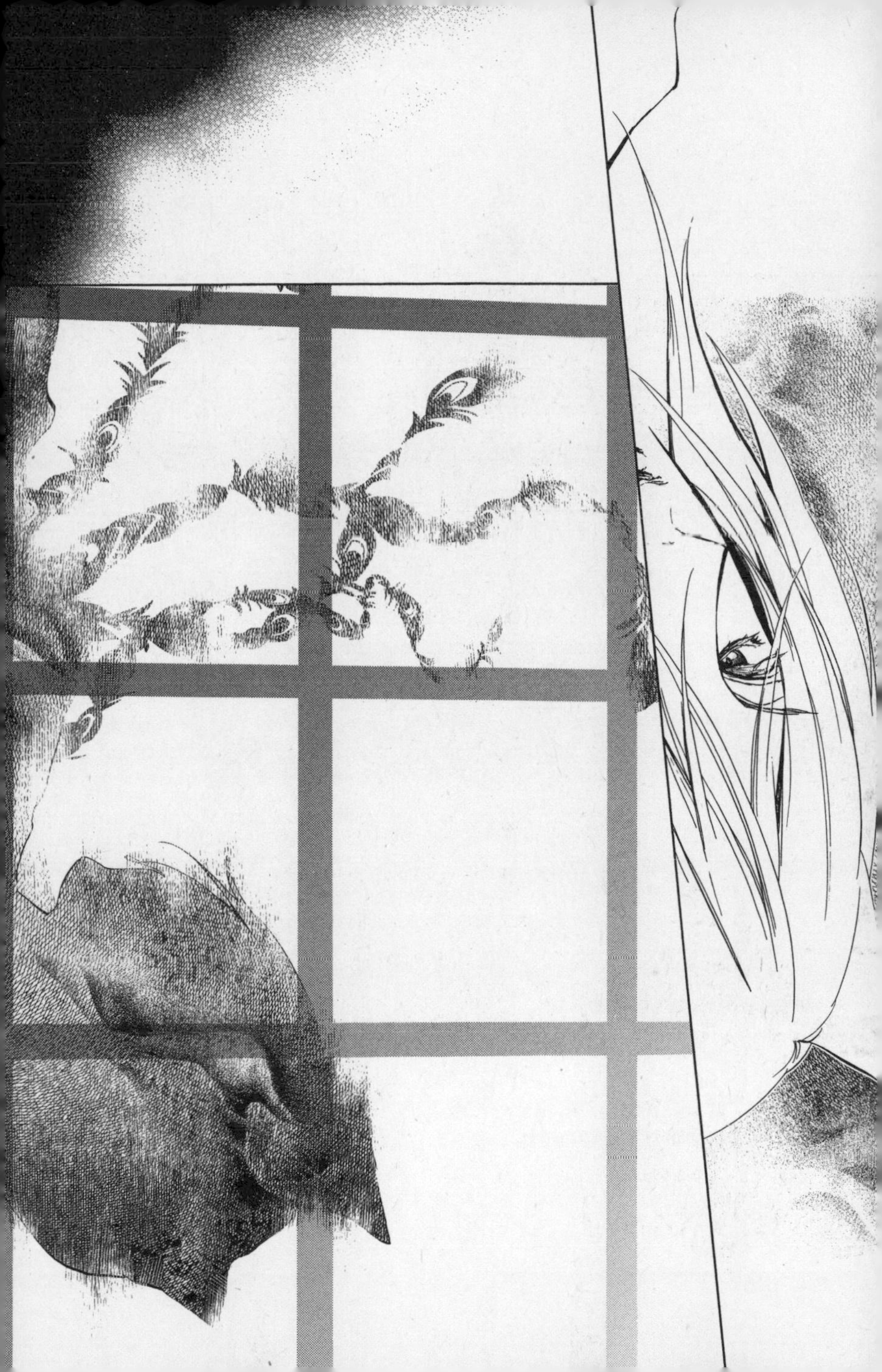

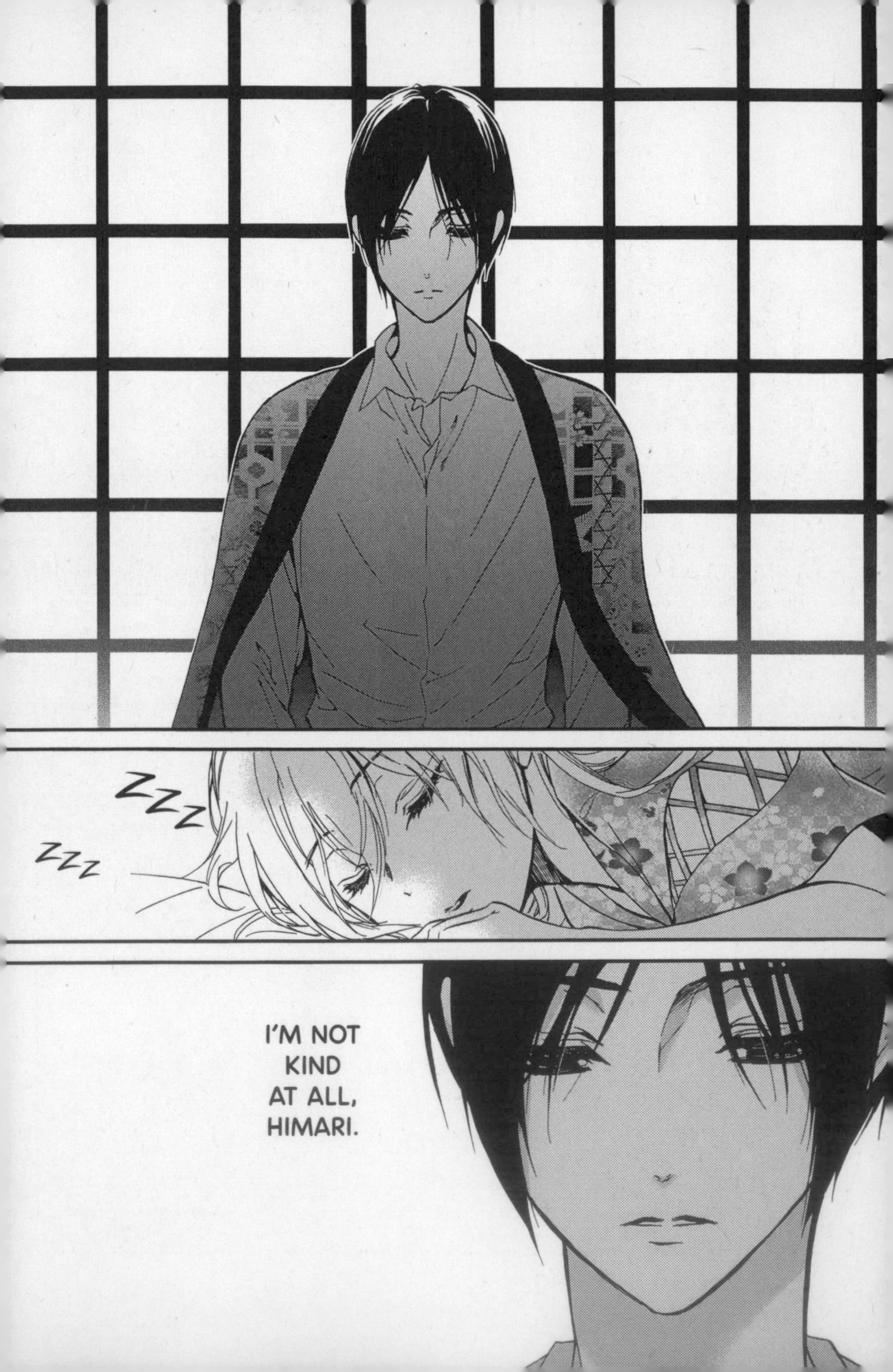
ZZZ
ZZZ
I'M NOT KIND AT ALL, HIMARI.

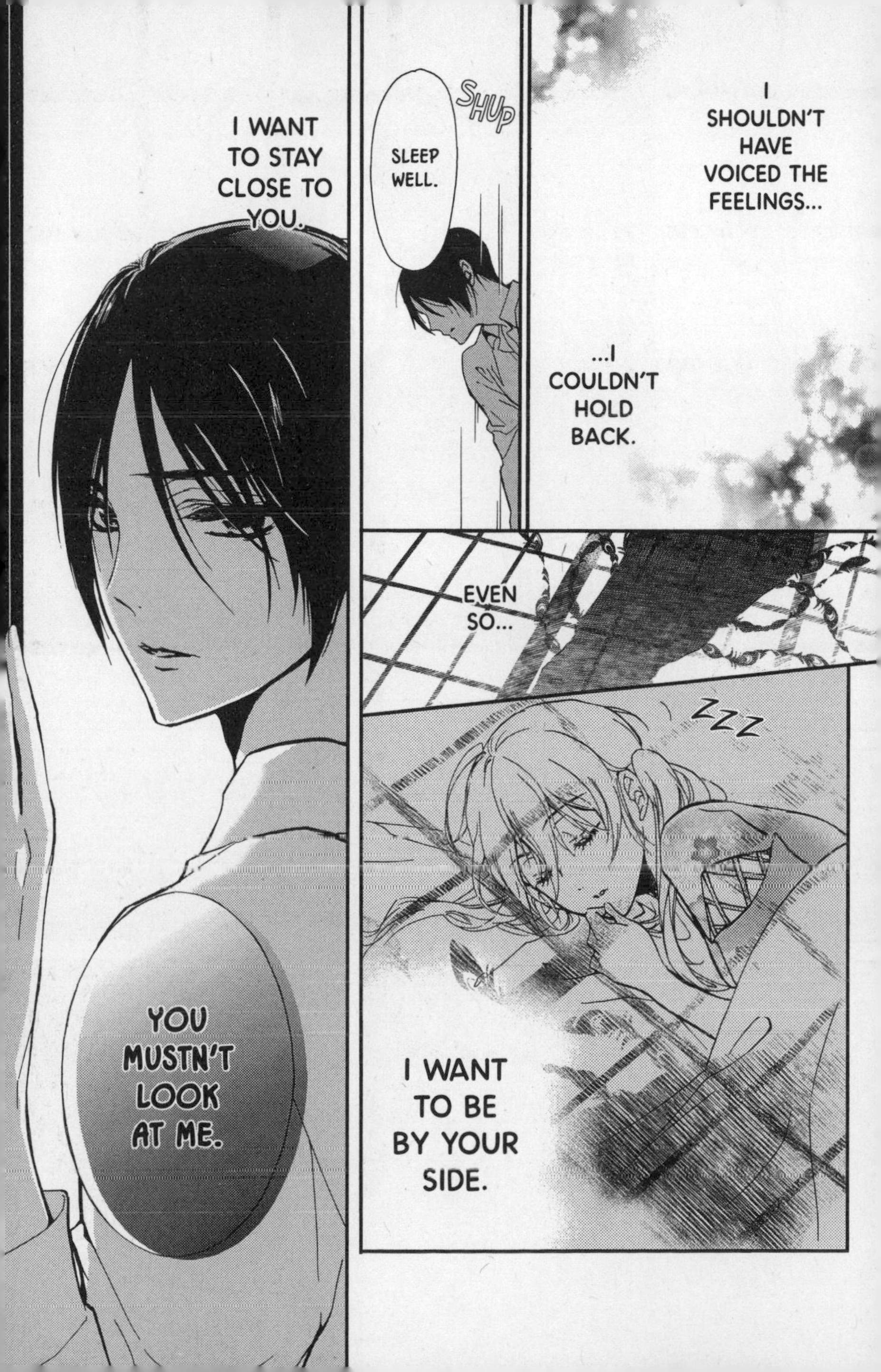
I SHOULDN'T HAVE VOICED THE FEELINGS...
...I COULDN'T HOLD BACK.
SHUP
SLEEP WELL.
EVEN SO...
ZZZ
I WANT TO BE BY YOUR SIDE.
I WANT TO STAY CLOSE TO YOU.
YOU MUSTN'T LOOK AT ME.

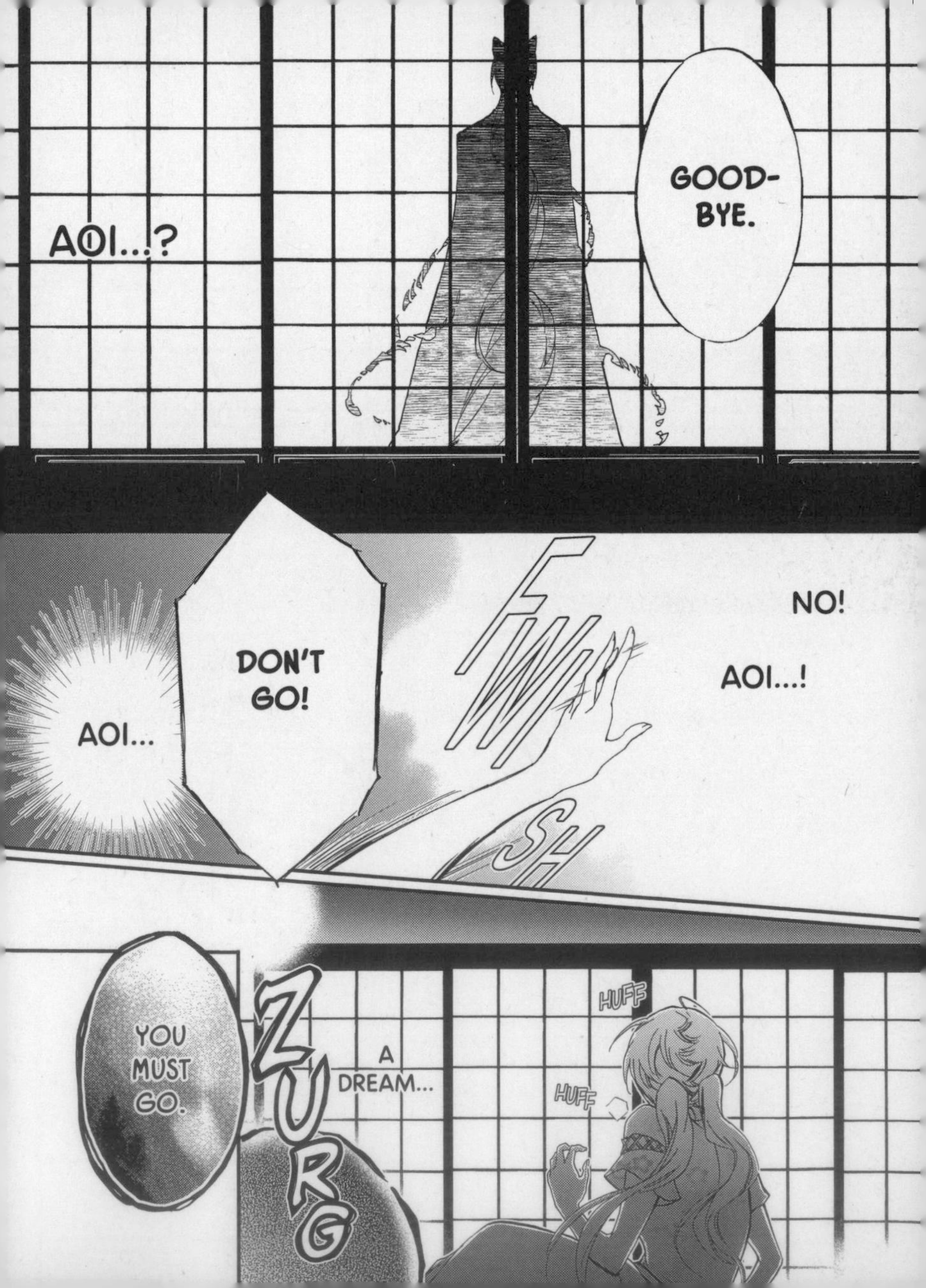
GOOD-BYE.
AOI...?
NO!
AOI...!
FWISH
DON'T GO!
AOI...
HUFF
HUFF
A DREAM...
ZURG
YOU MUST GO.

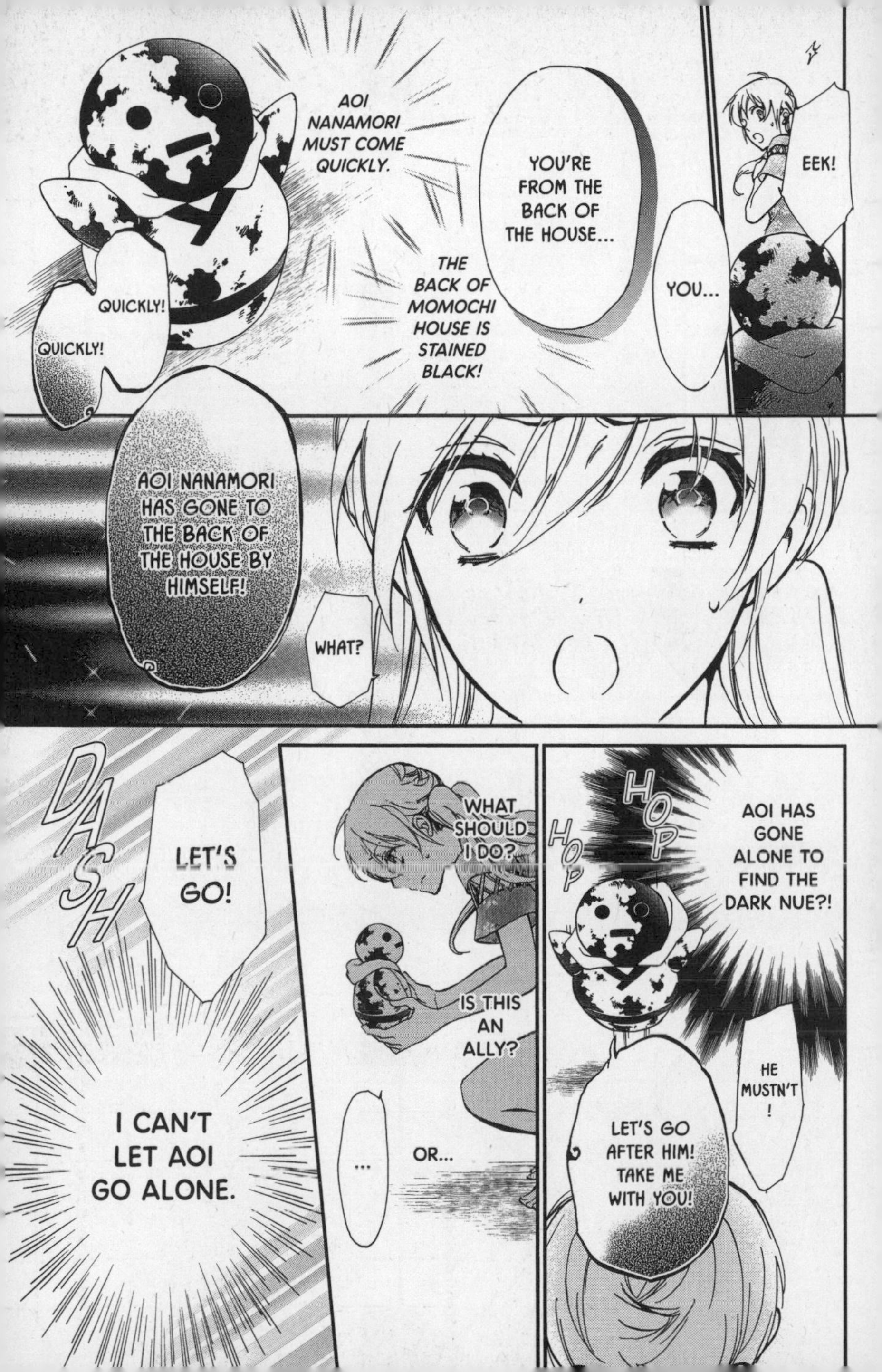
EEK!
YOU...
YOU'RE FROM THE BACK OF THE HOUSE...
THE BACK OF MOMOCHI HOUSE IS STAINED BLACK!
AOI NANAMORI MUST COME QUICKLY.
QUICKLY!
QUICKLY!
AOI NANAMORI HAS GONE TO THE BACK OF THE HOUSE BY HIMSELF!
WHAT?
HOP
HOP
AOI HAS GONE ALONE TO FIND THE DARK NUE?!
HE MUSTN'T!
LET'S GO AFTER HIM! TAKE ME WITH YOU!
WHAT SHOULD I DO?
IS THIS AN ALLY?
OR...
...
DASH
LET'S GO!
I CAN'T LET AOI GO ALONE.

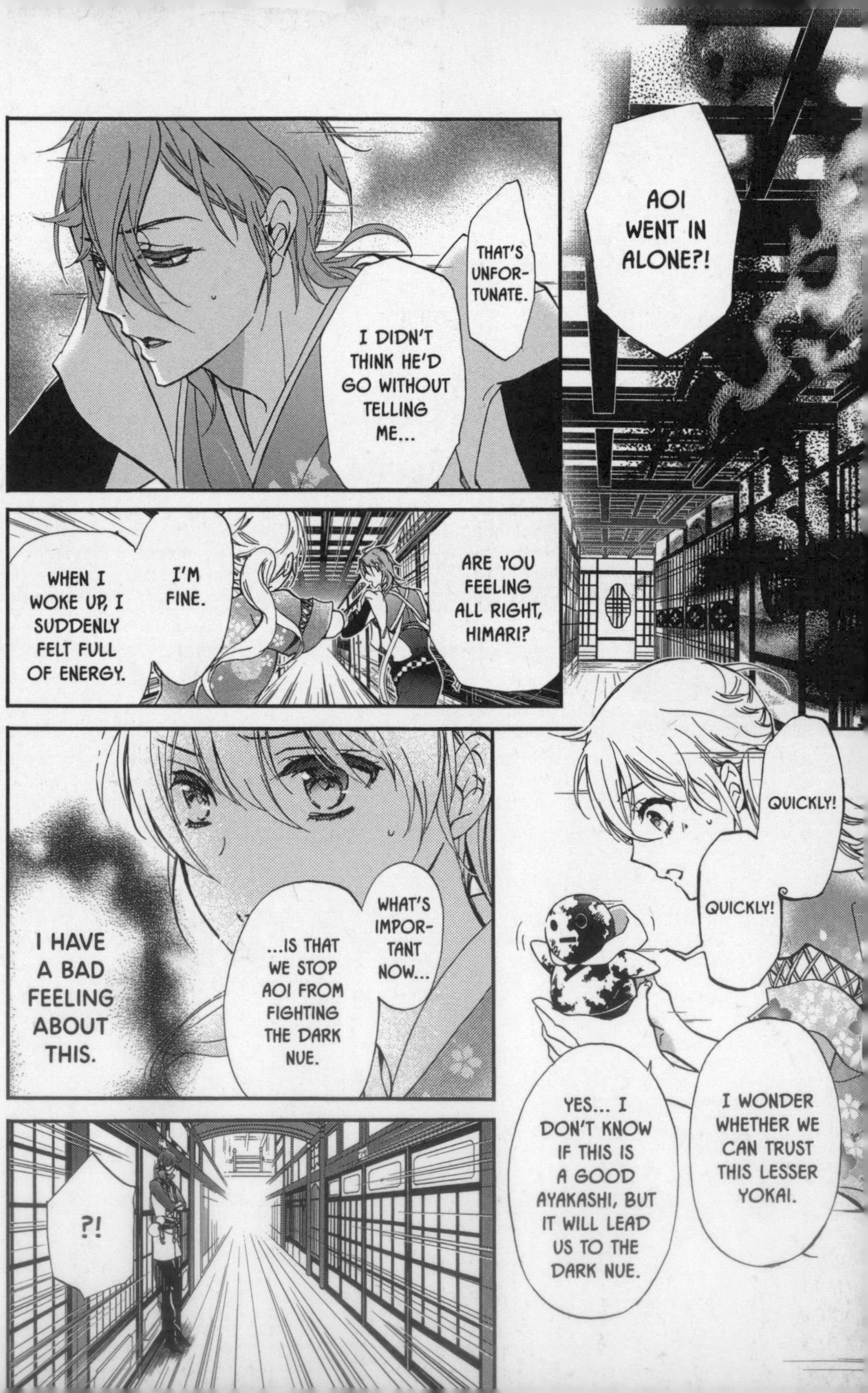
AOI WENT IN ALONE?!
THAT'S UNFOR-TUNATE.
I DIDN'T THINK HE'D GO WITHOUT TELLING ME...
ARE YOU FEELING ALL RIGHT, HIMARI?
I'M FINE.
WHEN I WOKE UP, I SUDDENLY FELT FULL OF ENERGY.
WHAT'S IMPOR-TANT NOW...
...IS THAT WE STOP AOI FROM FIGHTING THE DARK NUE.
I HAVE A BAD FEELING ABOUT THIS.
QUICKLY!
QUICKLY!
I WONDER WHETHER WE CAN TRUST THIS LESSER YOKAI.
YES... I DON'T KNOW IF THIS IS A GOOD AYAKASHI, BUT IT WILL LEAD US TO THE DARK NUE.
?!

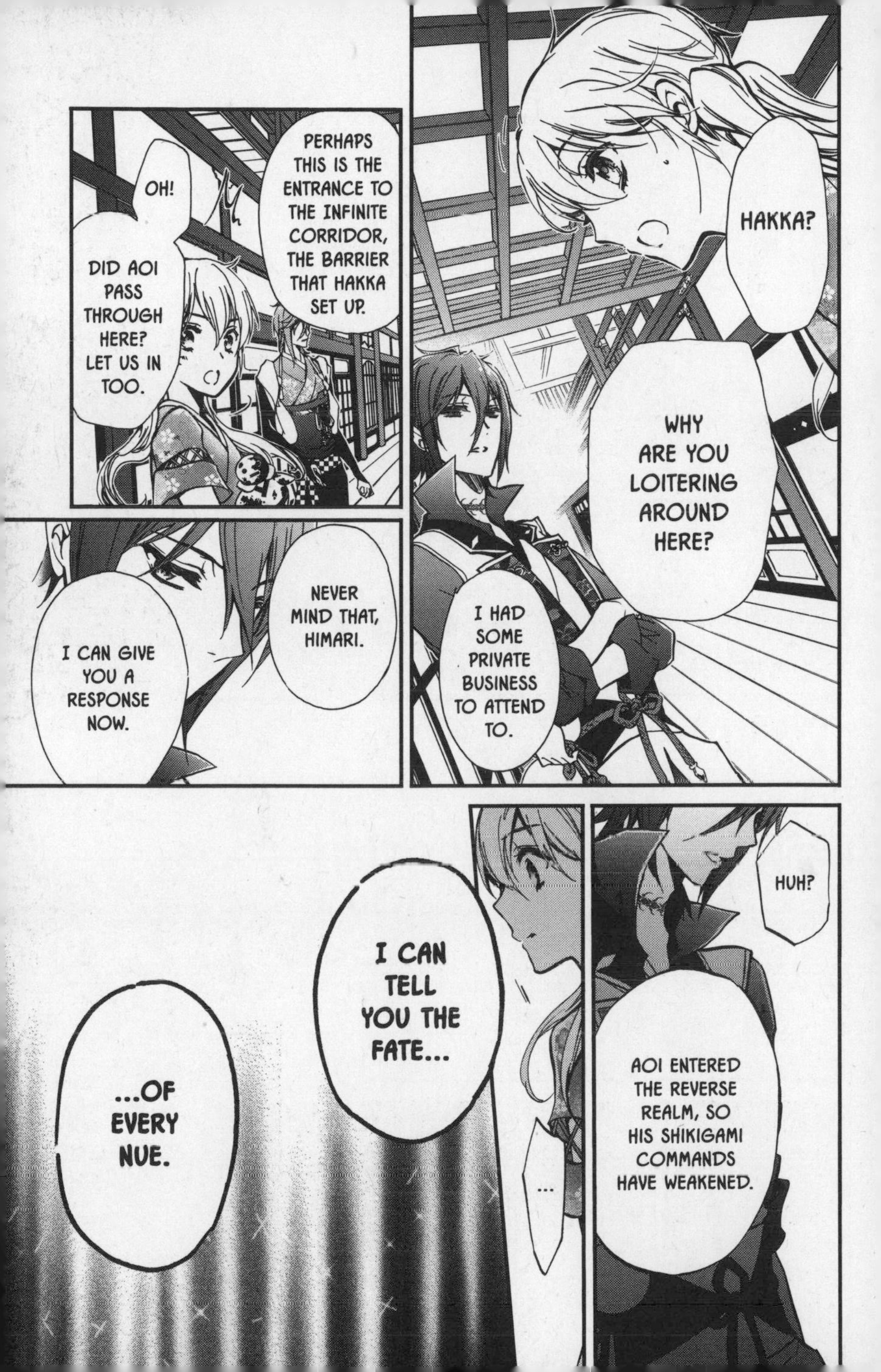
HAKKA?
WHY ARE YOU LOITERING AROUND HERE?
I HAD SOME PRIVATE BUSINESS TO ATTEND TO.
OH!
DID AOI PASS THROUGH HERE? LET US IN TOO.
PERHAPS THIS IS THE ENTRANCE TO THE INFINITE CORRIDOR, THE BARRIER THAT HAKKA SET UP.
NEVER MIND THAT, HIMARI.
I CAN GIVE YOU A RESPONSE NOW.
HUH?
AOI ENTERED THE REVERSE REALM, SO HIS SHIKIGAMI COMMANDS HAVE WEAKENED.
...
I CAN TELL YOU THE FATE...
...OF EVERY NUE.

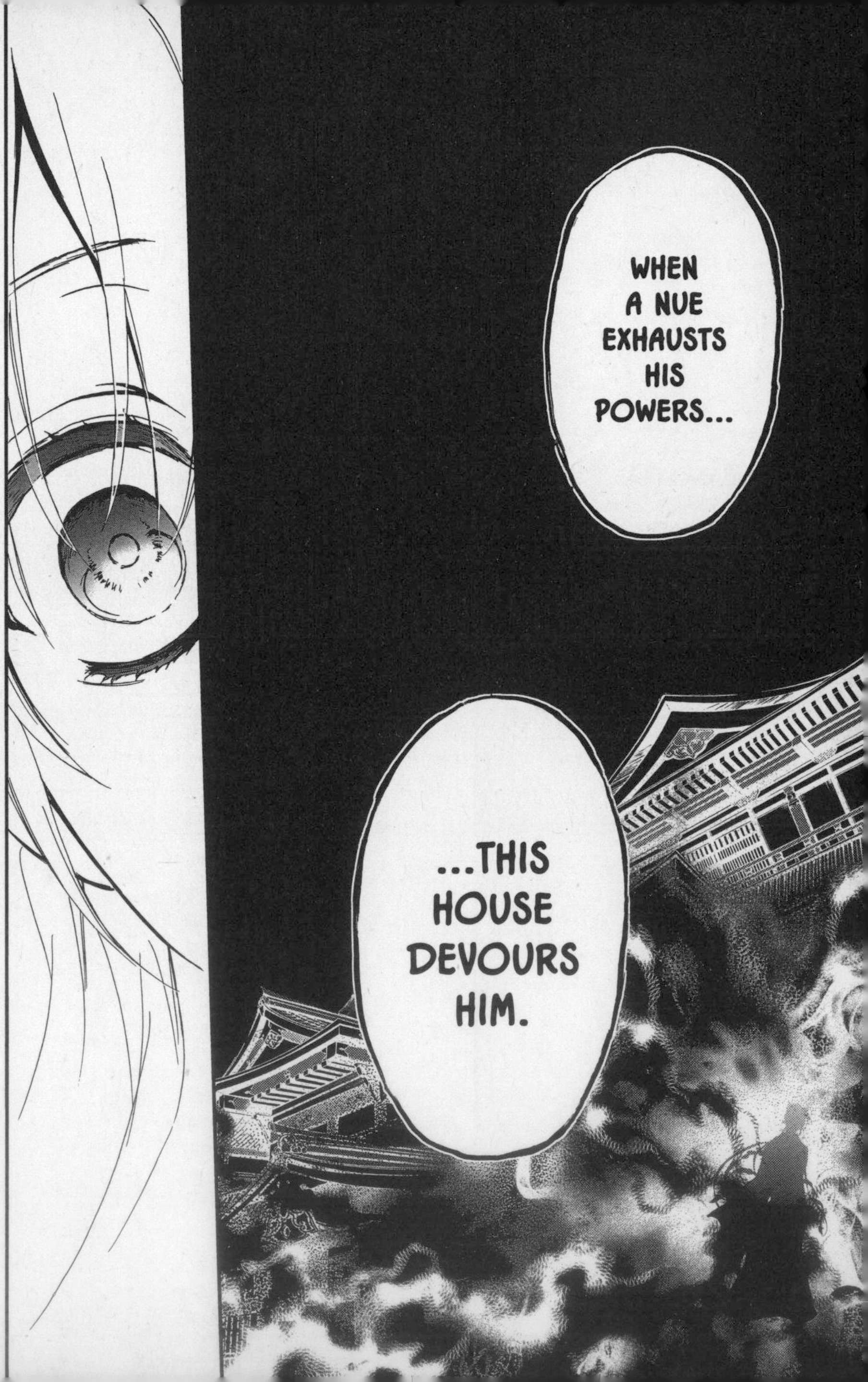
WHEN A NUE EXHAUSTS HIS POWERS...
...THIS HOUSE DEVOURS HIM.

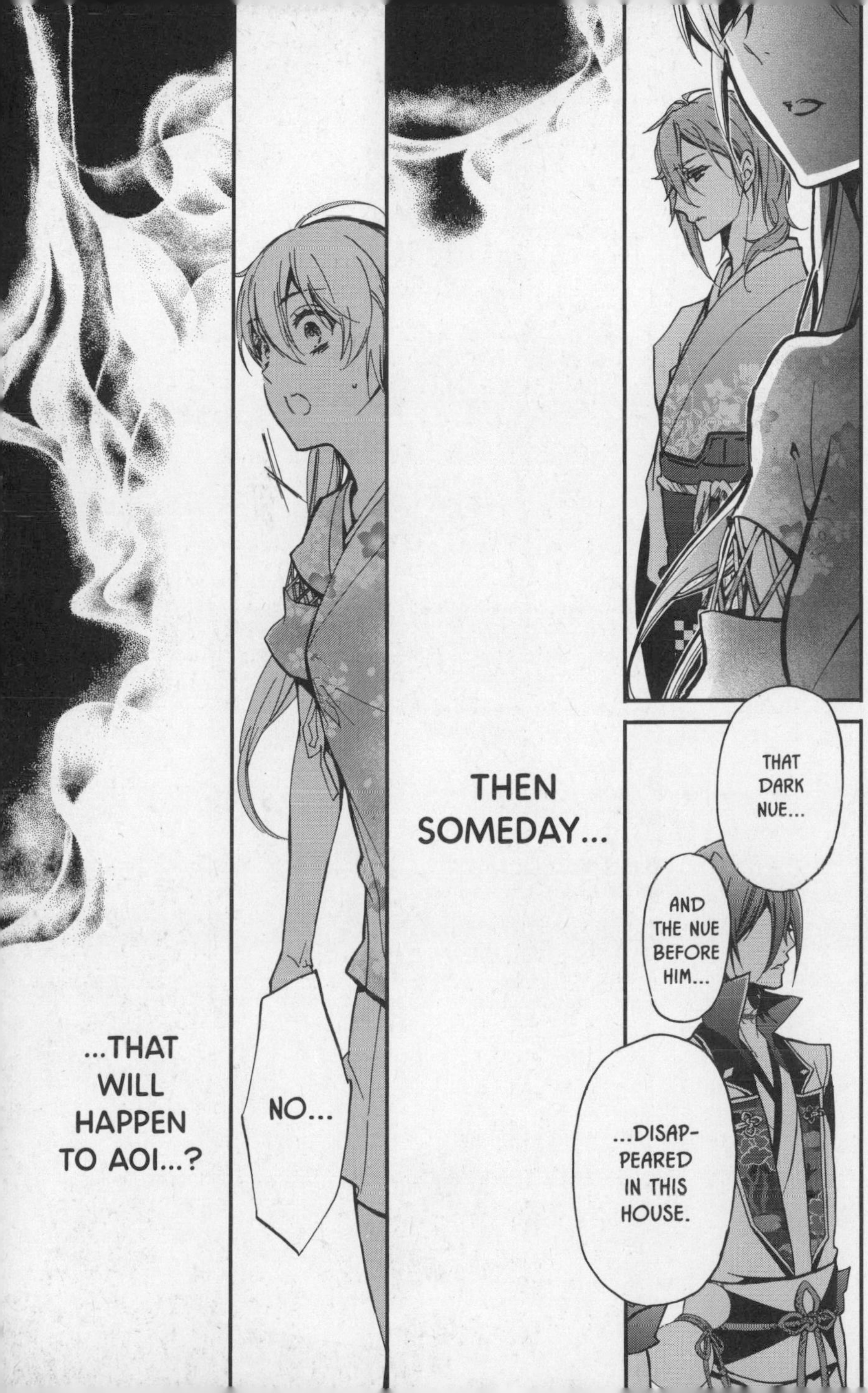
THAT DARK NUE...
AND THE NUE BEFORE HIM...
...DISAP-PEARED IN THIS HOUSE.
THEN SOMEDAY...
NO...
...THAT WILL HAPPEN TO AOI...?

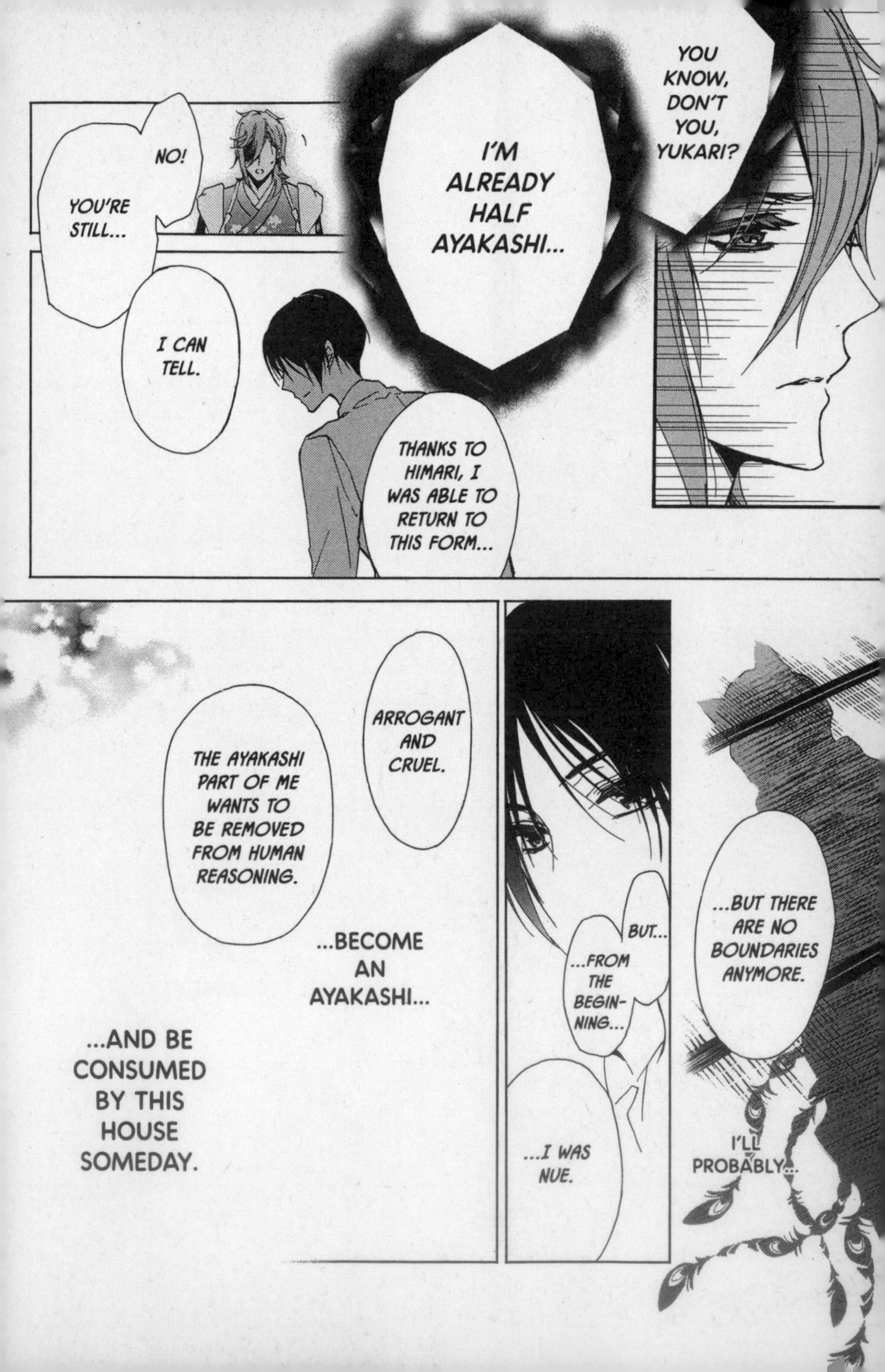
YOU KNOW, DON'T YOU, YUKARI?
I'M ALREADY HALF AYAKASHI...
NO!
YOU'RE STILL...
I CAN TELL.
THANKS TO HIMARI, I WAS ABLE TO RETURN TO THIS FORM...
...BUT THERE ARE NO BOUNDARIES ANYMORE.
I'LL PROBABLY...
BUT...
...FROM THE BEGIN-NING...
...I WAS NUE.
ARROGANT AND CRUEL.
THE AYAKASHI PART OF ME WANTS TO BE REMOVED FROM HUMAN REASONING.
...BECOME AN AYAKASHI...
...AND BE CONSUMED BY THIS HOUSE SOMEDAY.

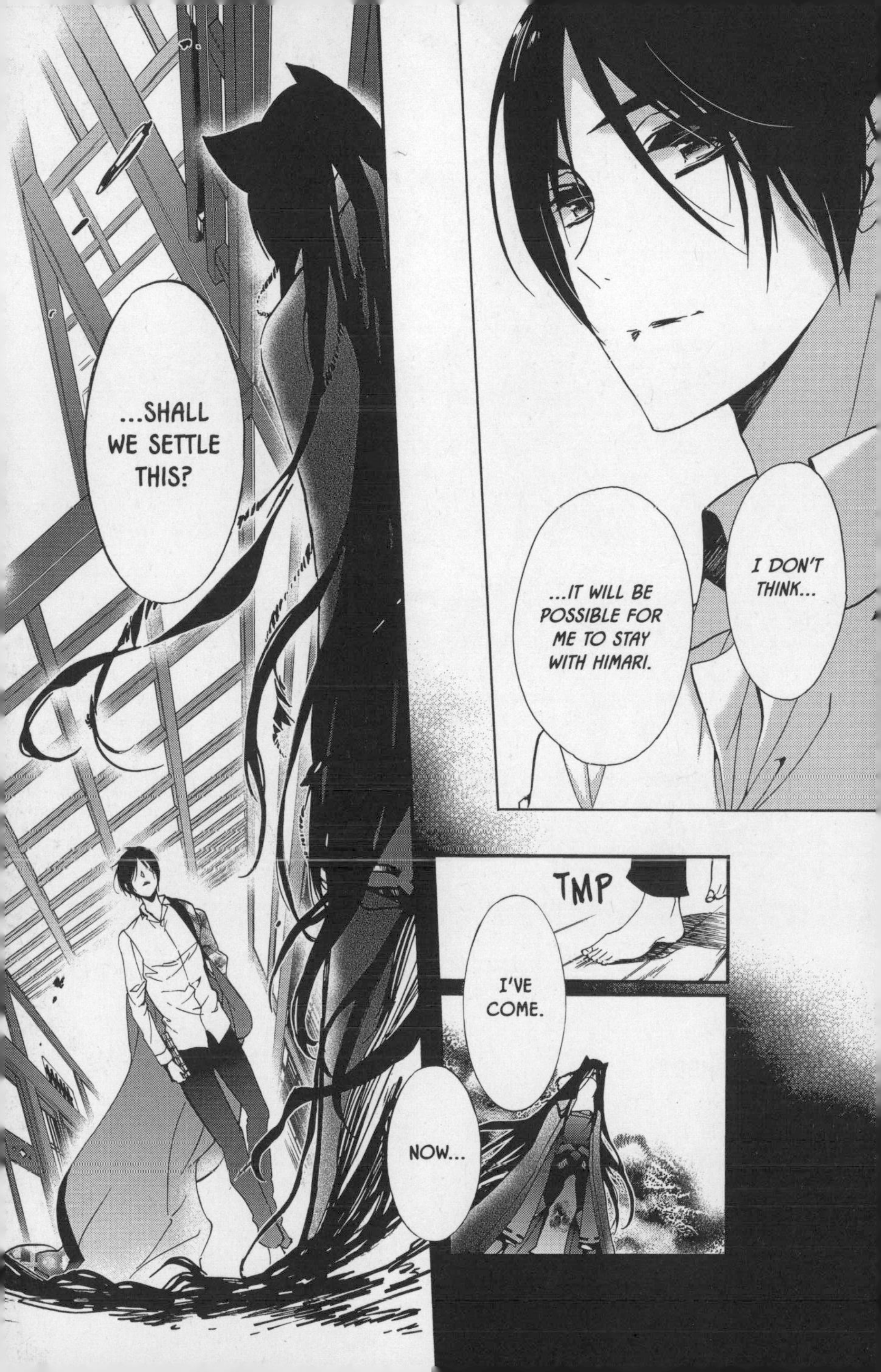
I DON'T THINK...
...IT WILL BE POSSIBLE FOR ME TO STAY WITH HIMARI.
TMP
I'VE COME.
NOW...
...SHALL WE SETTLE THIS?

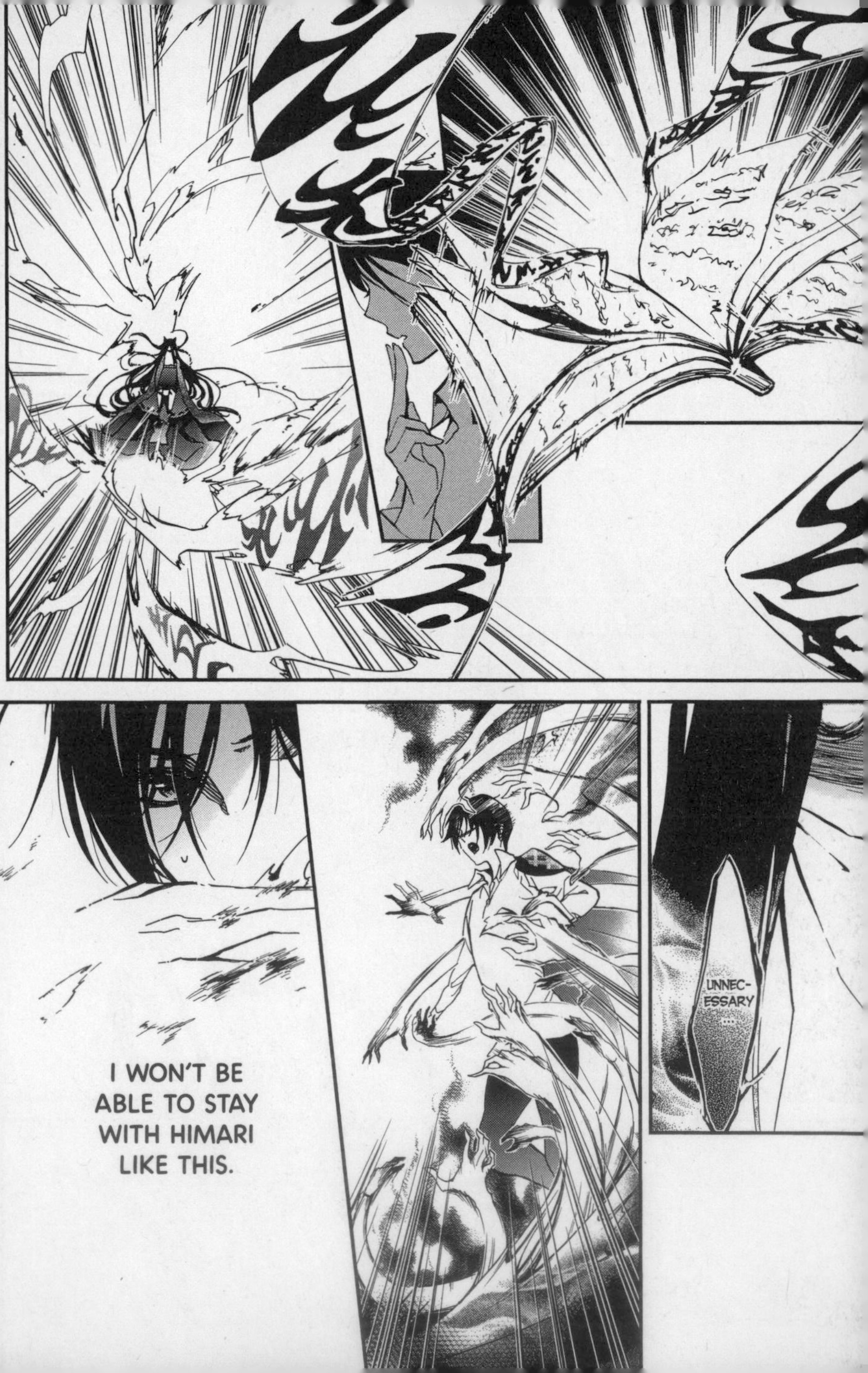
UNNEC-
ESSARY
...
I WON'T BE
ABLE TO STAY
WITH HIMARI
LIKE THIS.

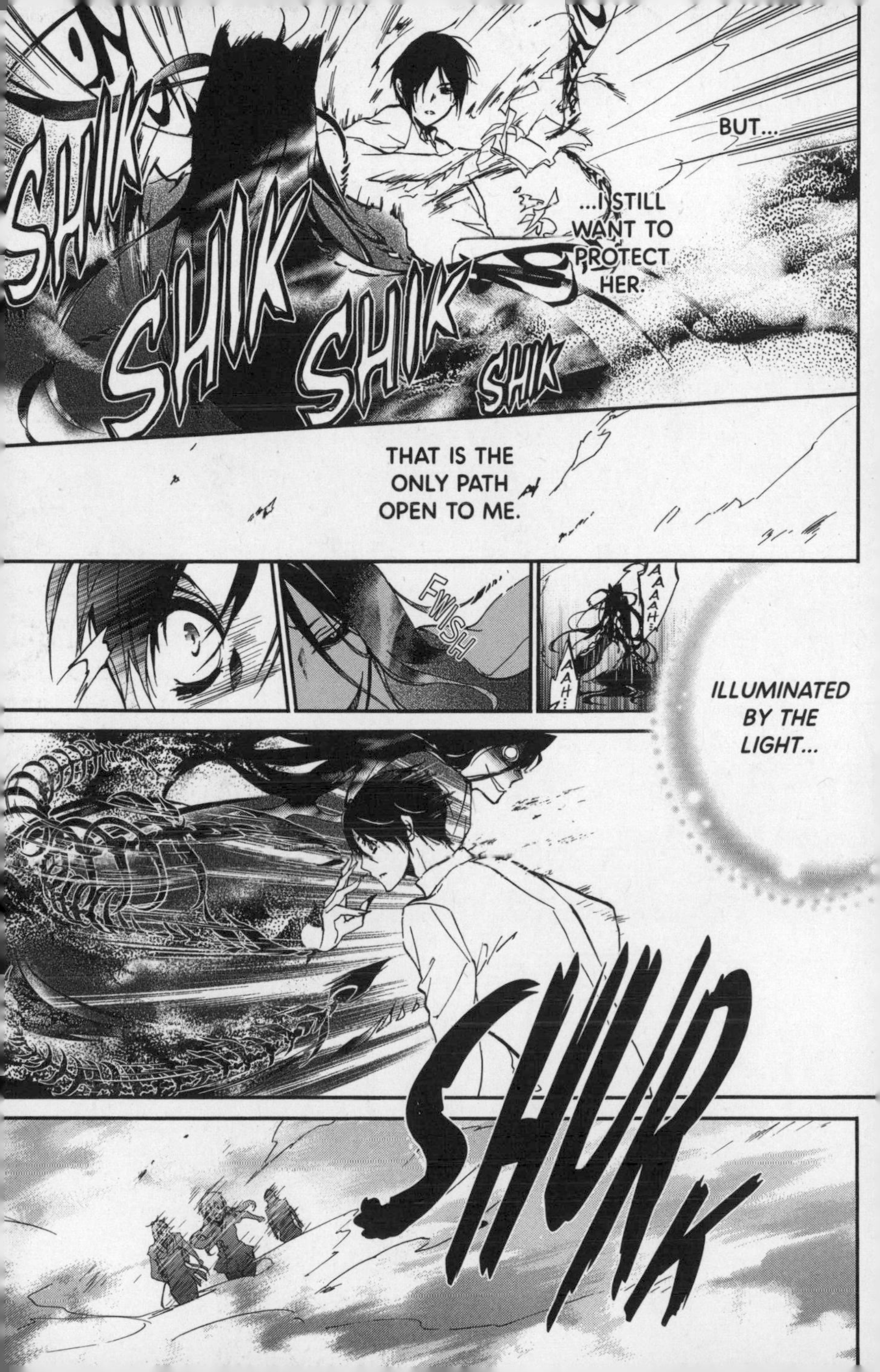
BUT...
...I STILL WANT TO PROTECT HER.
SHIK
SHIK
SHIK
SHIK
THAT IS THE ONLY PATH OPEN TO ME.
AAAAAH...
AAH...
FWISH
ILLUMINATED BY THE LIGHT...
SHUNK

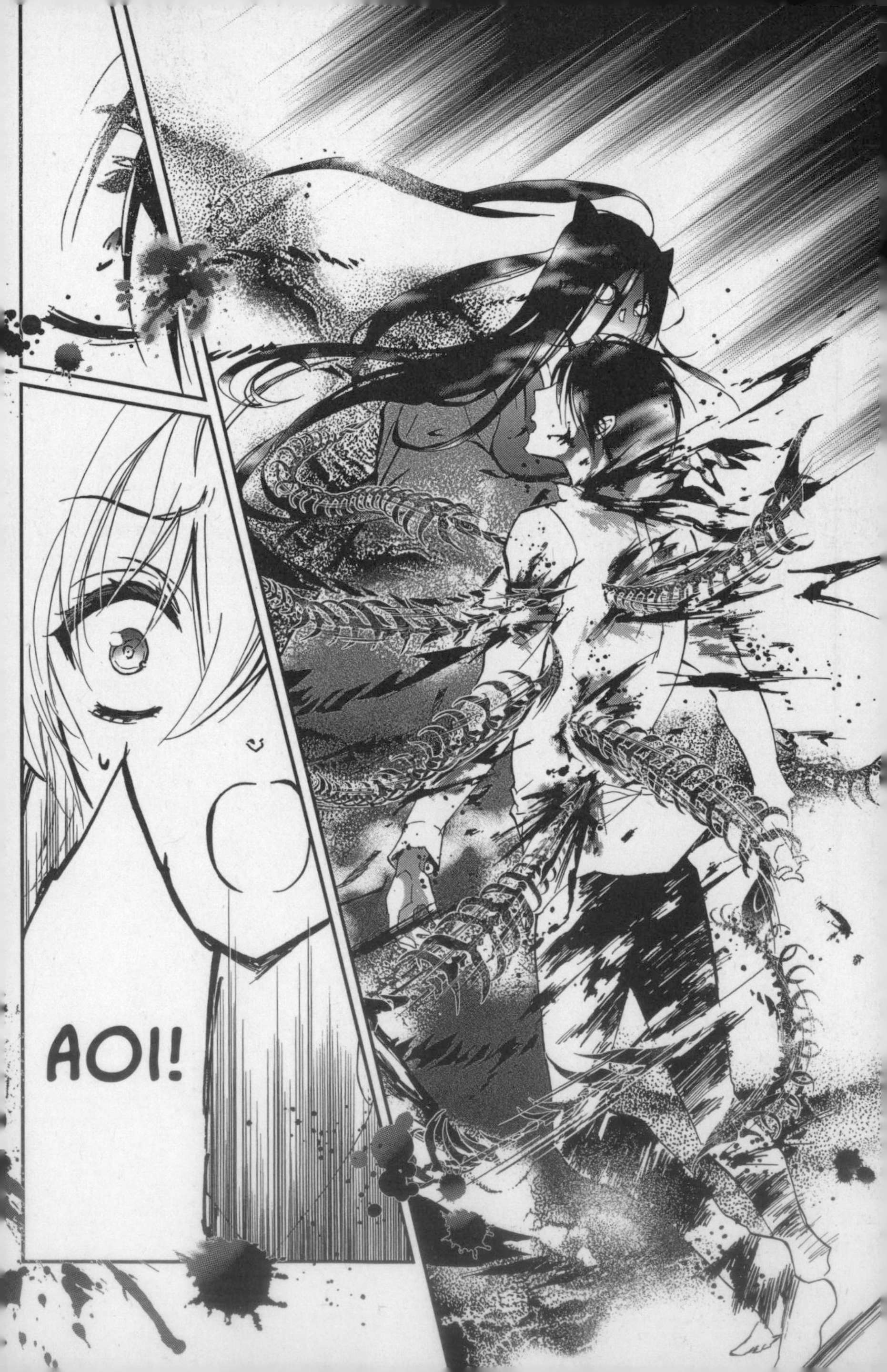
AOI!

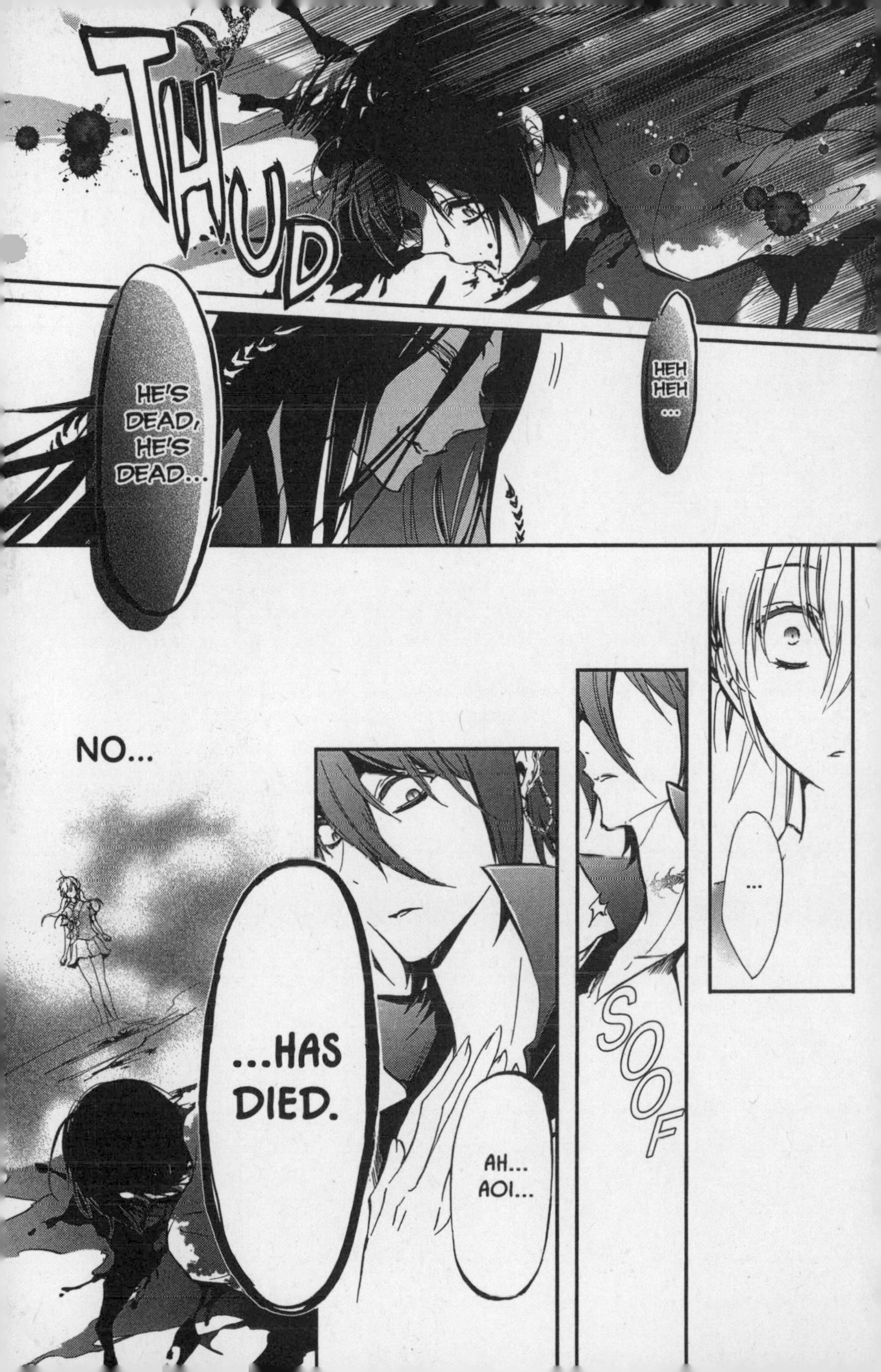
THUD
HEH HEH ...
HE'S DEAD, HE'S DEAD...
...
SOOF
AH... AOI...
...HAS DIED.
NO...

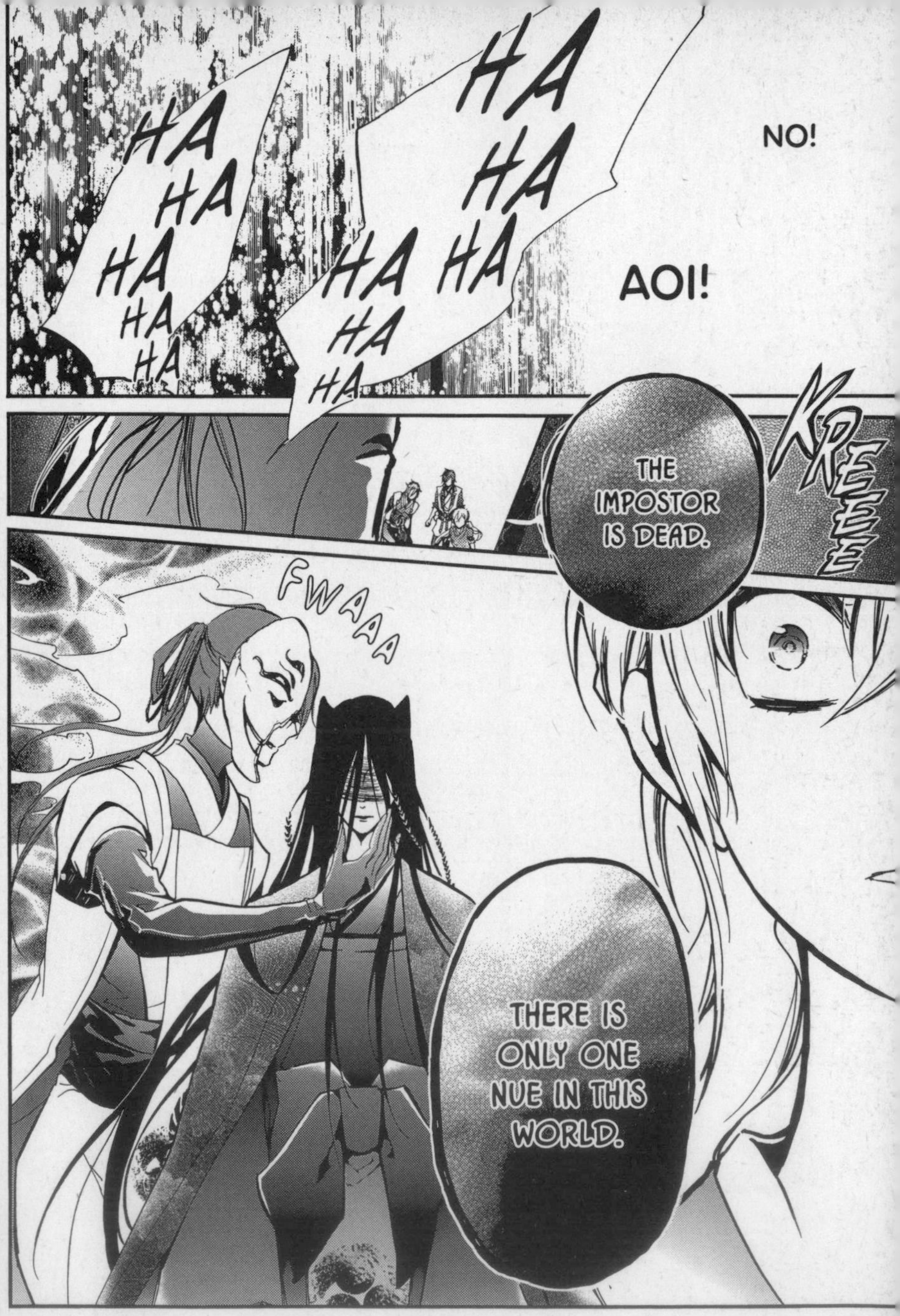
NO!
AOI!
HA HA HA HA HA HA
HA HA HA HA HA
KREEE
THE IMPOSTOR IS DEAD.
FWAAA
THERE IS ONLY ONE NUE IN THIS WORLD.

the DEMON PRINCE PRINCE of MOMOCHI HOUSE

The DEMON PRINCE of MOMOCHI HOUSE

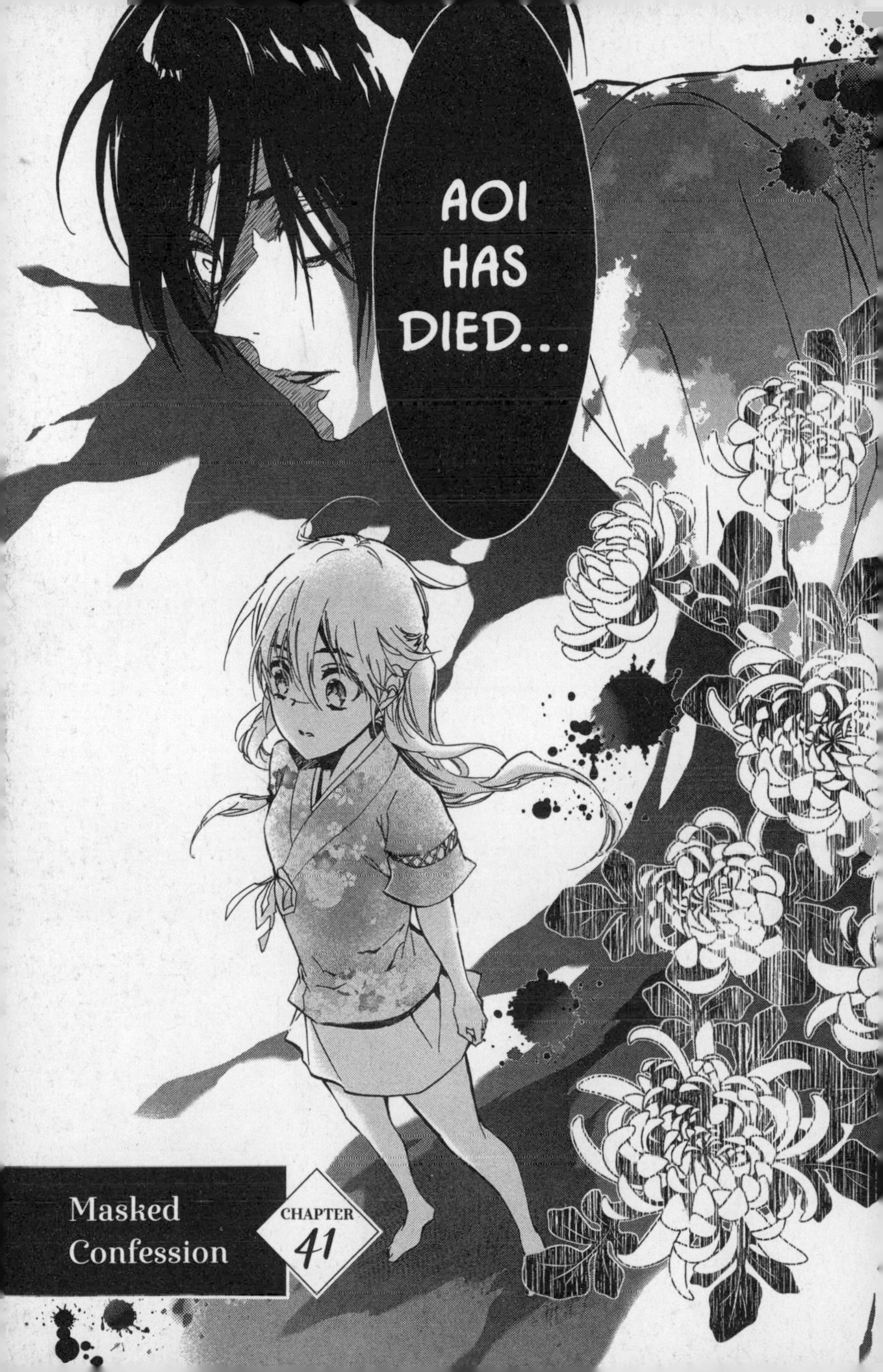
AOI HAS DIED...
CHAPTER 41
Masked Confession

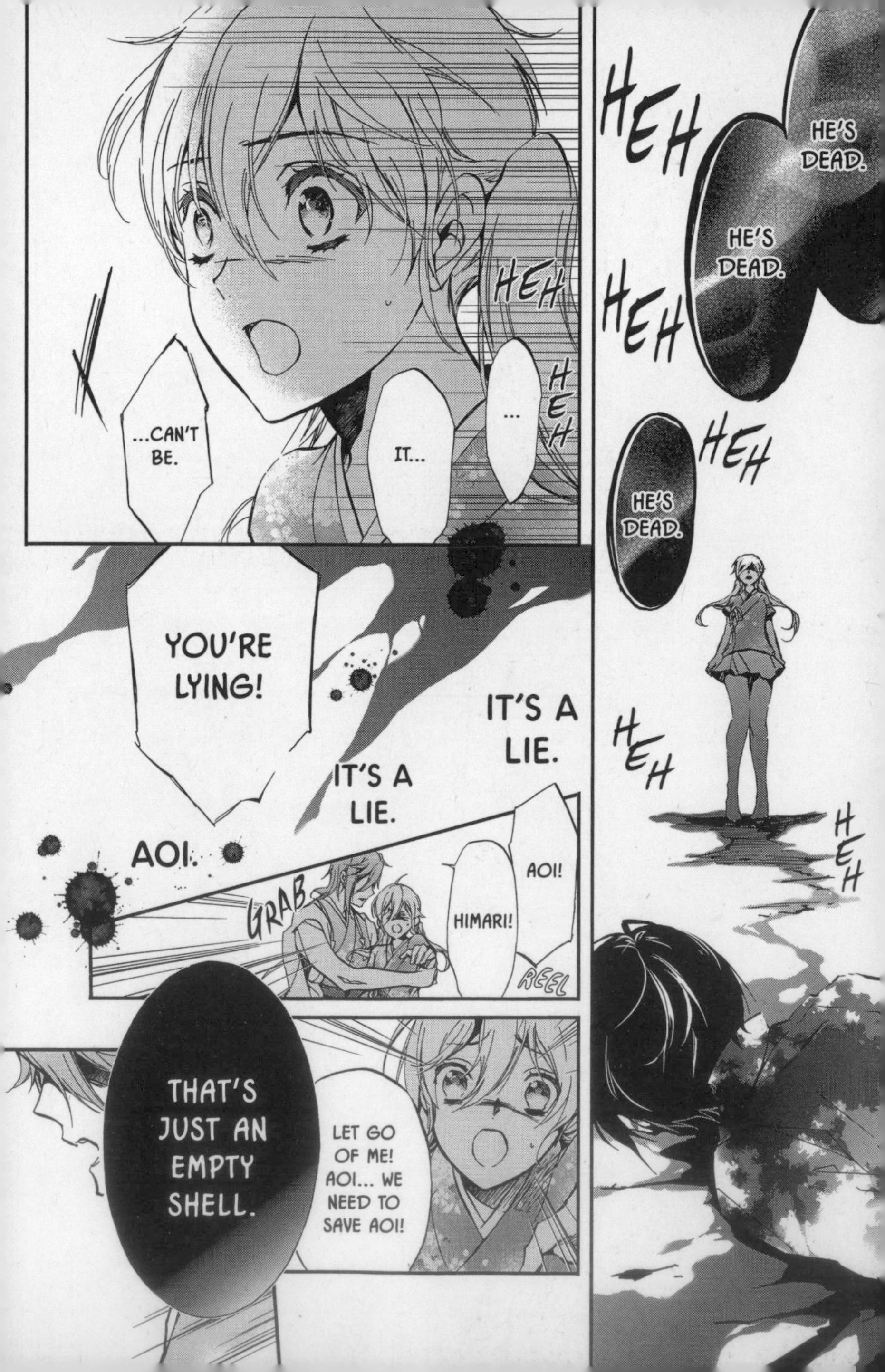
HEH
HE'S DEAD.
HEH
HE'S DEAD.
HEH
HE'S DEAD.
HEH
HEH
HEH
...
IT...
...CAN'T BE.
YOU'RE LYING!
IT'S A LIE.
IT'S A LIE.
AOI.
AOI!
HIMARI!
REEL
GRAB
LET GO OF ME! AOI... WE NEED TO SAVE AOI!
THAT'S JUST AN EMPTY SHELL.

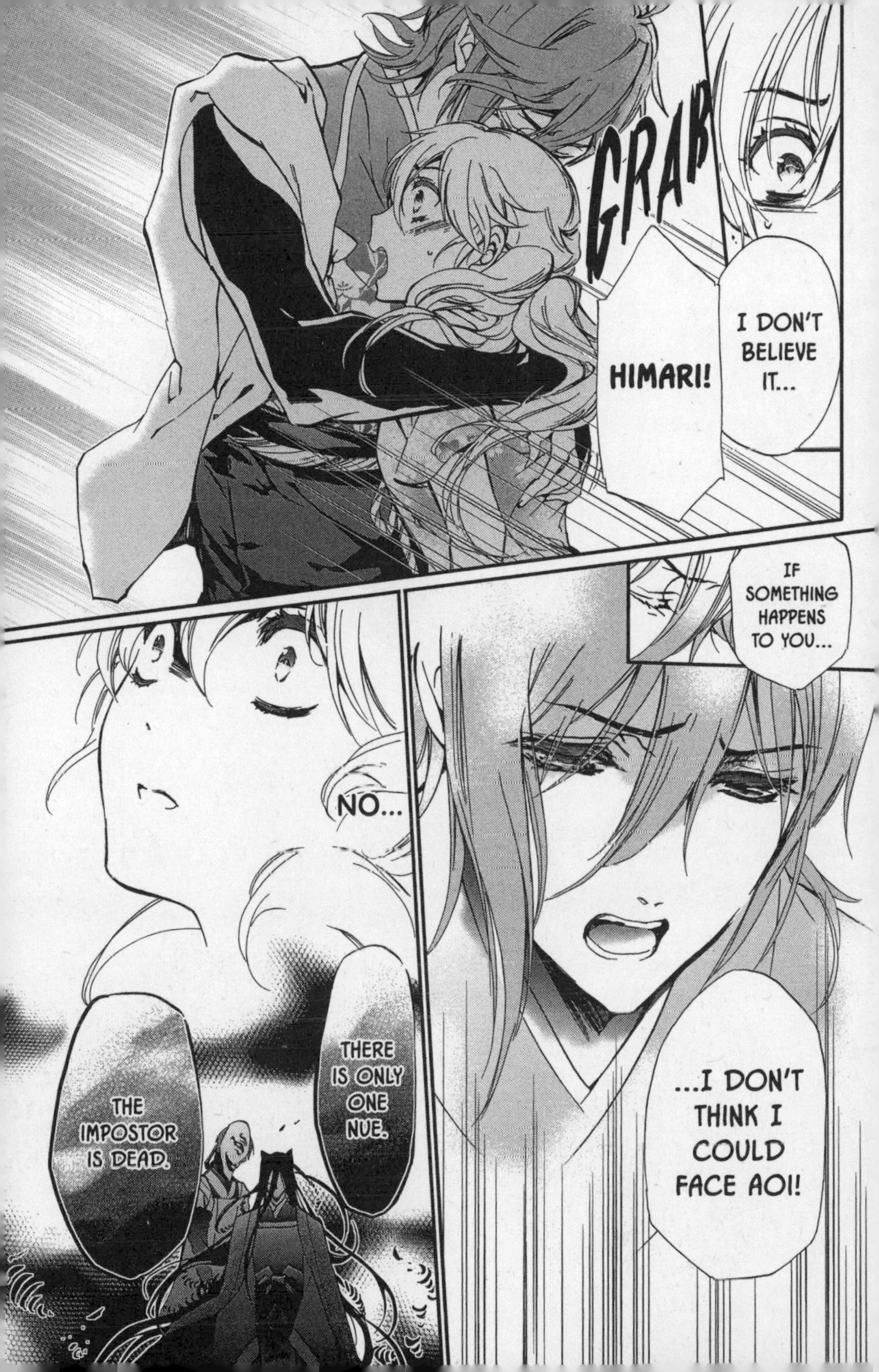
I DON'T BELIEVE IT...
HIMARI!
GRAB
IF SOMETHING HAPPENS TO YOU...
...I DON'T THINK I COULD FACE AOI!
NO...
THERE IS ONLY ONE NUE.
THE IMPOSTOR IS DEAD.

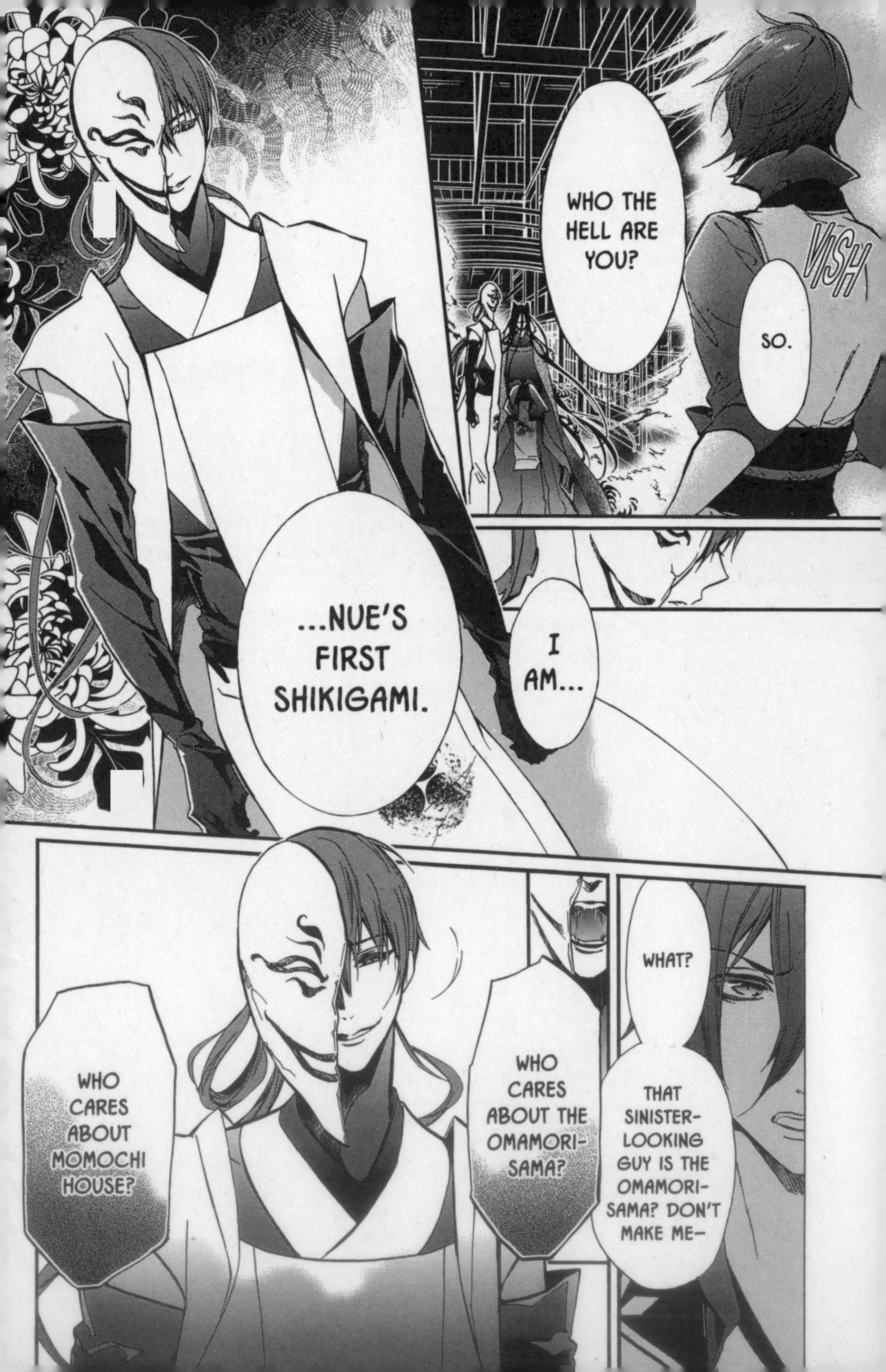
VISH
SO.
WHO THE HELL ARE YOU?
I AM...
...NUE'S FIRST SHIKIGAMI.
WHAT?
THAT SINISTER-LOOKING GUY IS THE OMAMORI-SAMA? DON'T MAKE ME–
WHO CARES ABOUT THE OMAMORI-SAMA?
WHO CARES ABOUT MOMOCHI HOUSE?

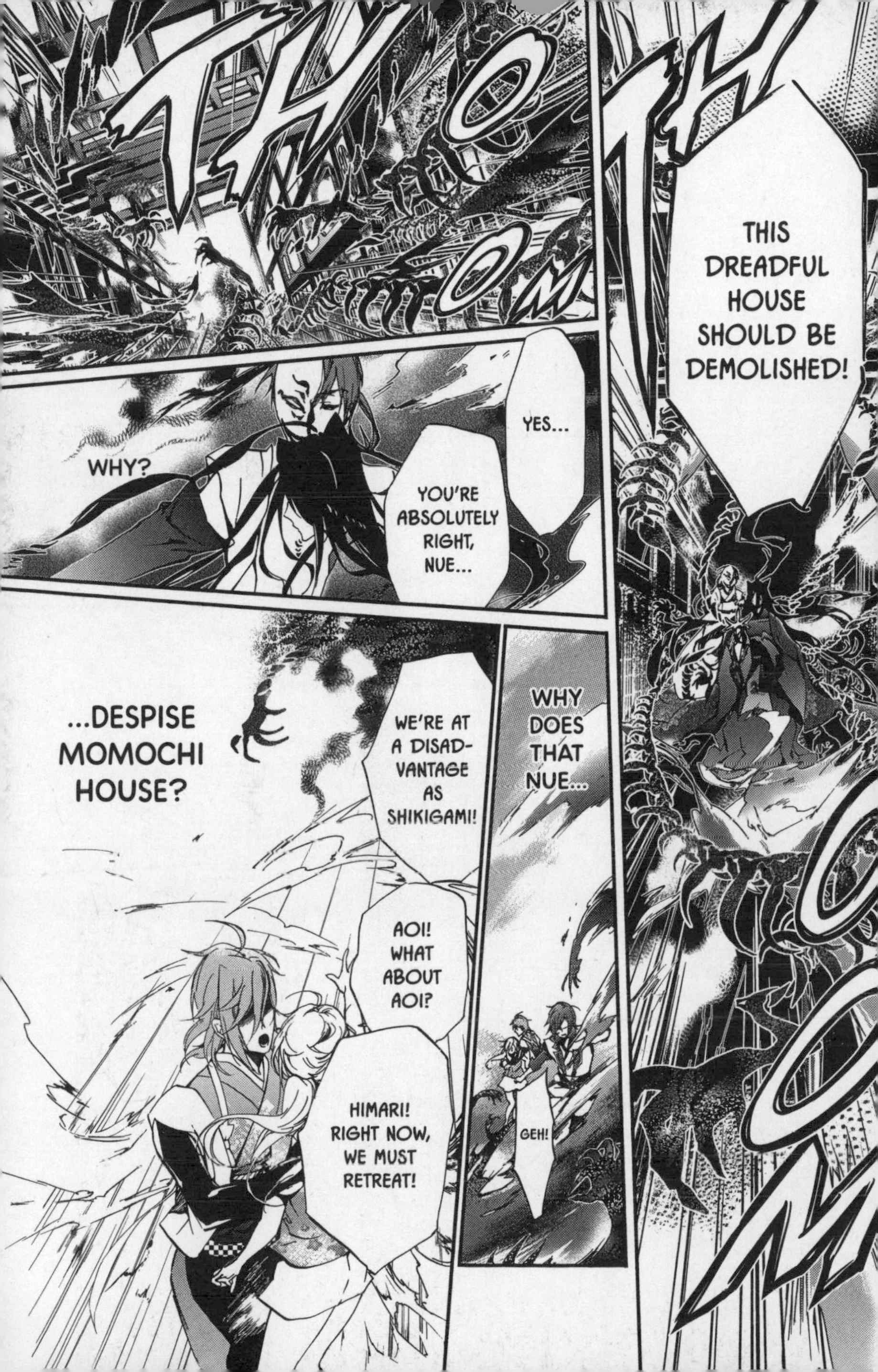
THIS DREADFUL HOUSE SHOULD BE DEMOLISHED!
THOOM
YES...
YOU'RE ABSOLUTELY RIGHT, NUE...
WHY?
WHY DOES THAT NUE...
GEH!
WE'RE AT A DISAD-VANTAGE AS SHIKIGAMI!
AOI! WHAT ABOUT AOI?
HIMARI! RIGHT NOW, WE MUST RETREAT!
...DESPISE MOMOCHI HOUSE?

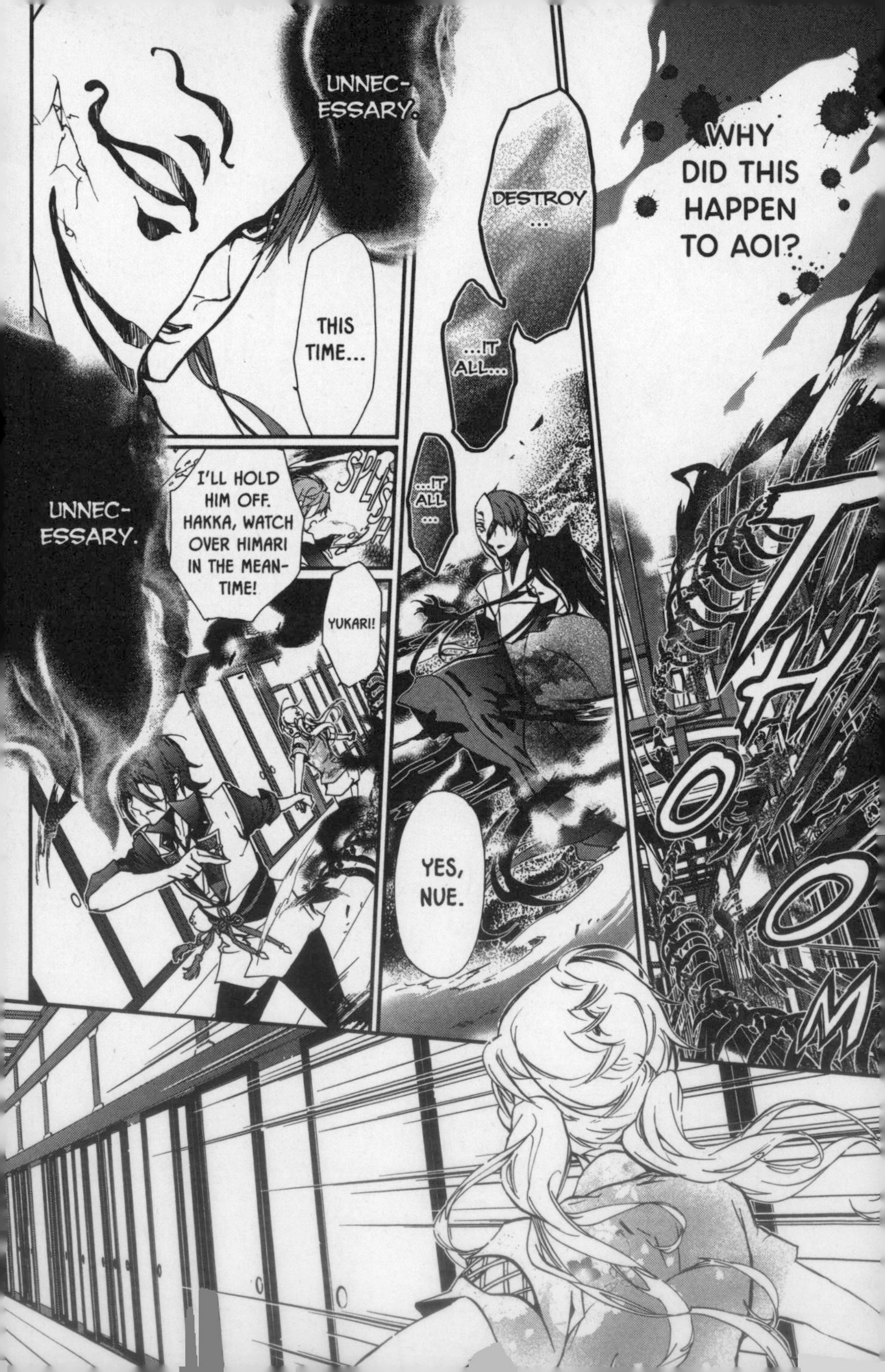
WHY DID THIS HAPPEN TO AOI?
DESTROY ...
...IT ALL...
...IT ALL ...
YES, NUE.
UNNEC- ESSARY.
THIS TIME...
SPLISH
I'LL HOLD HIM OFF. HAKKA, WATCH OVER HIMARI IN THE MEAN- TIME!
YUKARI!
UNNEC- ESSARY.

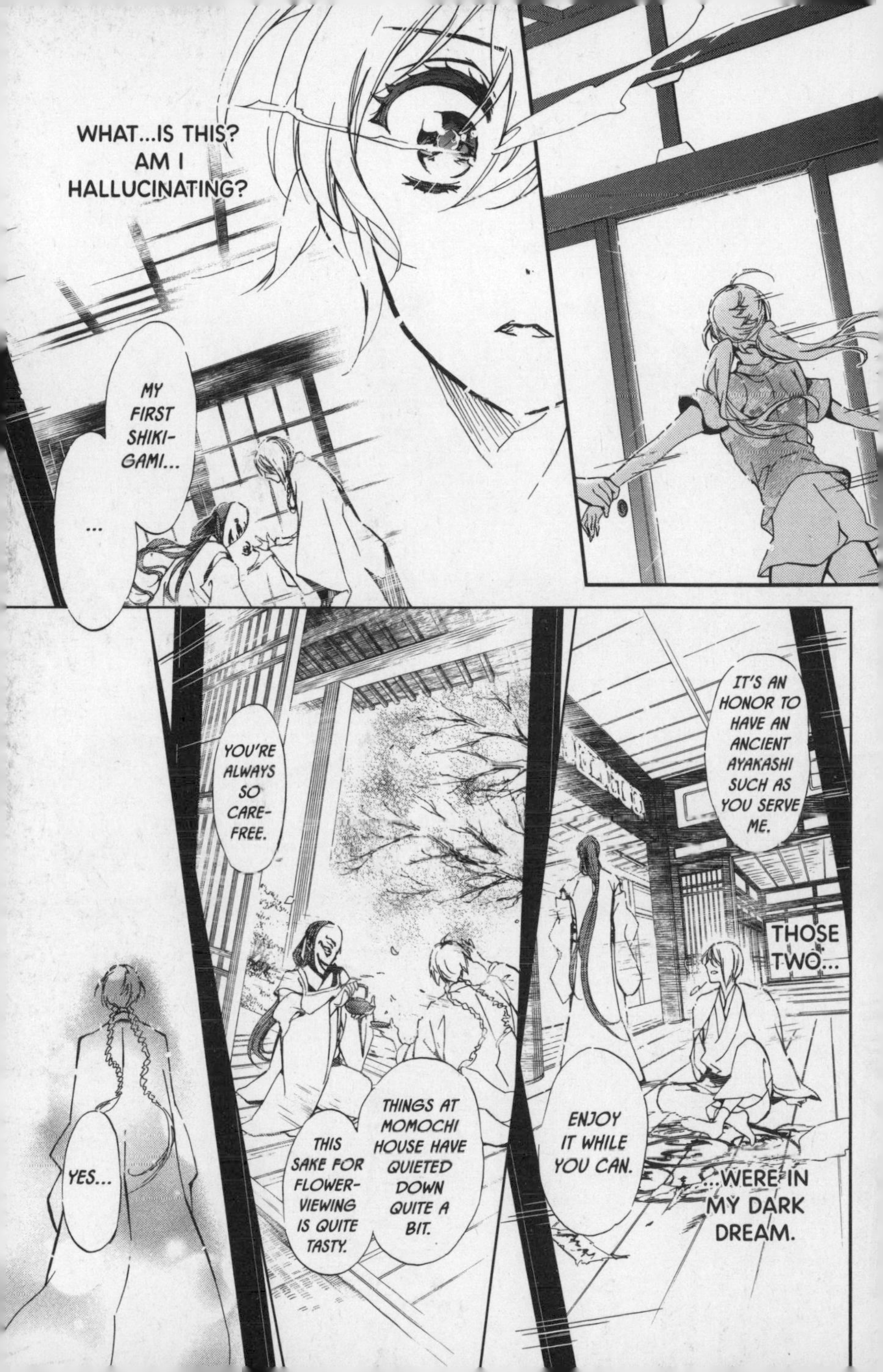
WHAT...IS THIS? AM I HALLUCINATING?
MY FIRST SHIKI-GAMI...
...
IT'S AN HONOR TO HAVE AN ANCIENT AYAKASHI SUCH AS YOU SERVE ME.
THOSE TWO...
ENJOY IT WHILE YOU CAN.
...WERE IN MY DARK DREAM.
YOU'RE ALWAYS SO CARE-FREE.
THINGS AT MOMOCHI HOUSE HAVE QUIETED DOWN QUITE A BIT.
THIS SAKE FOR FLOWER-VIEWING IS QUITE TASTY.
YES...

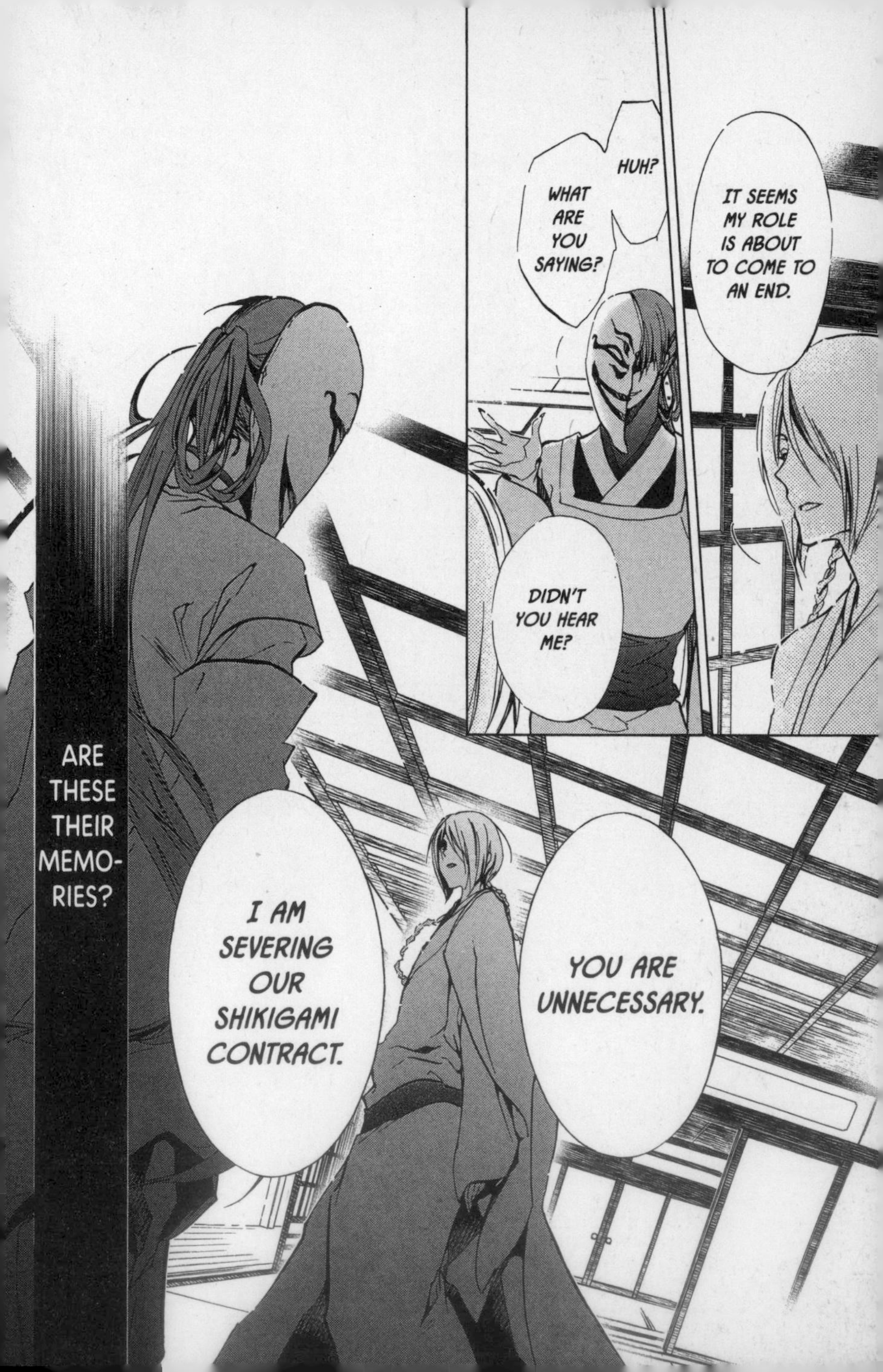
IT SEEMS MY ROLE IS ABOUT TO COME TO AN END.
HUH?
WHAT ARE YOU SAYING?
DIDN'T YOU HEAR ME?
YOU ARE UNNECESSARY.
I AM SEVERING OUR SHIKIGAMI CONTRACT.
ARE THESE THEIR MEMO-RIES?

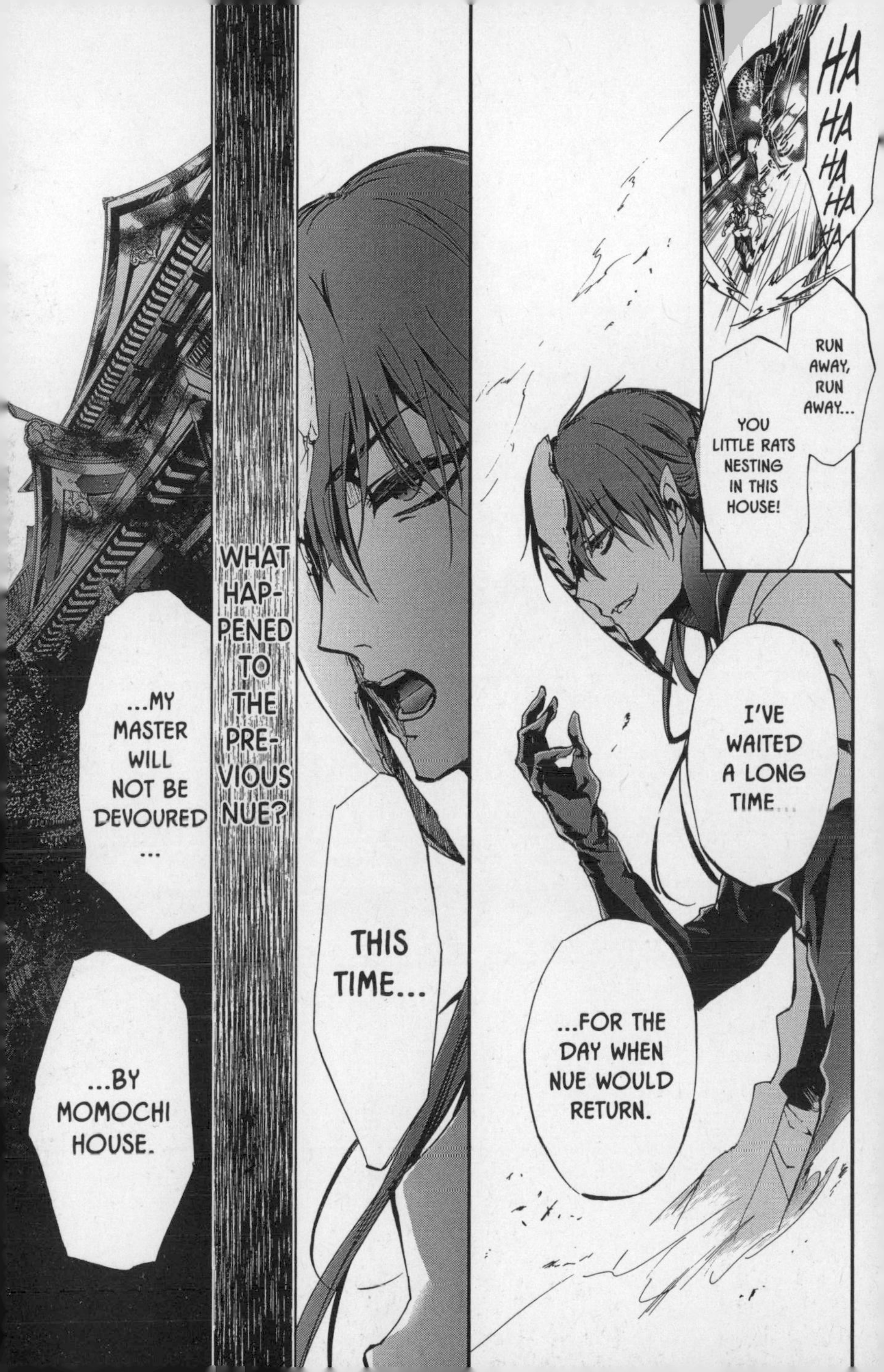
HA HA HA HA HA
RUN AWAY, RUN AWAY...
YOU LITTLE RATS NESTING IN THIS HOUSE!
I'VE WAITED A LONG TIME...
...FOR THE DAY WHEN NUE WOULD RETURN.
WHAT HAPPENED TO THE PREVIOUS NUE?
THIS TIME...
...MY MASTER WILL NOT BE DEVOURED...
...BY MOMOCHI HOUSE.

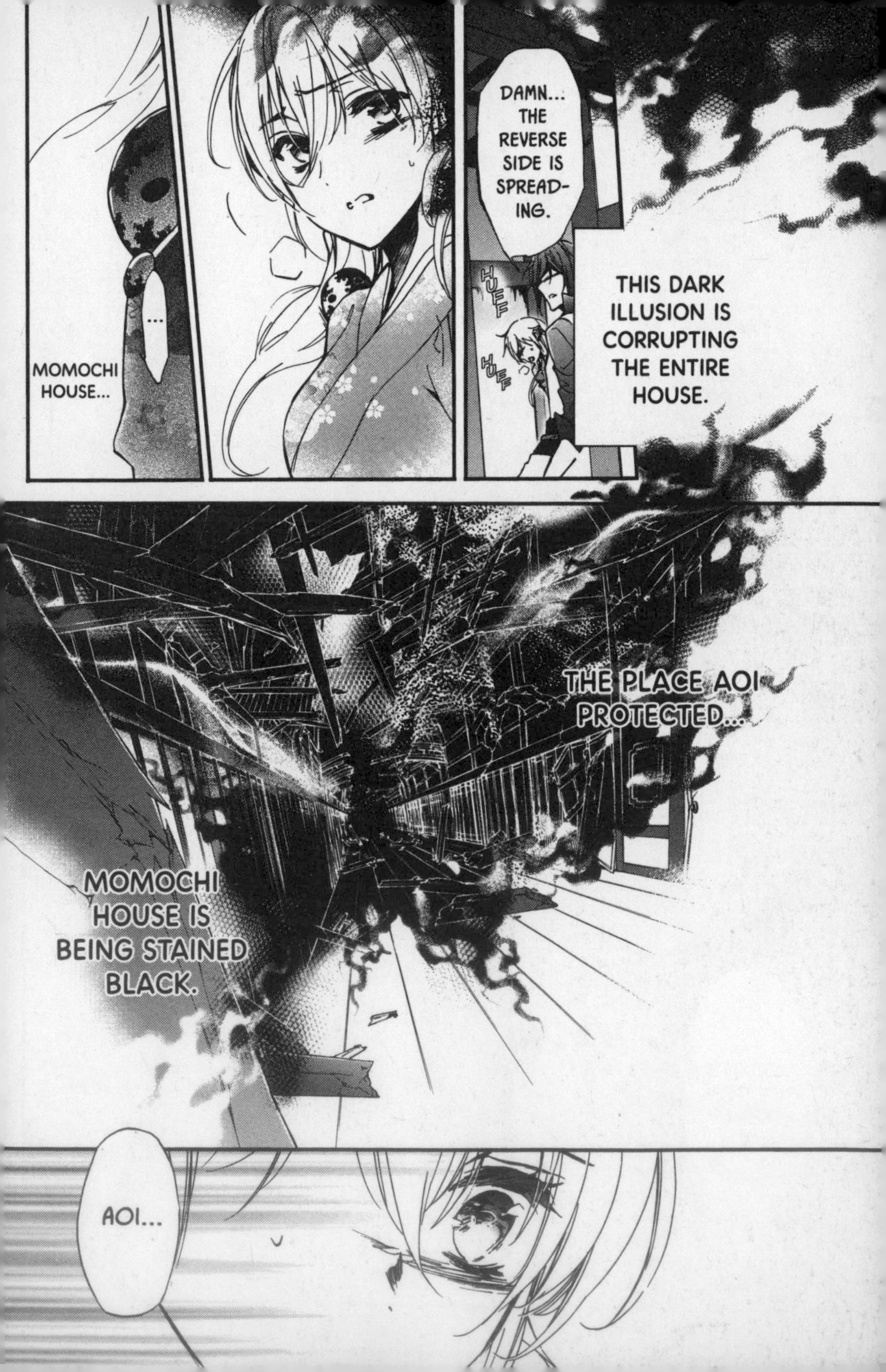
THIS DARK ILLUSION IS CORRUPTING THE ENTIRE HOUSE.
HUFF HUFF
DAMN... THE REVERSE SIDE IS SPREAD-ING.
...
MOMOCHI HOUSE...
THE PLACE AOI PROTECTED...
MOMOCHI HOUSE IS BEING STAINED BLACK.
AOI...

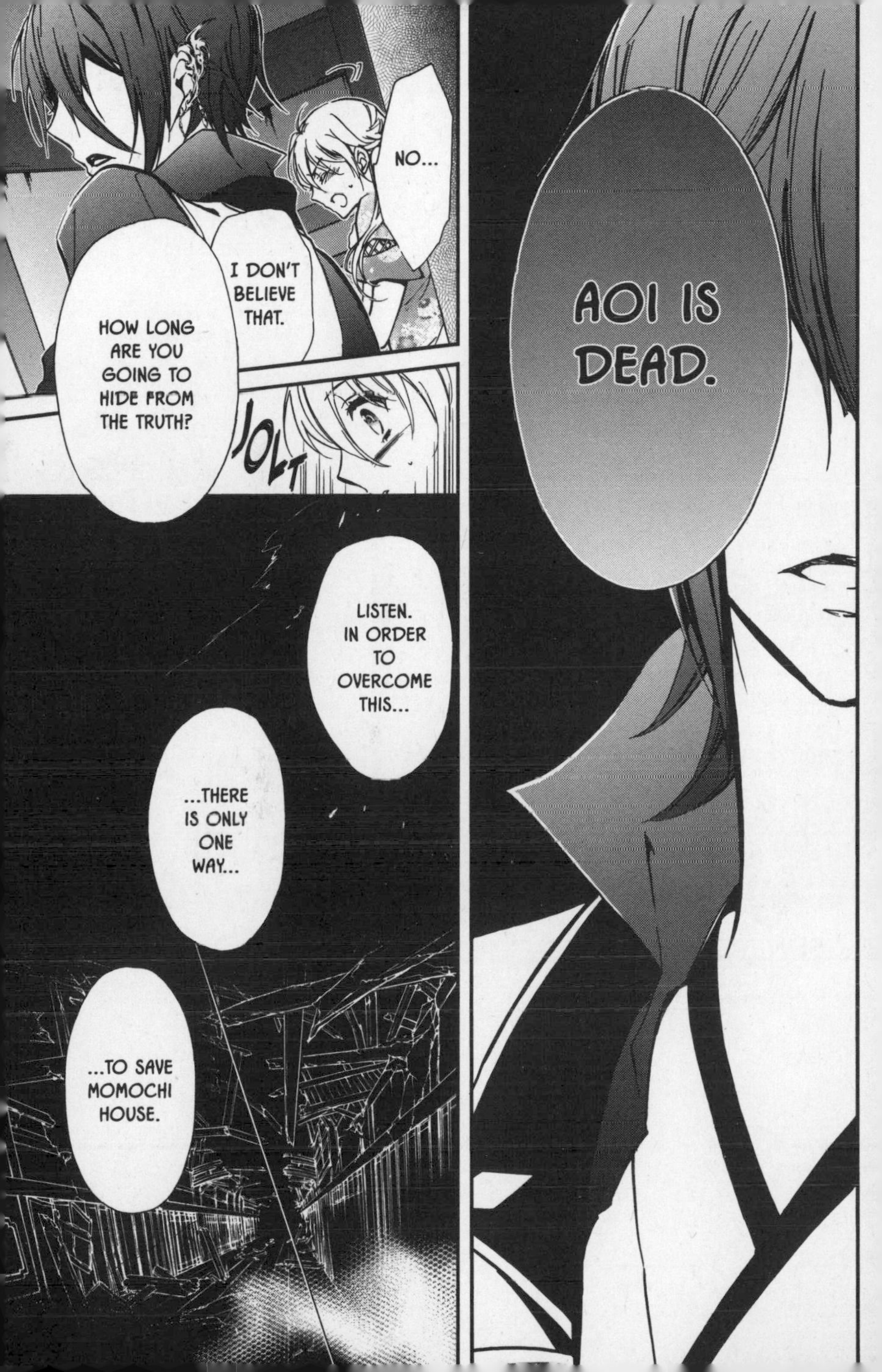
AOI IS DEAD.
NO...
I DON'T BELIEVE THAT.
HOW LONG ARE YOU GOING TO HIDE FROM THE TRUTH?
JOLT
LISTEN. IN ORDER TO OVERCOME THIS...
...THERE IS ONLY ONE WAY...
...TO SAVE MOMOCHI HOUSE.

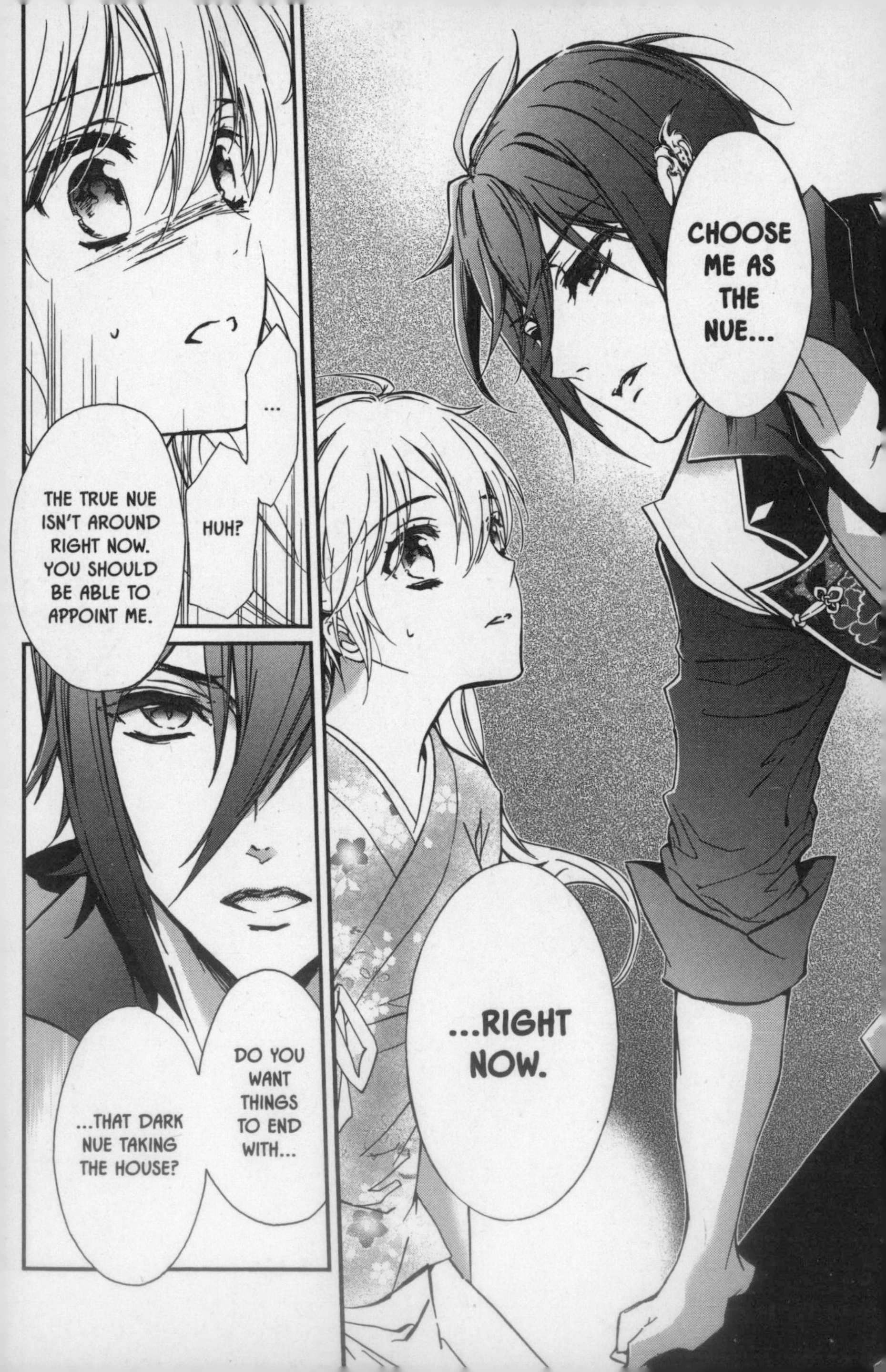
CHOOSE ME AS THE NUE...
...RIGHT NOW.
...
HUH?
THE TRUE NUE ISN'T AROUND RIGHT NOW. YOU SHOULD BE ABLE TO APPOINT ME.
DO YOU WANT THINGS TO END WITH...
...THAT DARK NUE TAKING THE HOUSE?

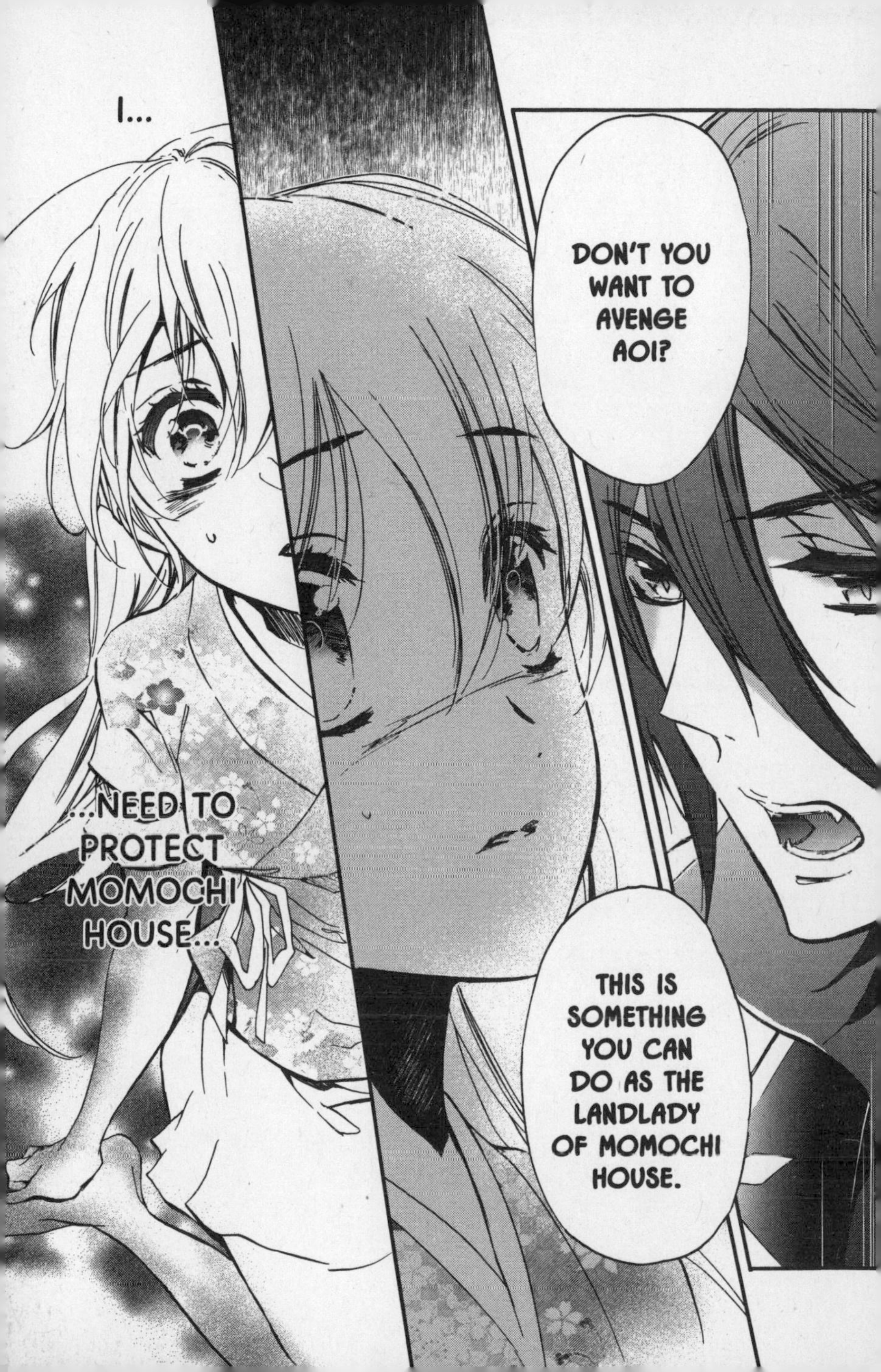
DON'T YOU WANT TO AVENGE AOI?
THIS IS SOMETHING YOU CAN DO AS THE LANDLADY OF MOMOCHI HOUSE.
I...
...NEED TO PROTECT MOMOCHI HOUSE...

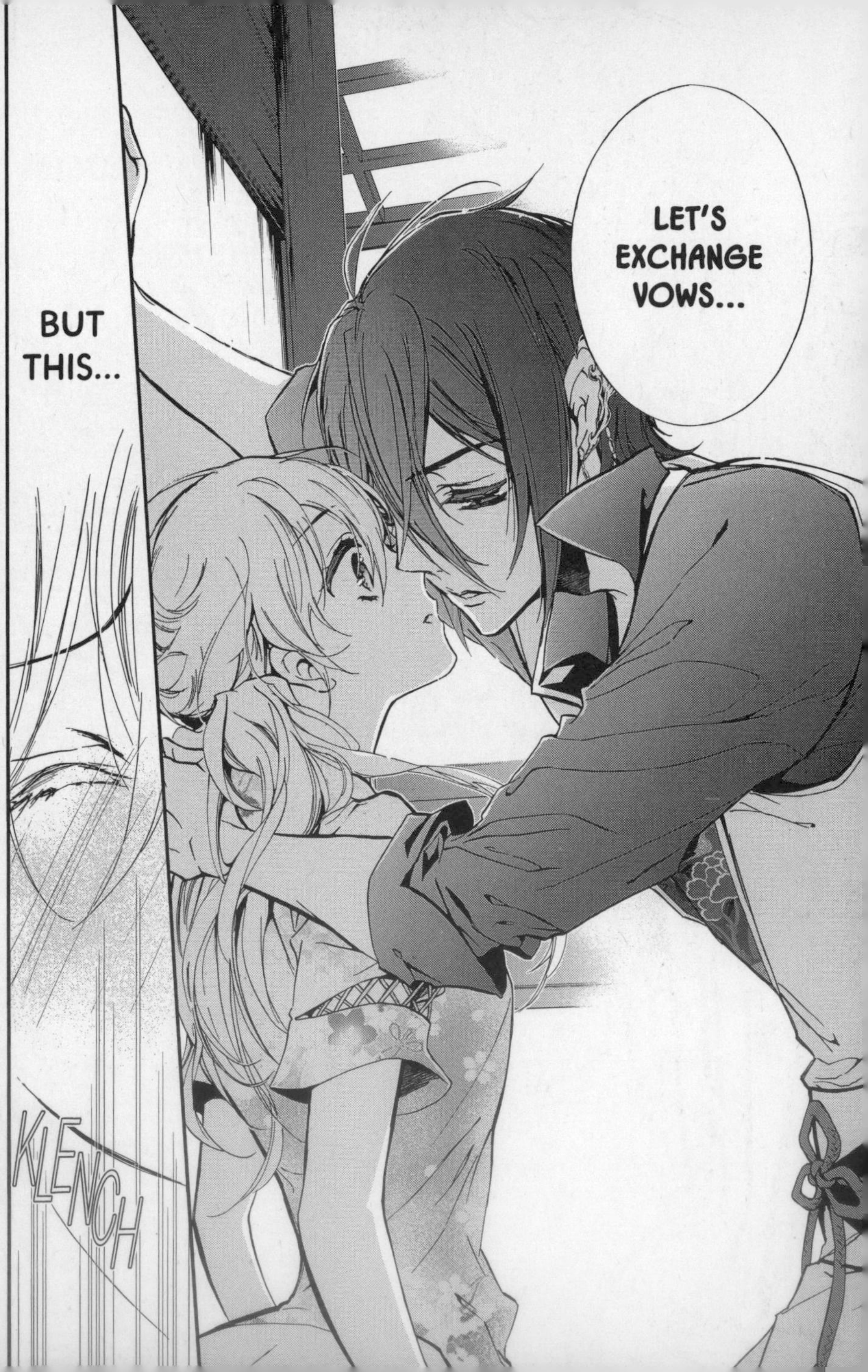
LET'S EXCHANGE VOWS...
BUT THIS...
KLENCH

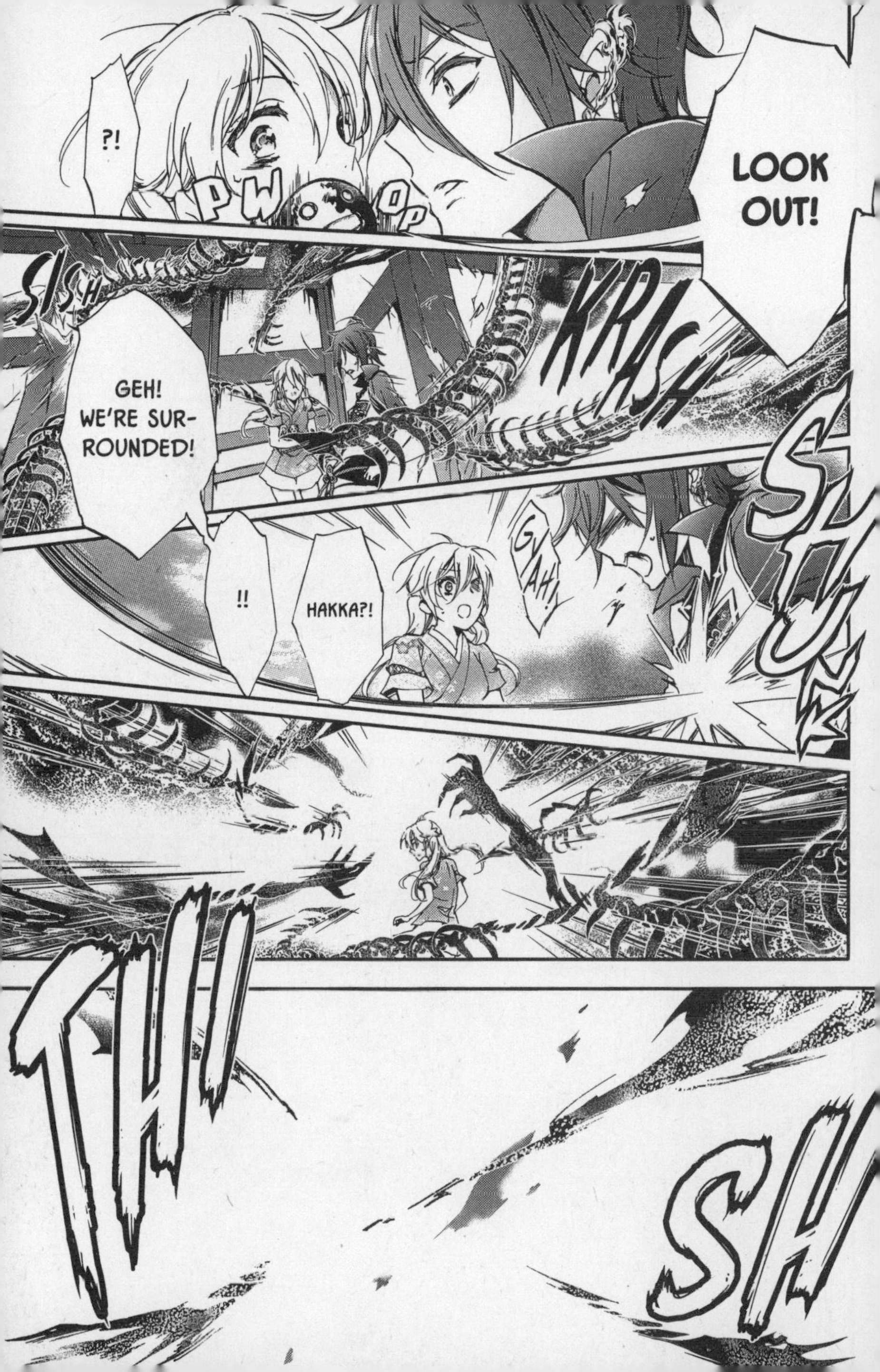
LOOK OUT!
?!
PWOOP
KRASH
SISH
GEH! WE'RE SUR-ROUNDED!
SHUK
GYAH!
HAKKA?!
!!
THWSH

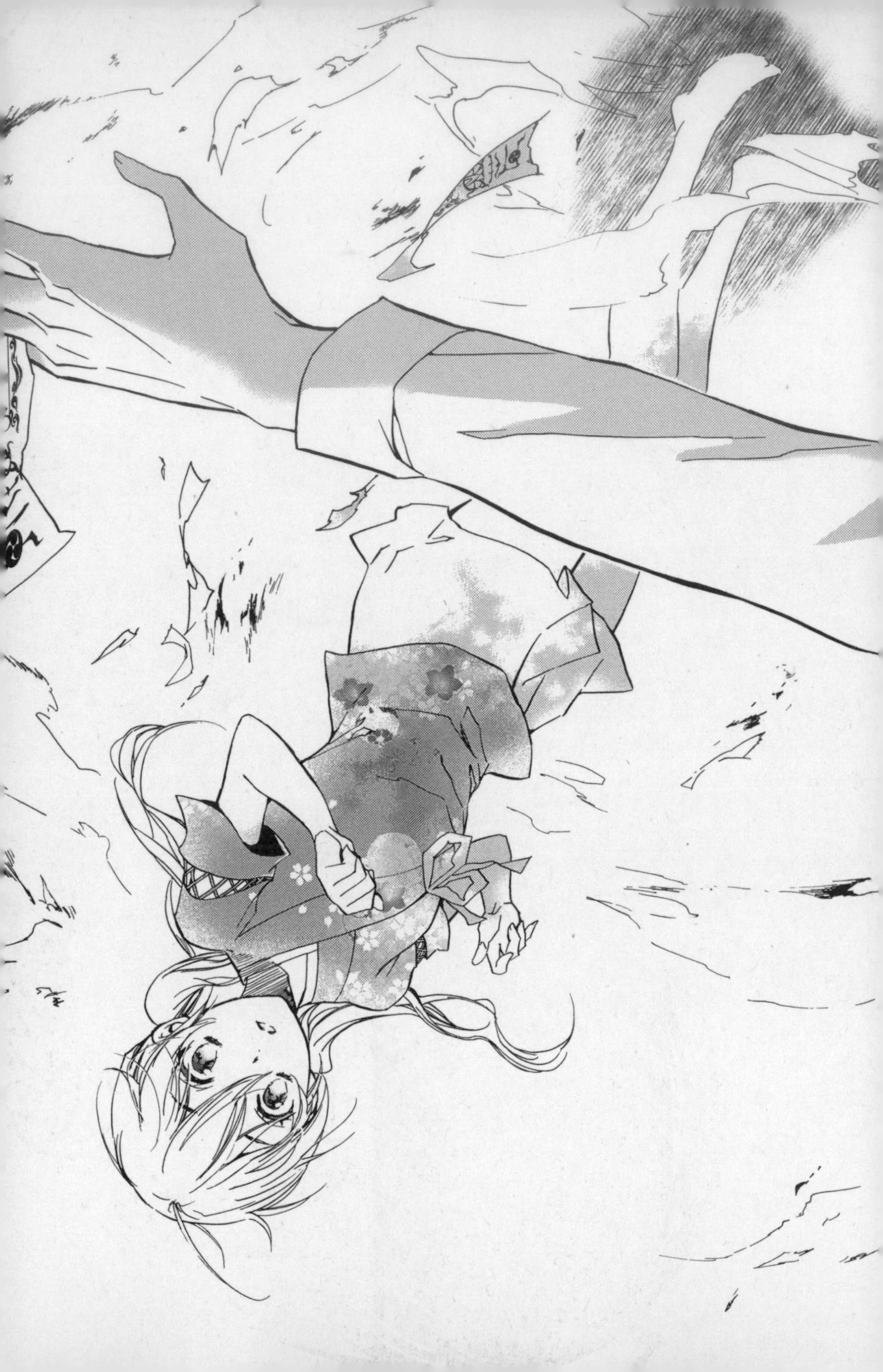

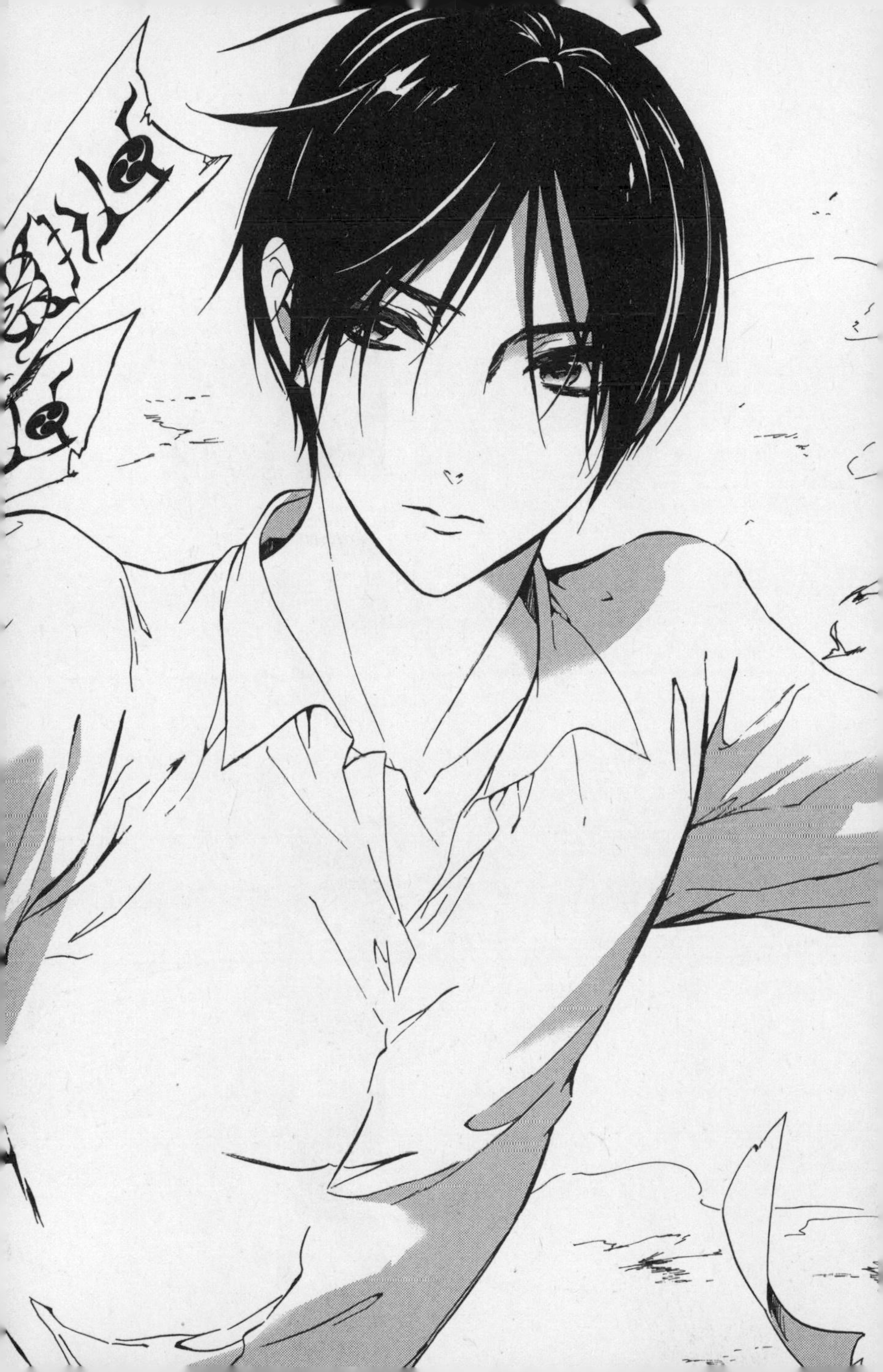

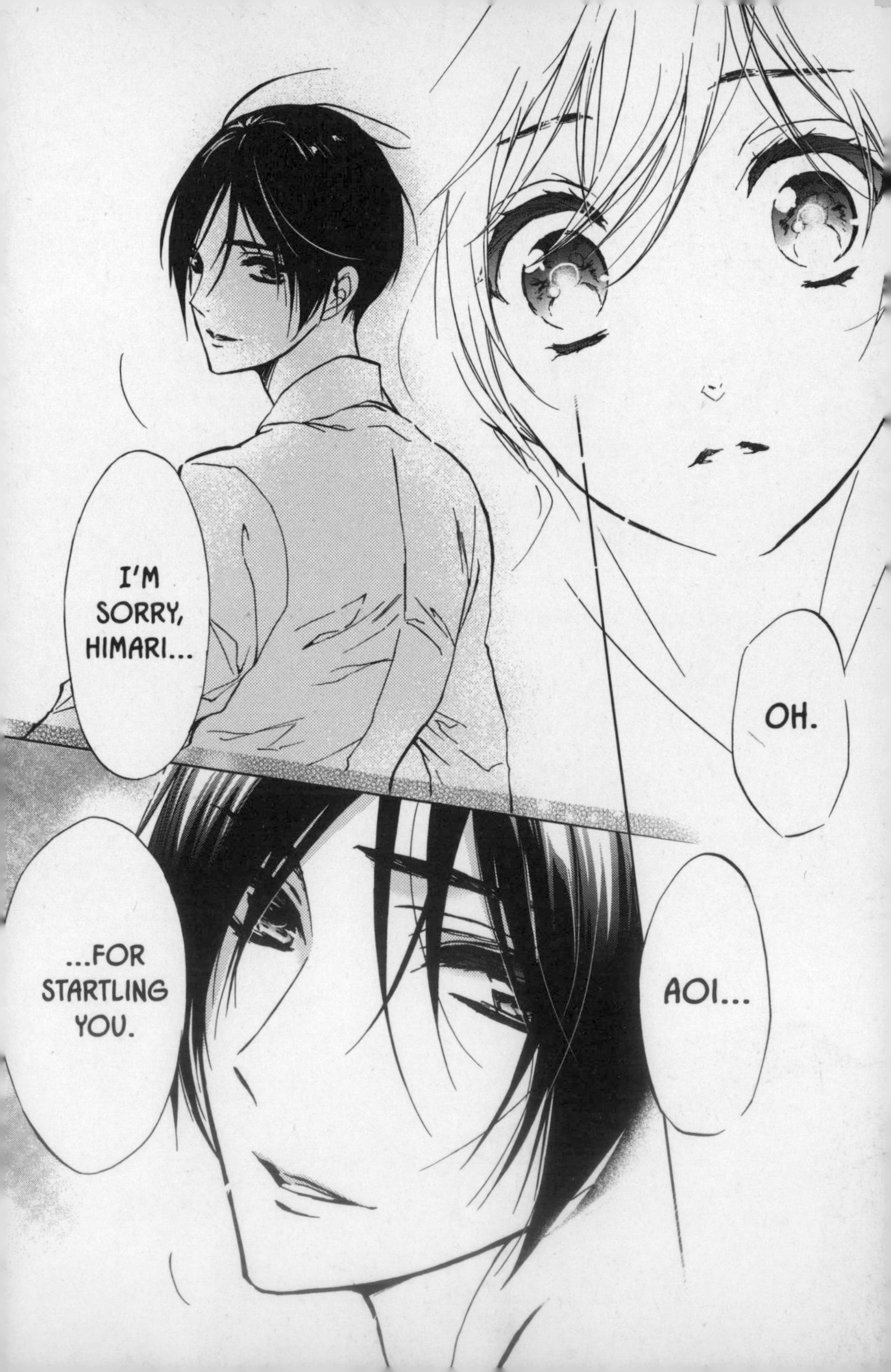
OH.
I'M SORRY, HIMARI...
AOI...
...FOR STARTLING YOU.

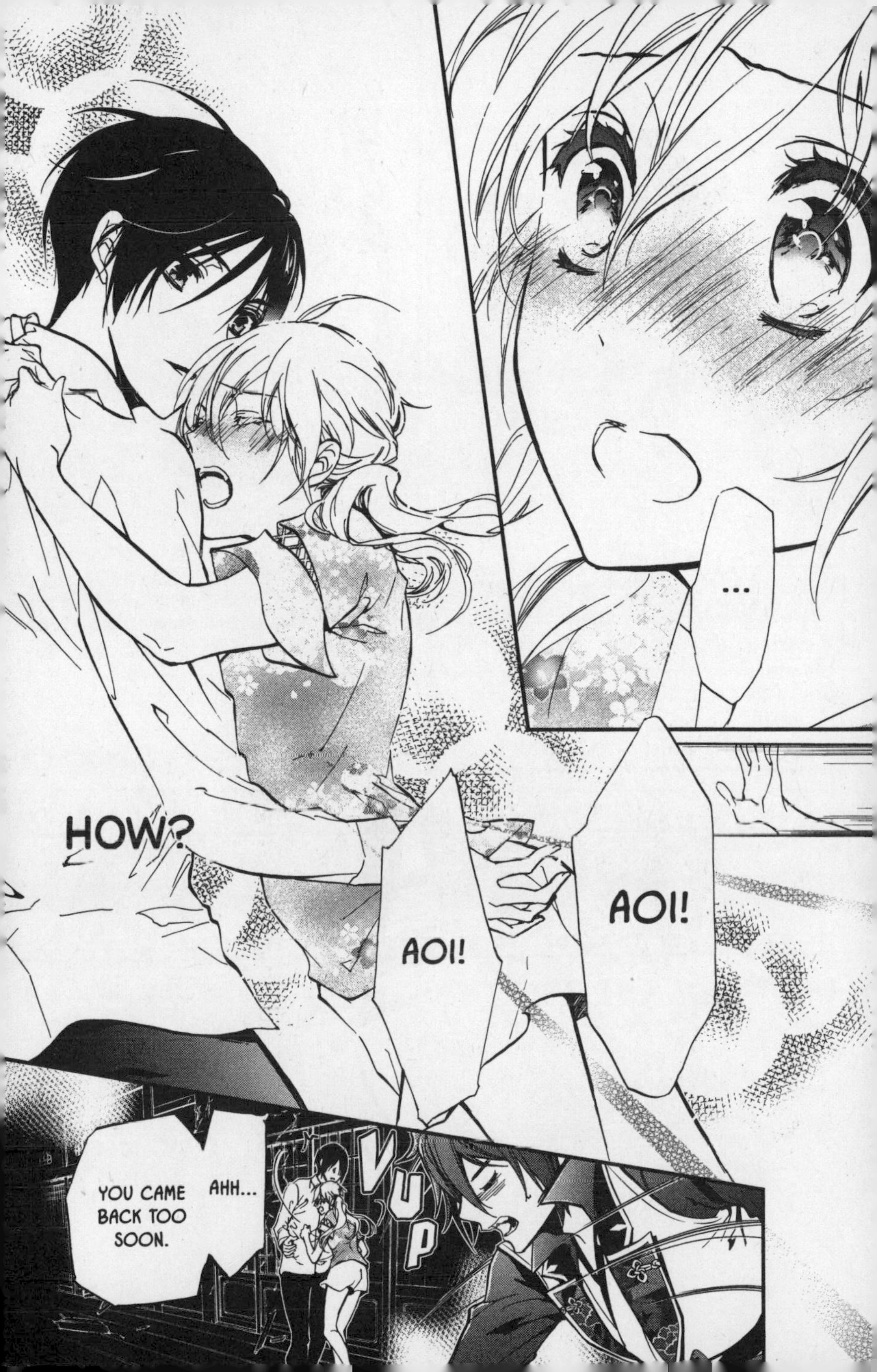
...
AOI!
AOI!
HOW?
VUP
AHH...
YOU CAME BACK TOO SOON.

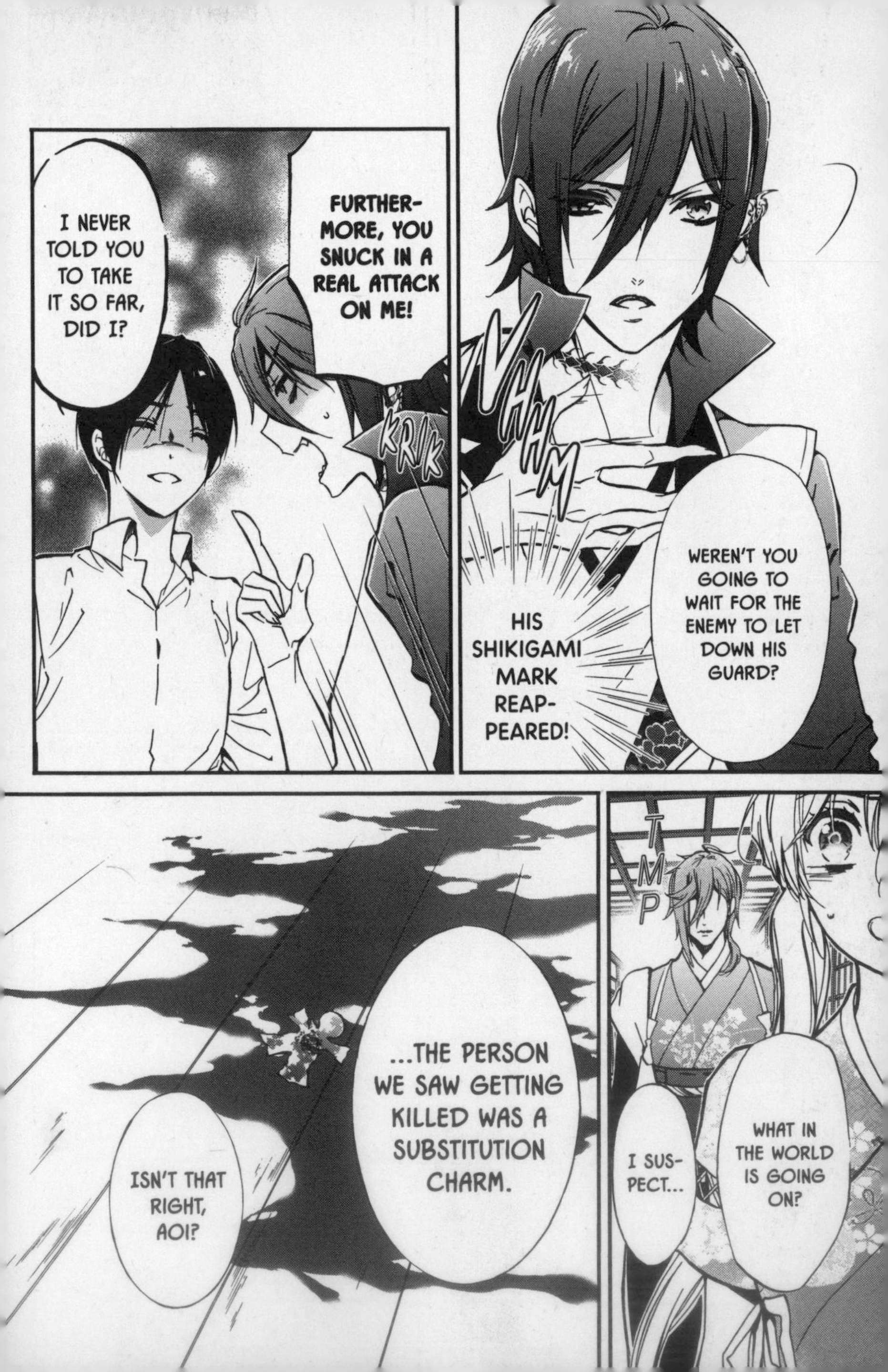
VHHM
WEREN'T YOU GOING TO WAIT FOR THE ENEMY TO LET DOWN HIS GUARD?
HIS SHIKIGAMI MARK REAP-PEARED!
KRIK
FURTHER-MORE, YOU SNUCK IN A REAL ATTACK ON ME!
I NEVER TOLD YOU TO TAKE IT SO FAR, DID I?
TMP
WHAT IN THE WORLD IS GOING ON?
I SUS-PECT...
...THE PERSON WE SAW GETTING KILLED WAS A SUBSTITUTION CHARM.
ISN'T THAT RIGHT, AOI?

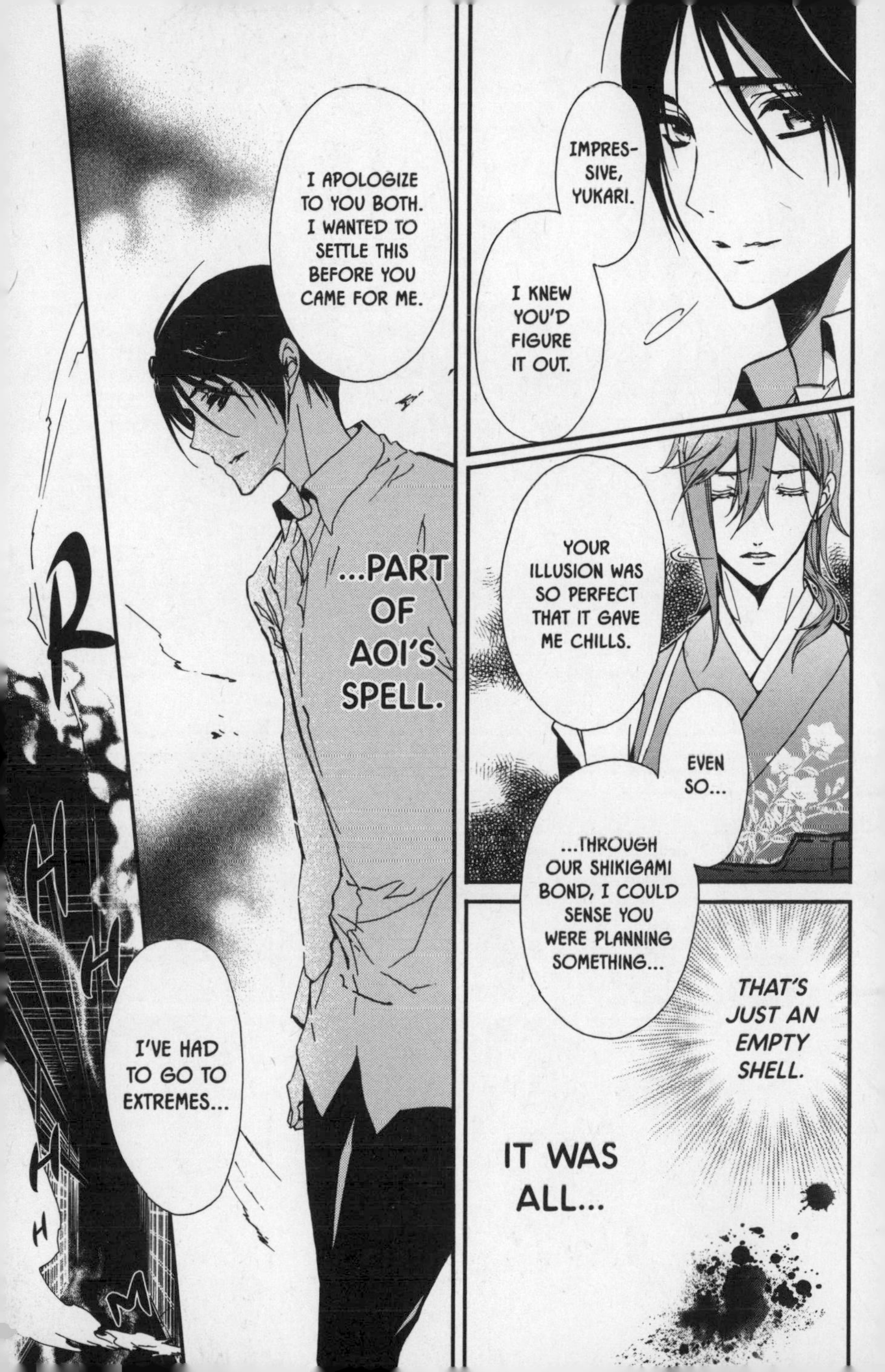
IMPRES-SIVE, YUKARI.
I KNEW YOU'D FIGURE IT OUT.
YOUR ILLUSION WAS SO PERFECT THAT IT GAVE ME CHILLS.
EVEN SO...
...THROUGH OUR SHIKIGAMI BOND, I COULD SENSE YOU WERE PLANNING SOMETHING...
THAT'S JUST AN EMPTY SHELL.
IT WAS ALL...
I APOLOGIZE TO YOU BOTH. I WANTED TO SETTLE THIS BEFORE YOU CAME FOR ME.
...PART OF AOI'S SPELL.
I'VE HAD TO GO TO EXTREMES...

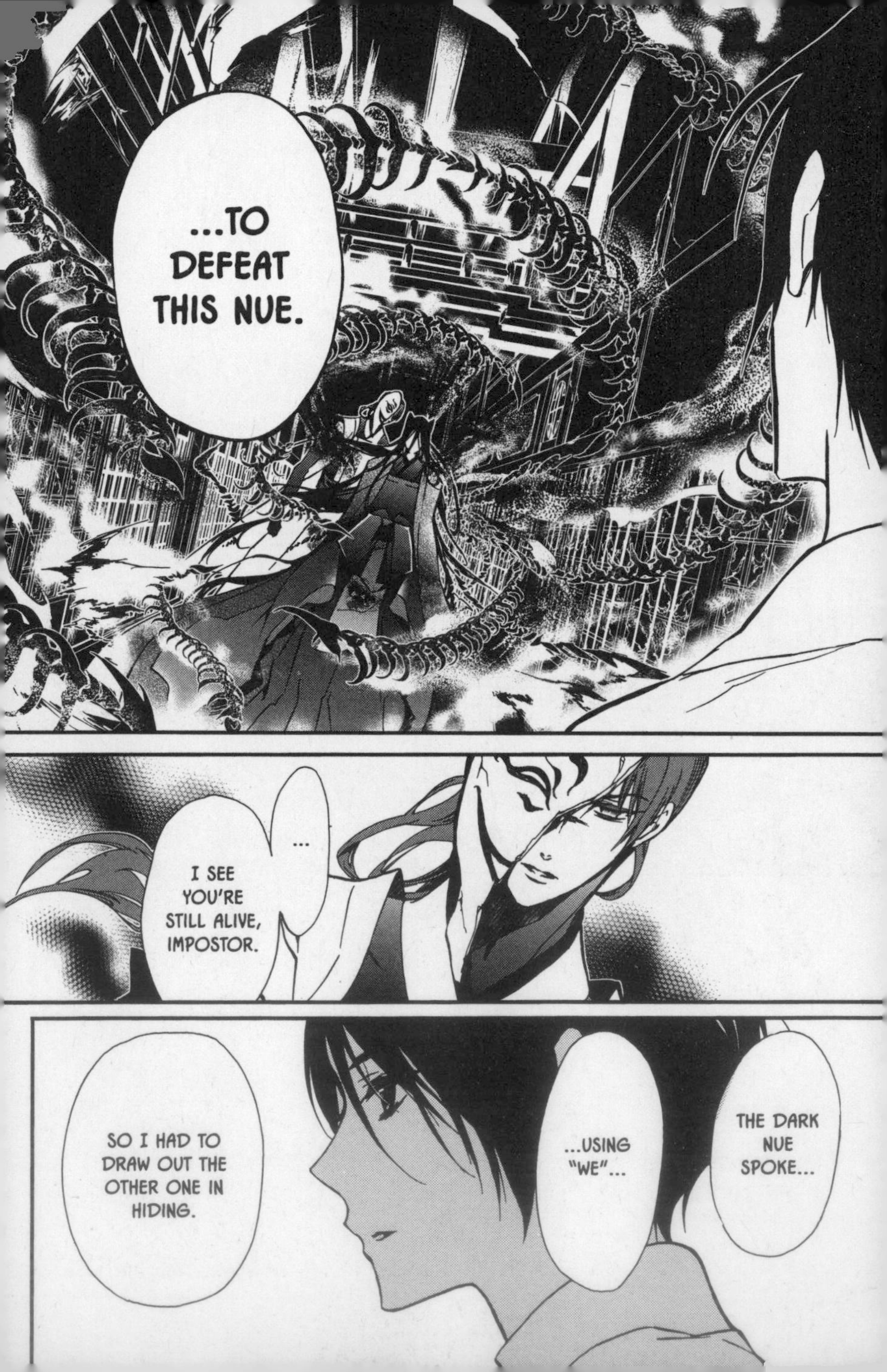
...TO DEFEAT THIS NUE.
...
I SEE YOU'RE STILL ALIVE, IMPOSTOR.
THE DARK NUE SPOKE...
...USING "WE"...
SO I HAD TO DRAW OUT THE OTHER ONE IN HIDING.

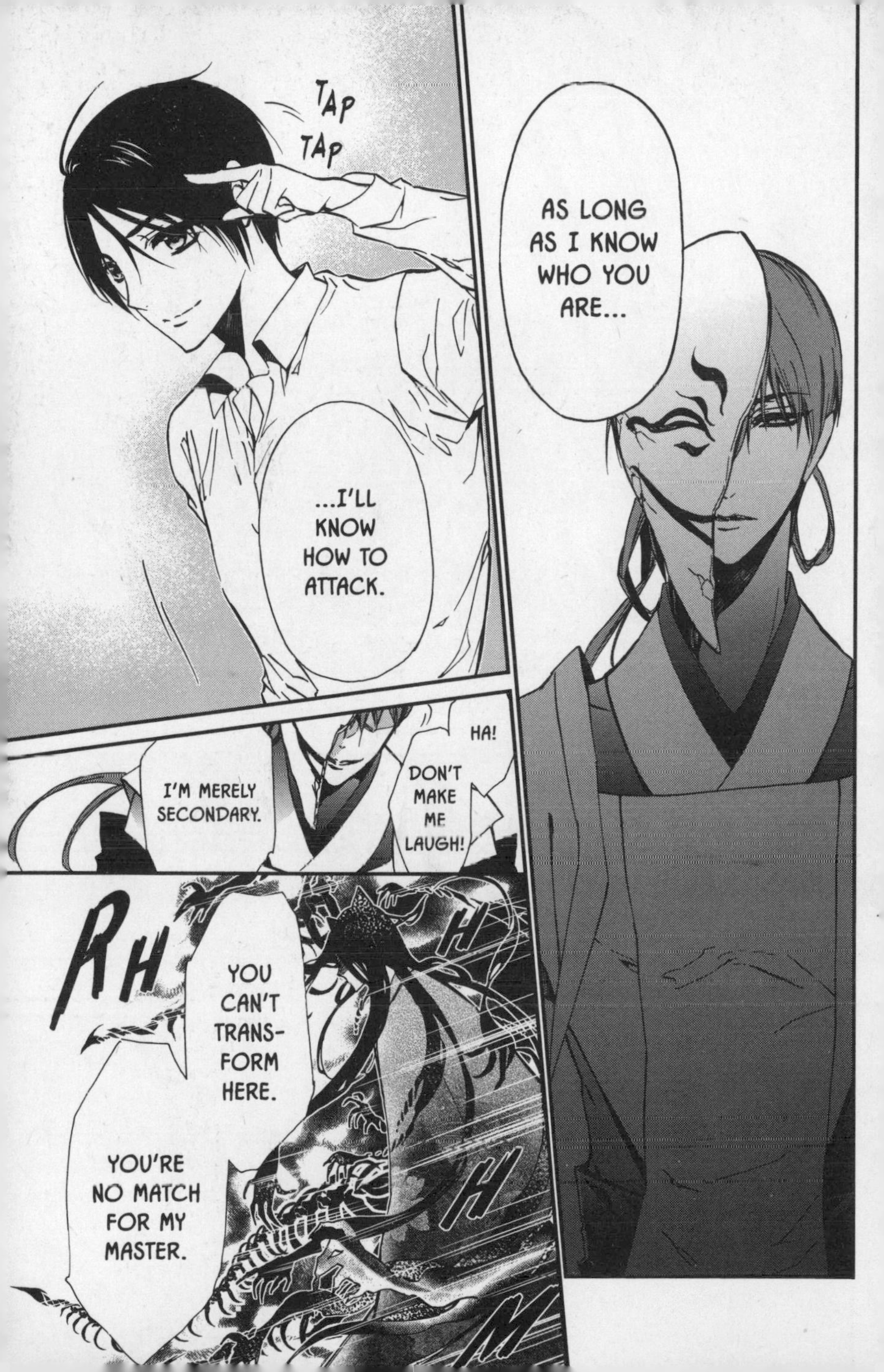
AS LONG AS I KNOW WHO YOU ARE...
TAP TAP
...I'LL KNOW HOW TO ATTACK.
HA!
DON'T MAKE ME LAUGH!
I'M MERELY SECONDARY.
RH
H
YOU CAN'T TRANS- FORM HERE.
H
YOU'RE NO MATCH FOR MY MASTER.
M

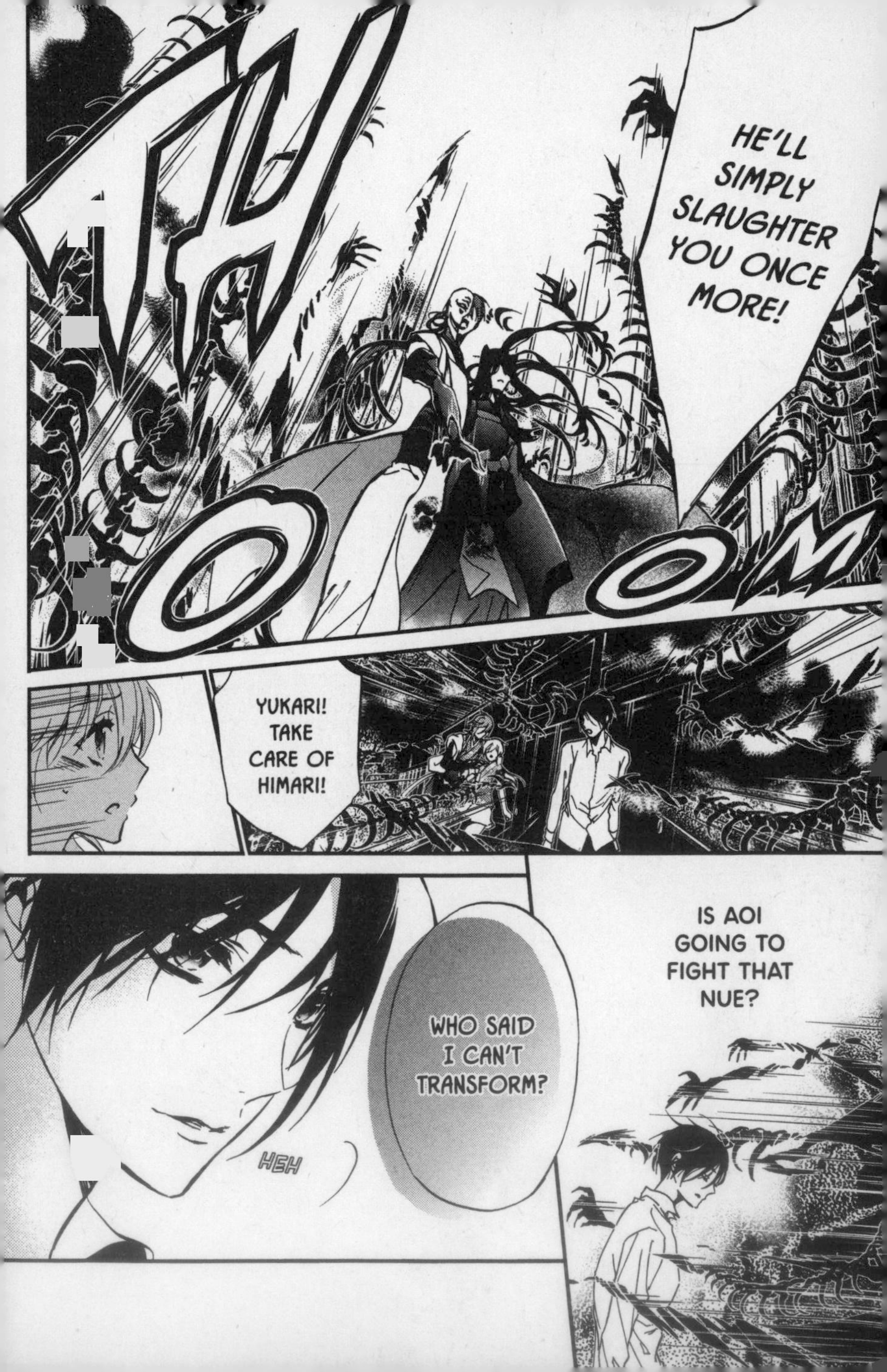
HE'LL SIMPLY SLAUGHTER YOU ONCE MORE!
YUKARI! TAKE CARE OF HIMARI!
IS AOI GOING TO FIGHT THAT NUE?
WHO SAID I CAN'T TRANSFORM?
HEH

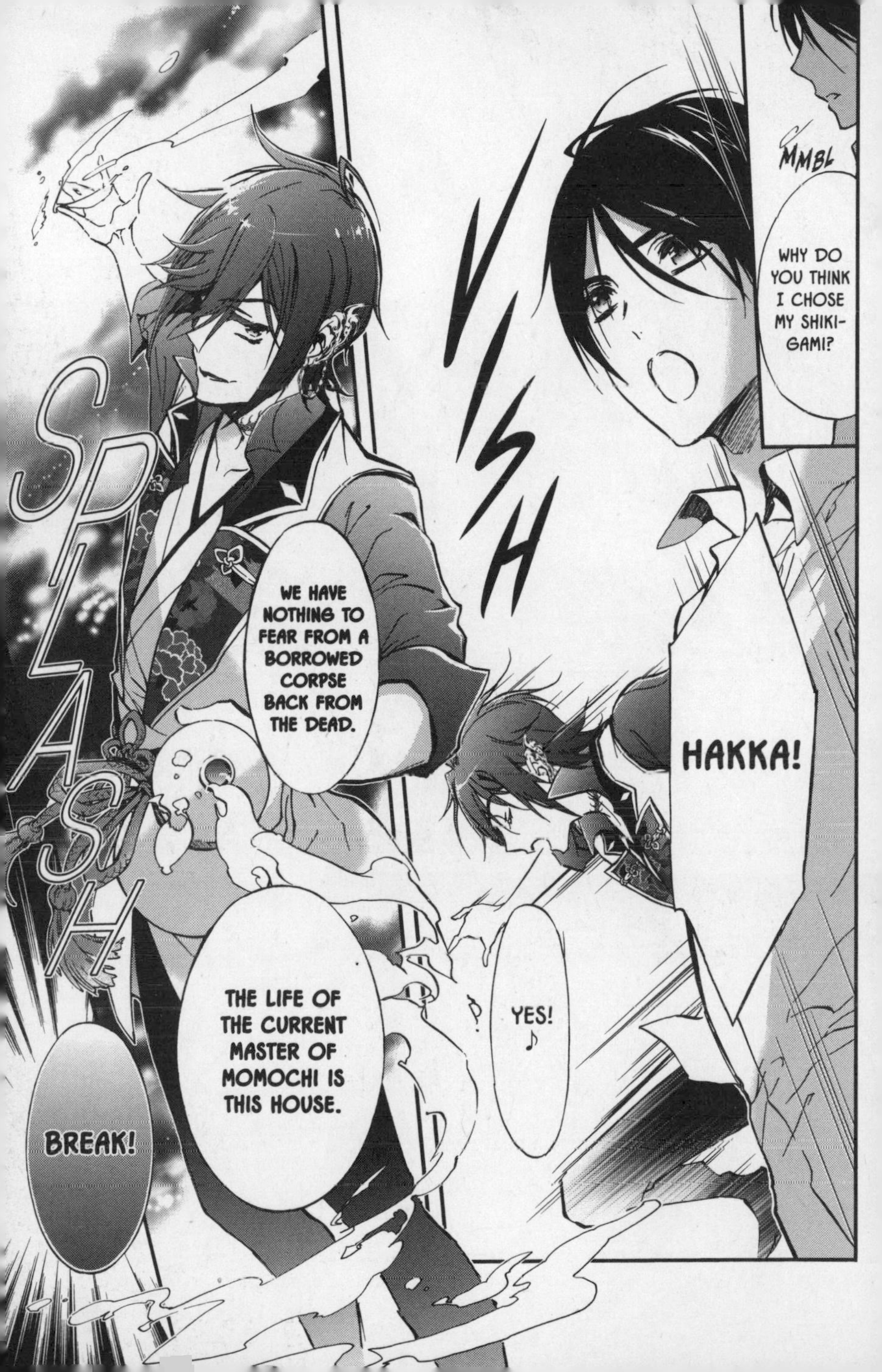
MMBL
WHY DO YOU THINK I CHOSE MY SHIKI-GAMI?
VISH
HAKKA!
YES! ♪
WE HAVE NOTHING TO FEAR FROM A BORROWED CORPSE BACK FROM THE DEAD.
THE LIFE OF THE CURRENT MASTER OF MOMOCHI IS THIS HOUSE.
SPLASH
BREAK!

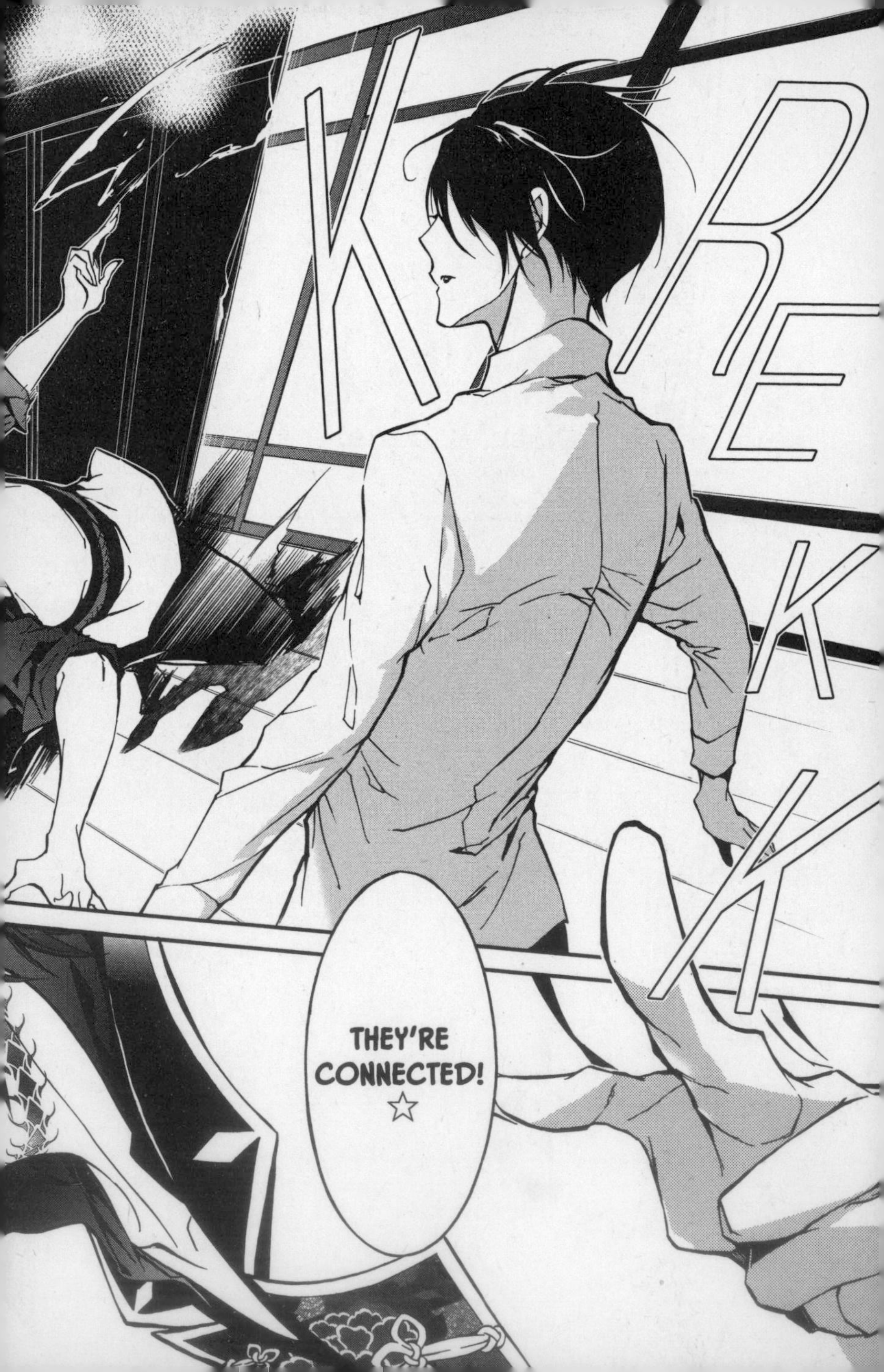
KREKK
THEY'RE CONNECTED! ☆

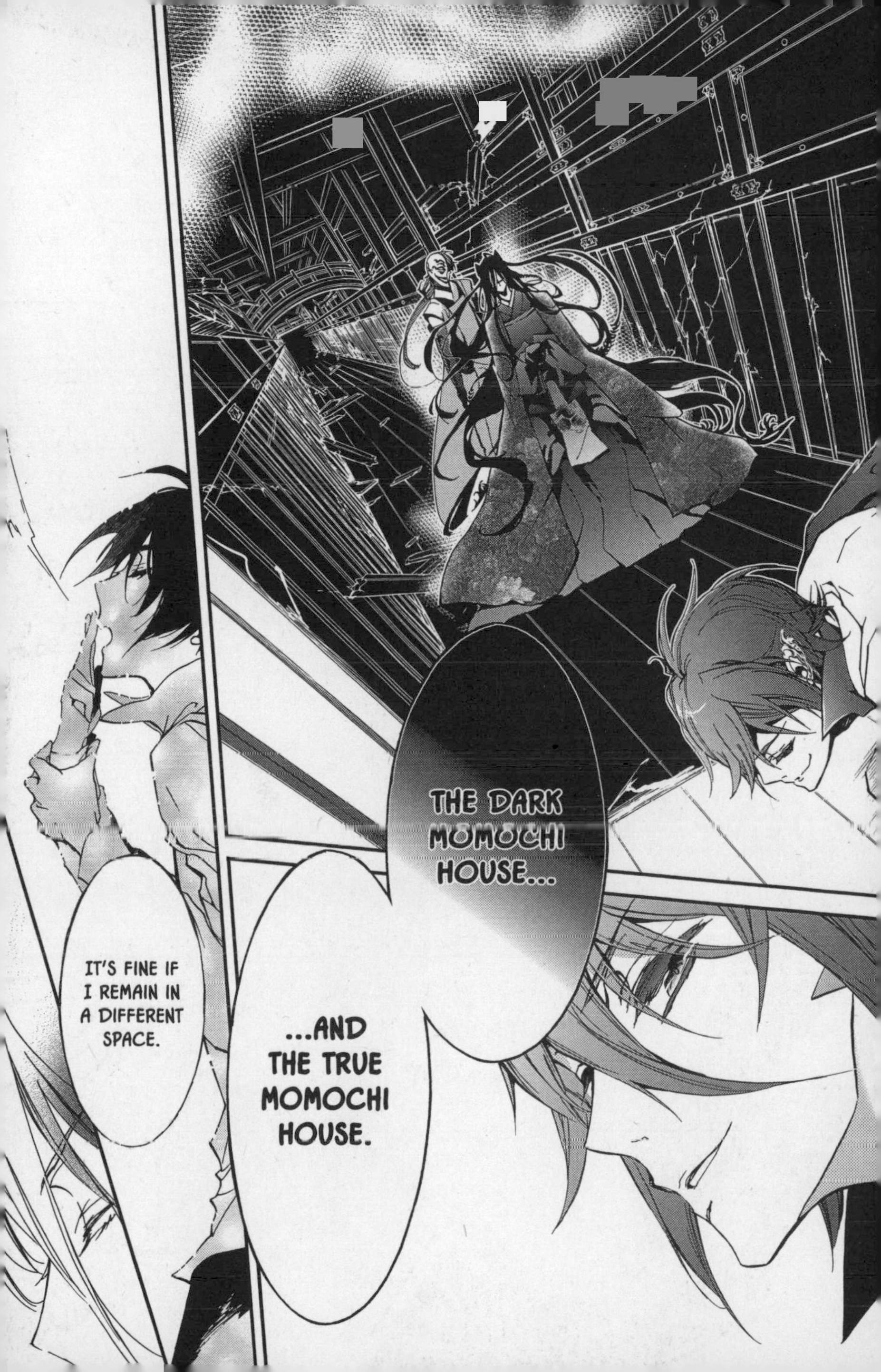
THE DARK MOMOCHI HOUSE...
...AND THE TRUE MOMOCHI HOUSE.
IT'S FINE IF I REMAIN IN A DIFFERENT SPACE.

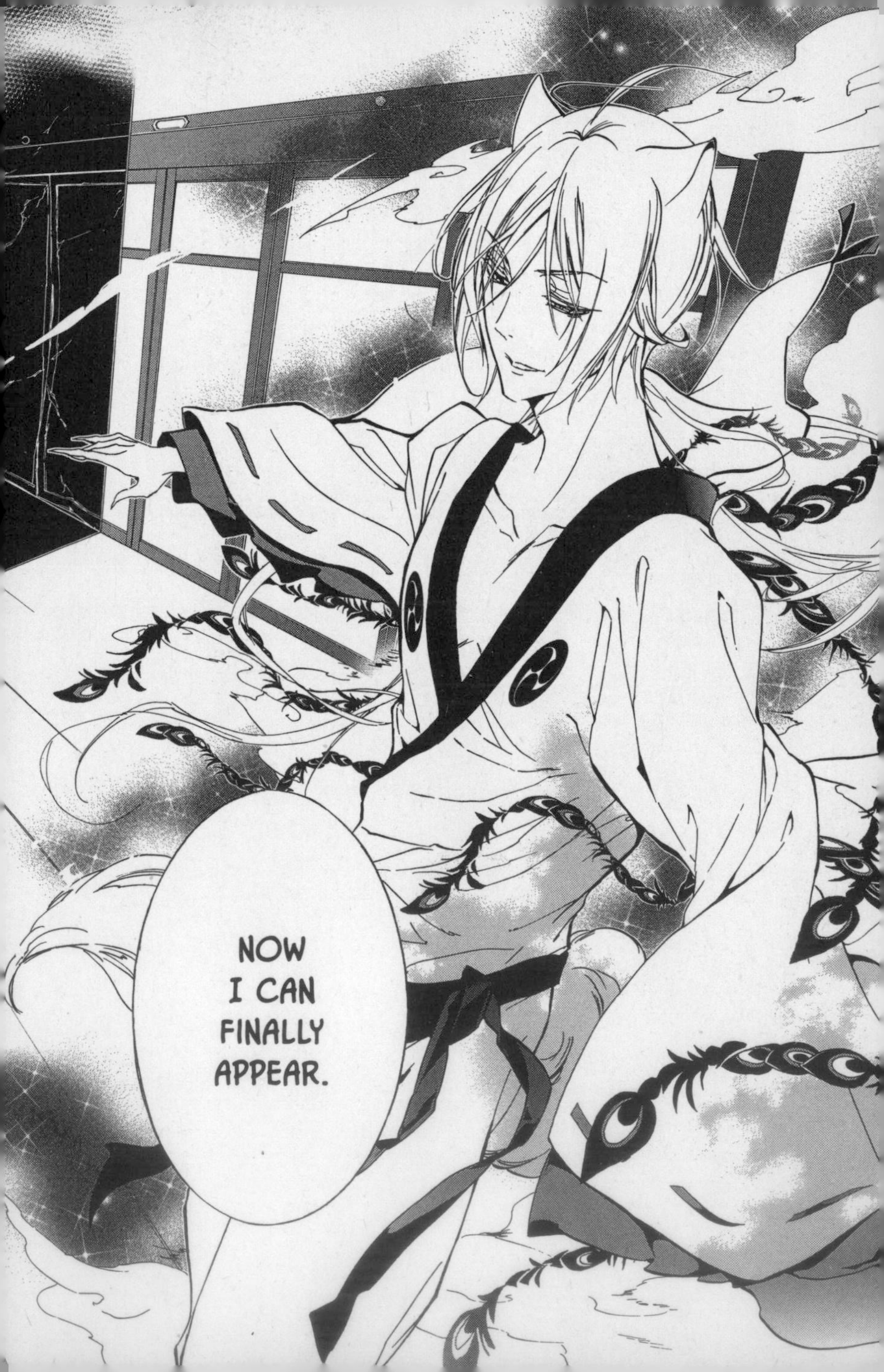
NOW I CAN FINALLY APPEAR.

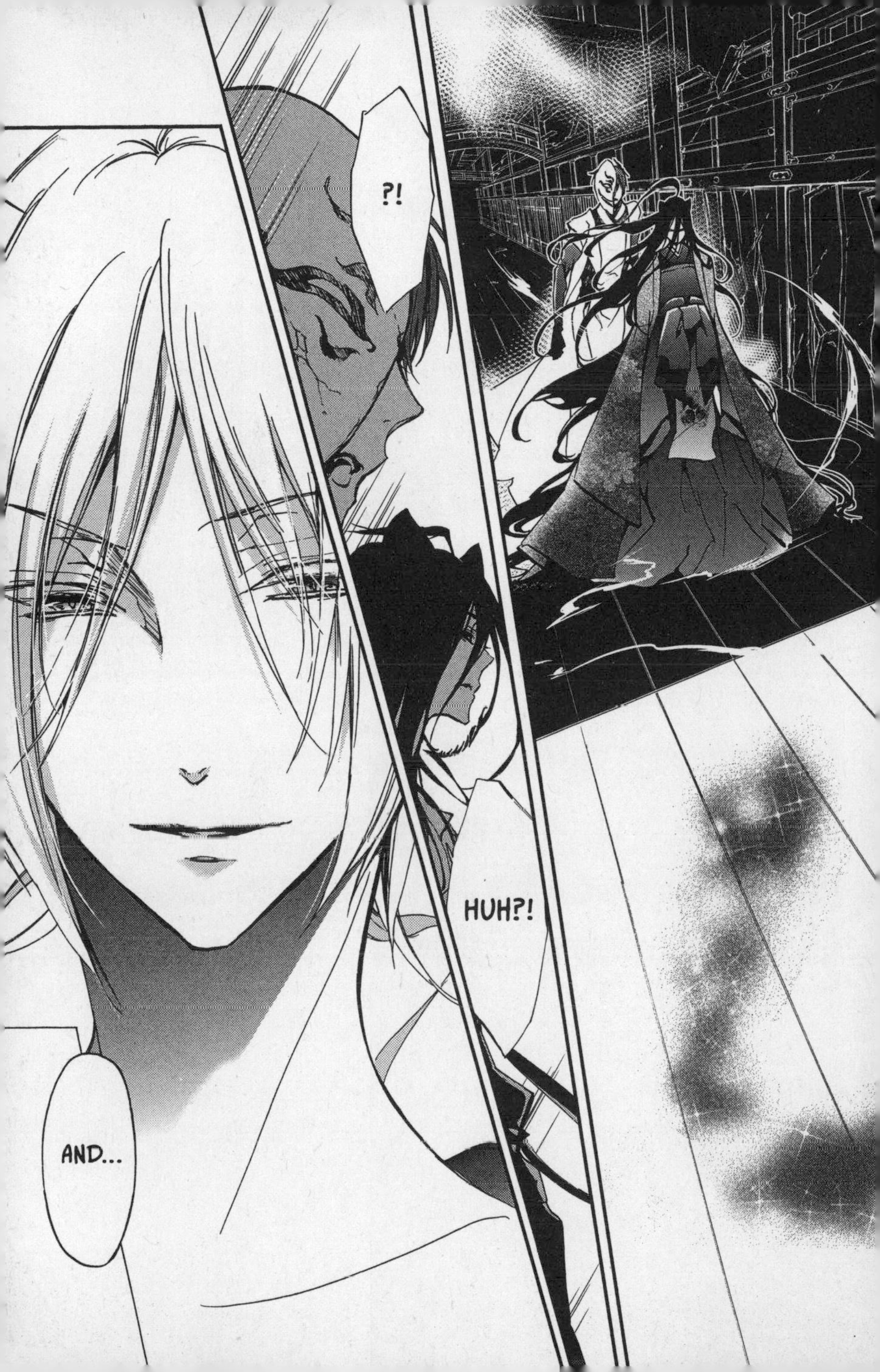
HUH?!
?!
AND...

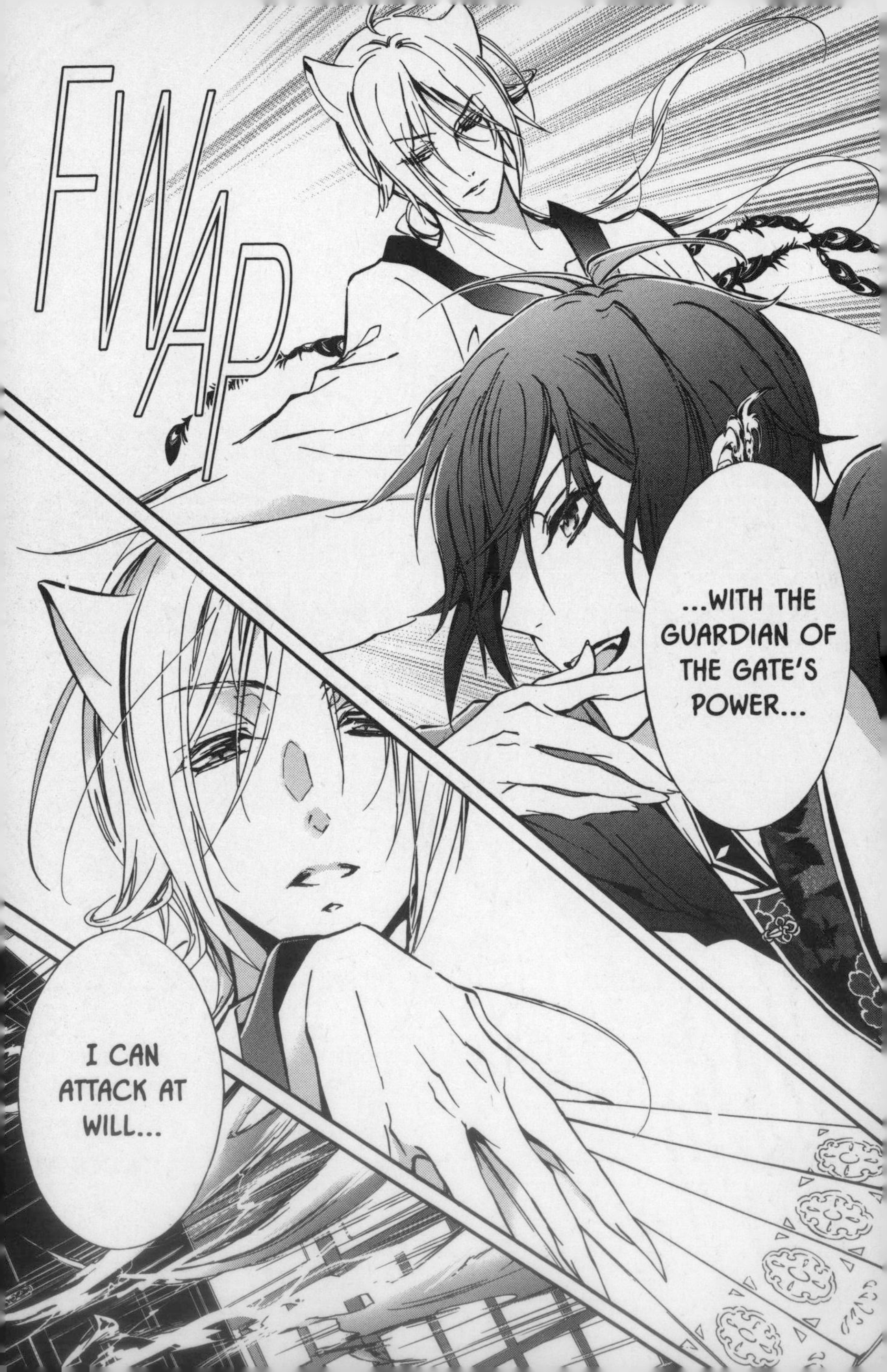
...WITH THE GUARDIAN OF THE GATE'S POWER...
FWAP
I CAN ATTACK AT WILL...

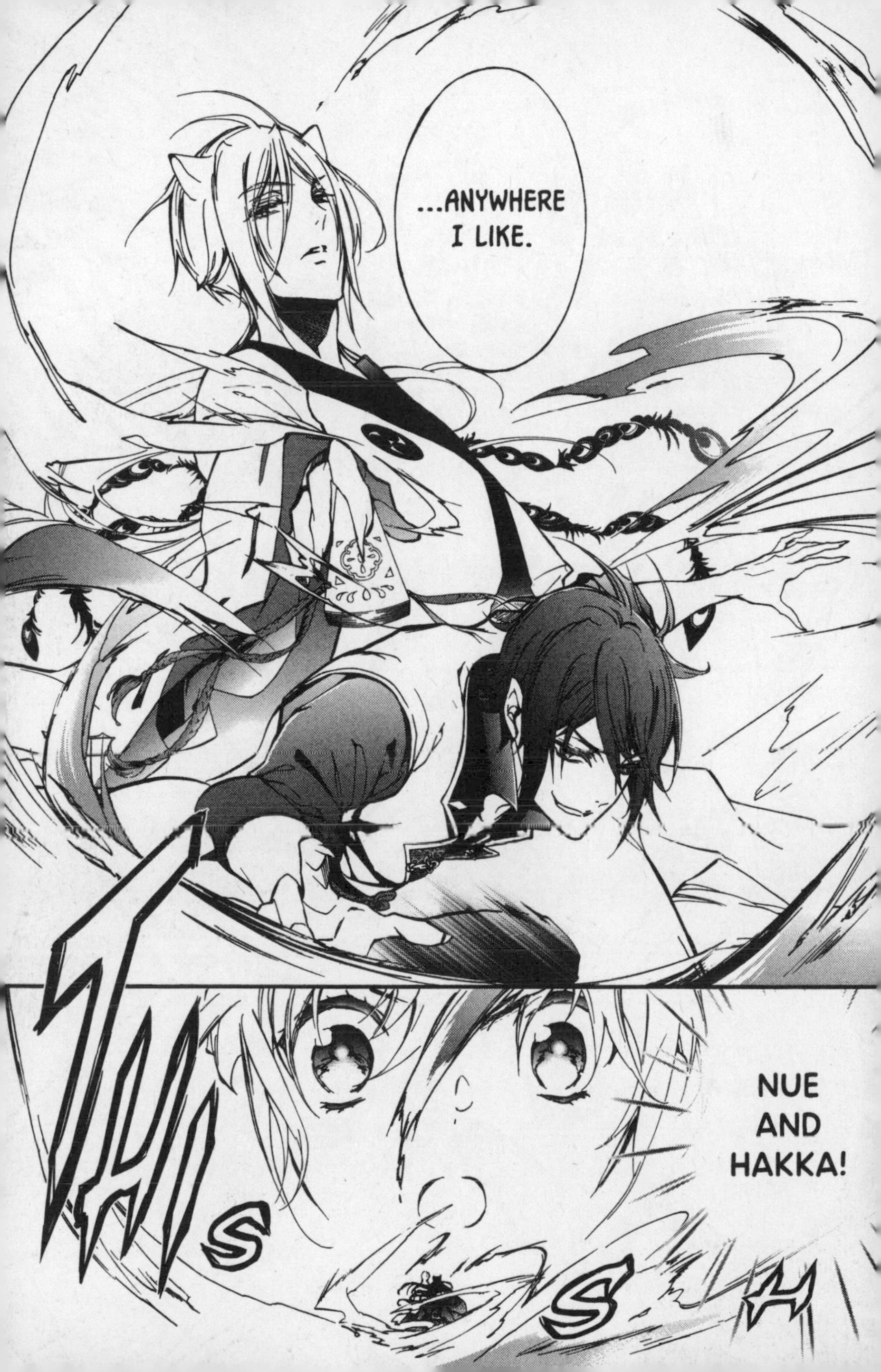
...ANYWHERE I LIKE.
NUE AND HAKKA!
SHHSSSH

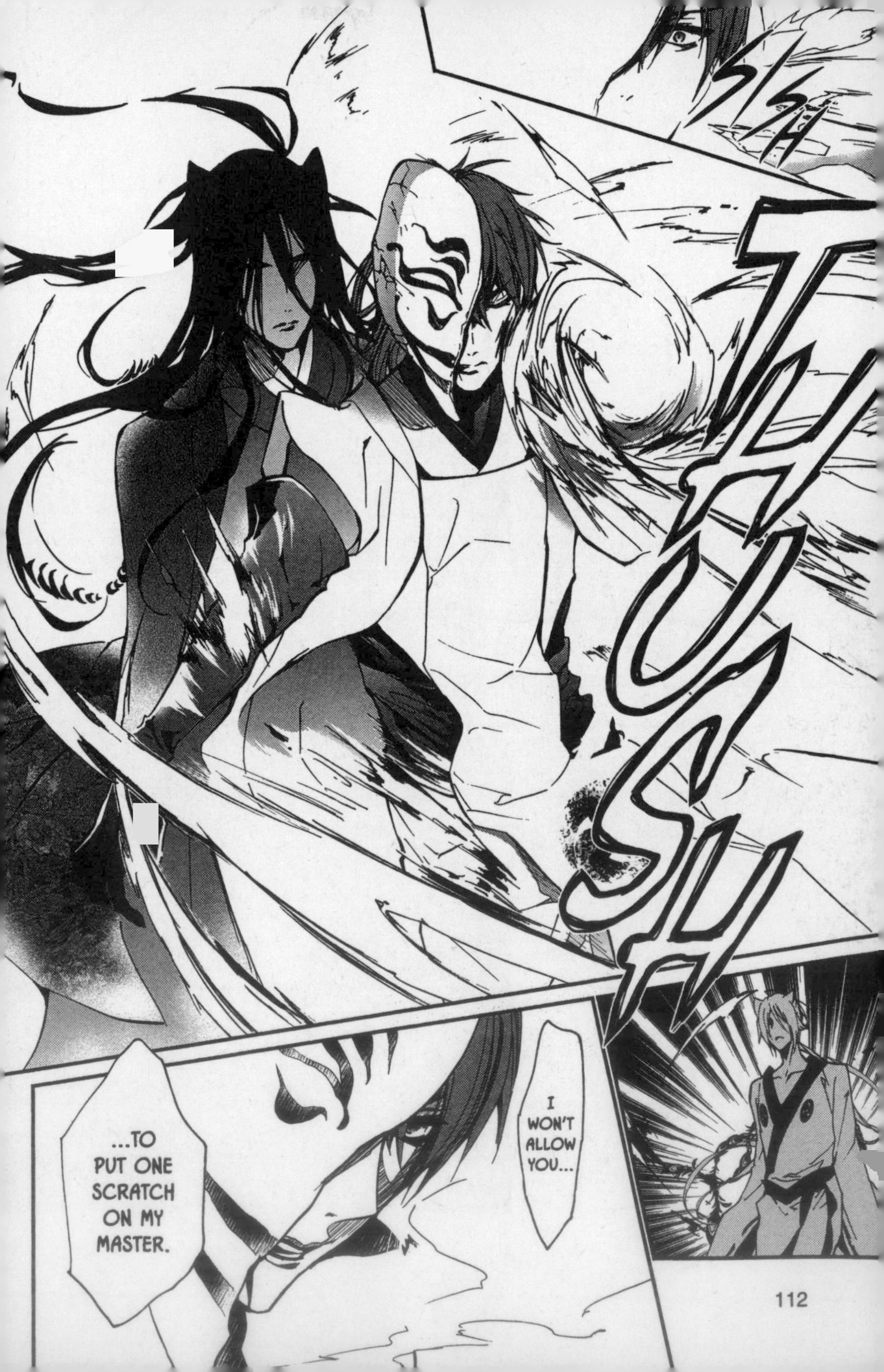
SLISH
THUSH
I WON'T ALLOW YOU...
...TO PUT ONE SCRATCH ON MY MASTER.

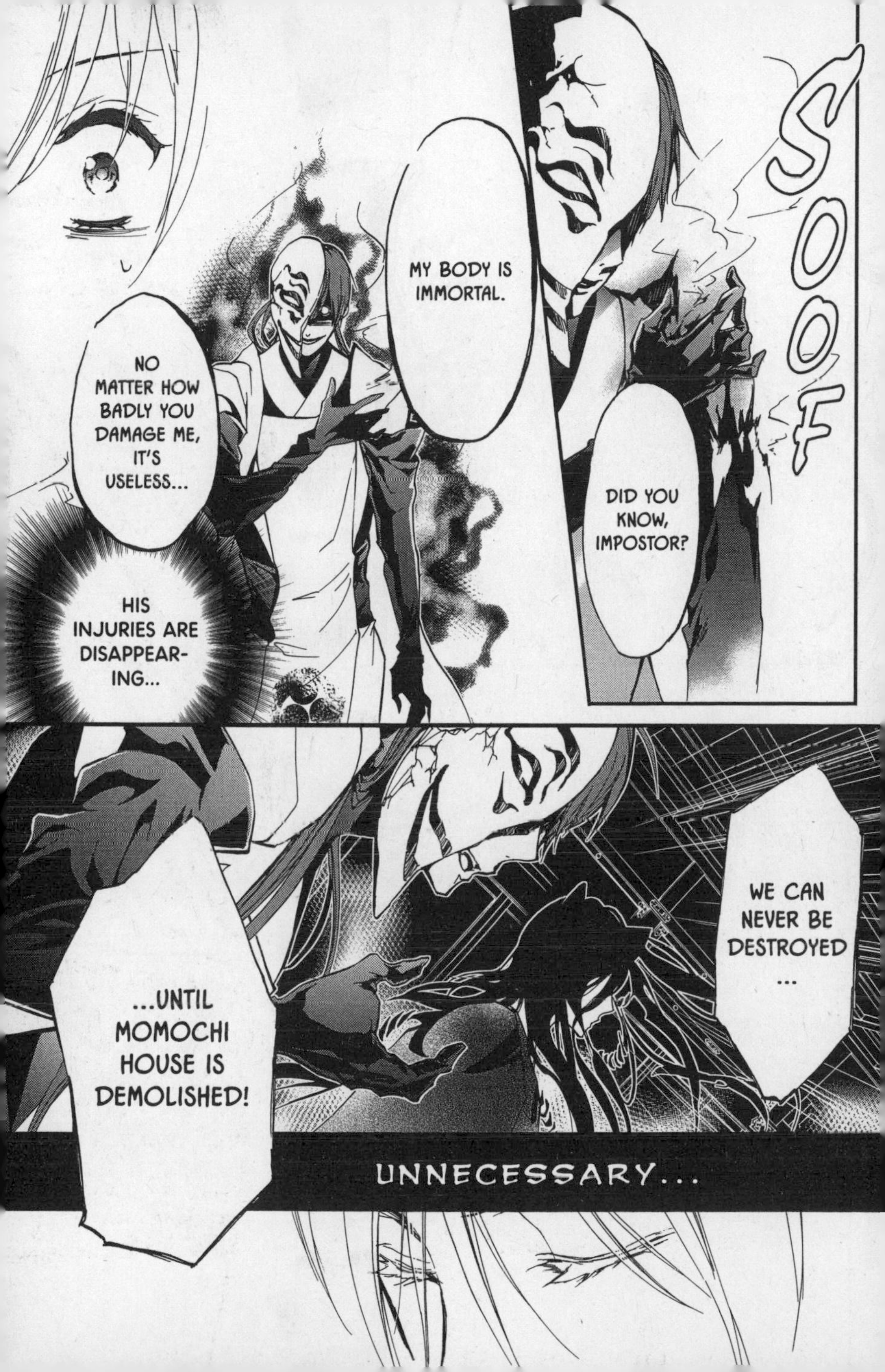
SOOF
DID YOU KNOW, IMPOSTOR?
MY BODY IS IMMORTAL.
NO MATTER HOW BADLY YOU DAMAGE ME, IT'S USELESS...
HIS INJURIES ARE DISAPPEARING...
WE CAN NEVER BE DESTROYED...
...UNTIL MOMOCHI HOUSE IS DEMOLISHED!
UNNECESSARY...

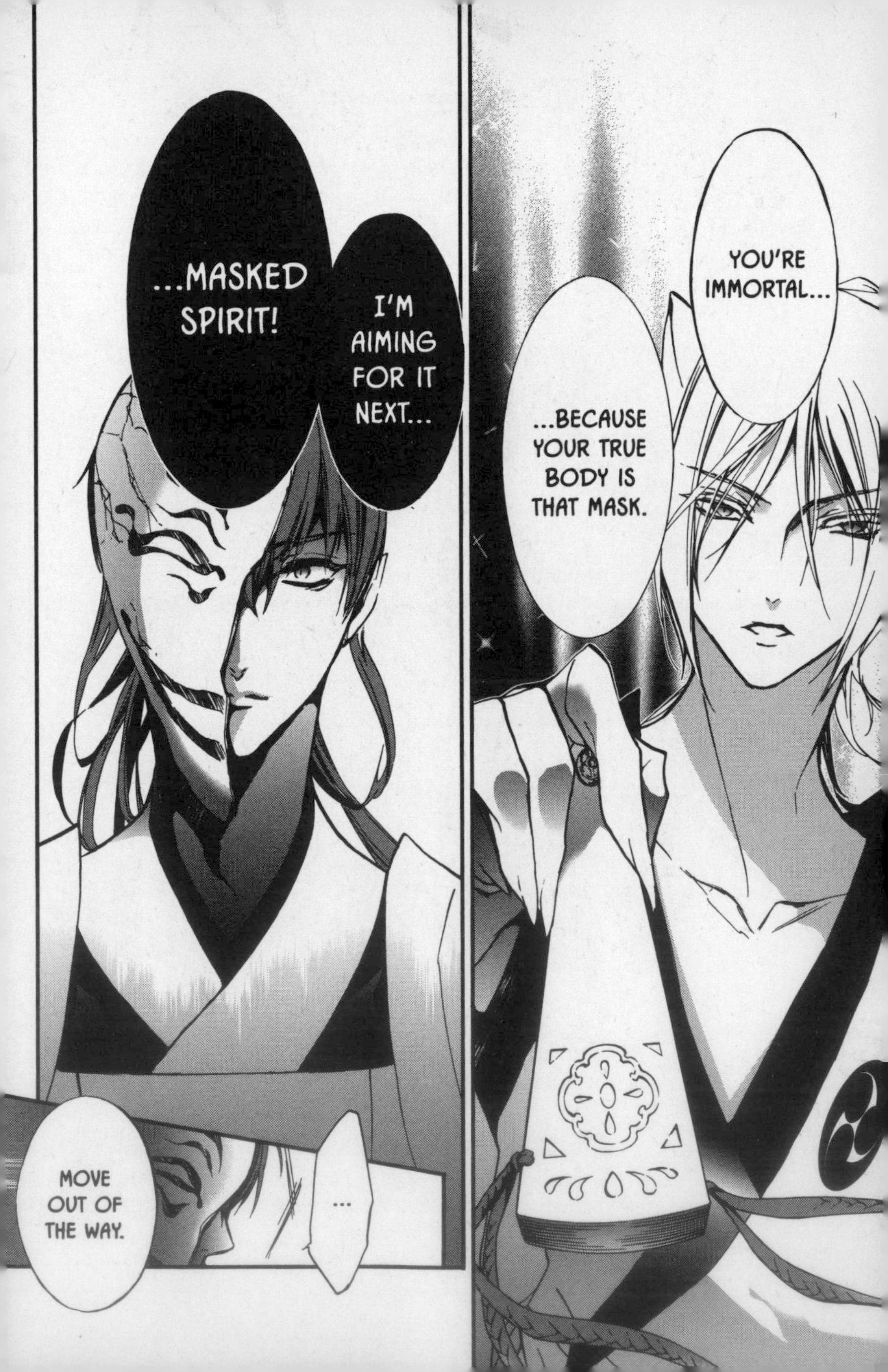
YOU'RE IMMORTAL...
...BECAUSE YOUR TRUE BODY IS THAT MASK.
...MASKED SPIRIT!
I'M AIMING FOR IT NEXT...
...
MOVE OUT OF THE WAY.

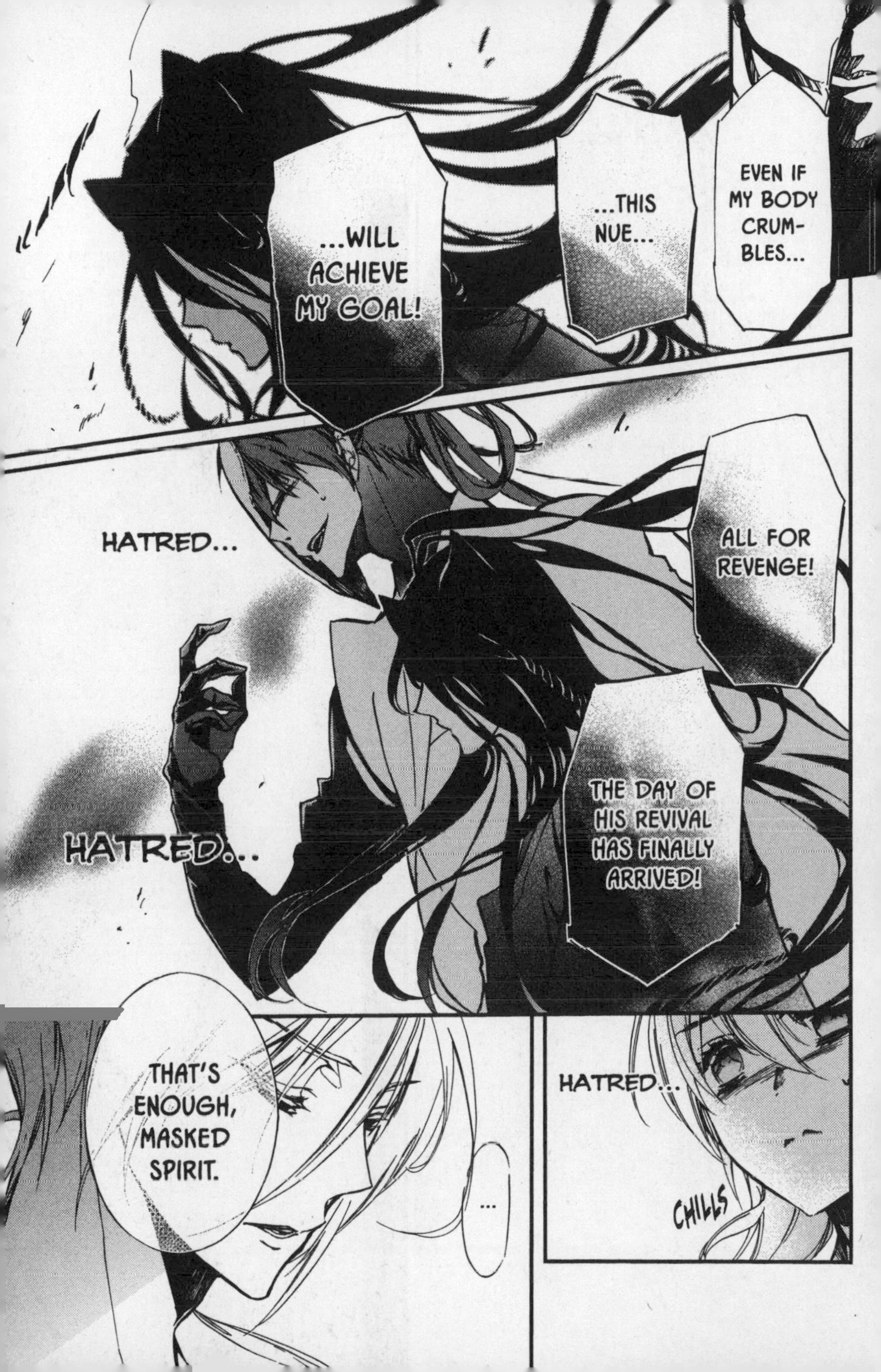
EVEN IF MY BODY CRUMBLES...
...THIS NUE...
...WILL ACHIEVE MY GOAL!
ALL FOR REVENGE!
THE DAY OF HIS REVIVAL HAS FINALLY ARRIVED!
HATRED...
HATRED...
HATRED...
CHILLS
THAT'S ENOUGH, MASKED SPIRIT.
...

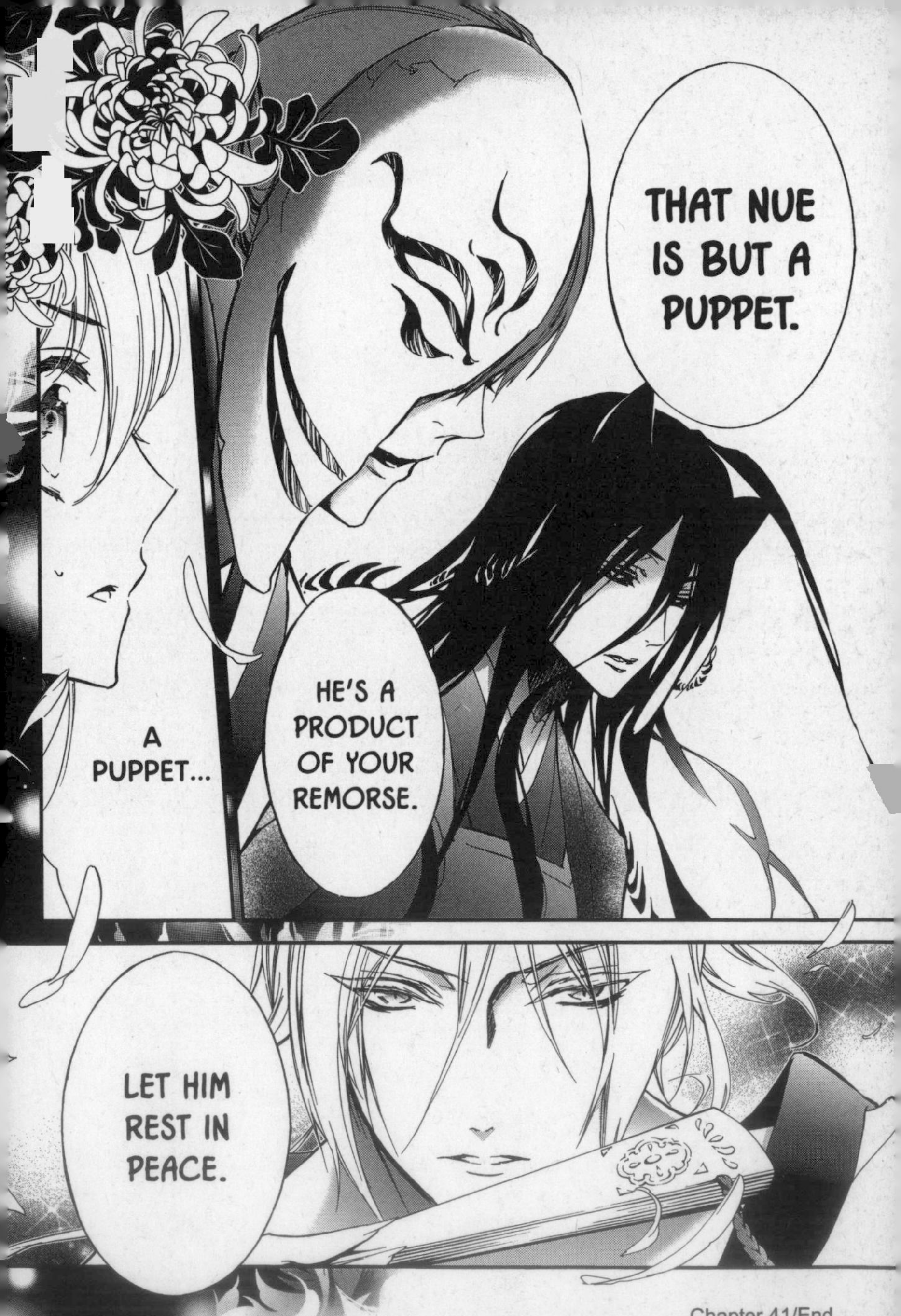
THAT NUE IS BUT A PUPPET.
HE'S A PRODUCT OF YOUR REMORSE.
A PUPPET...
LET HIM REST IN PEACE.

Chapter 41/End

The
DEMON
PRINCE
of MOMOCHI
HOUSE

The DEMON PRINCE of MOMOCHI HOUSE

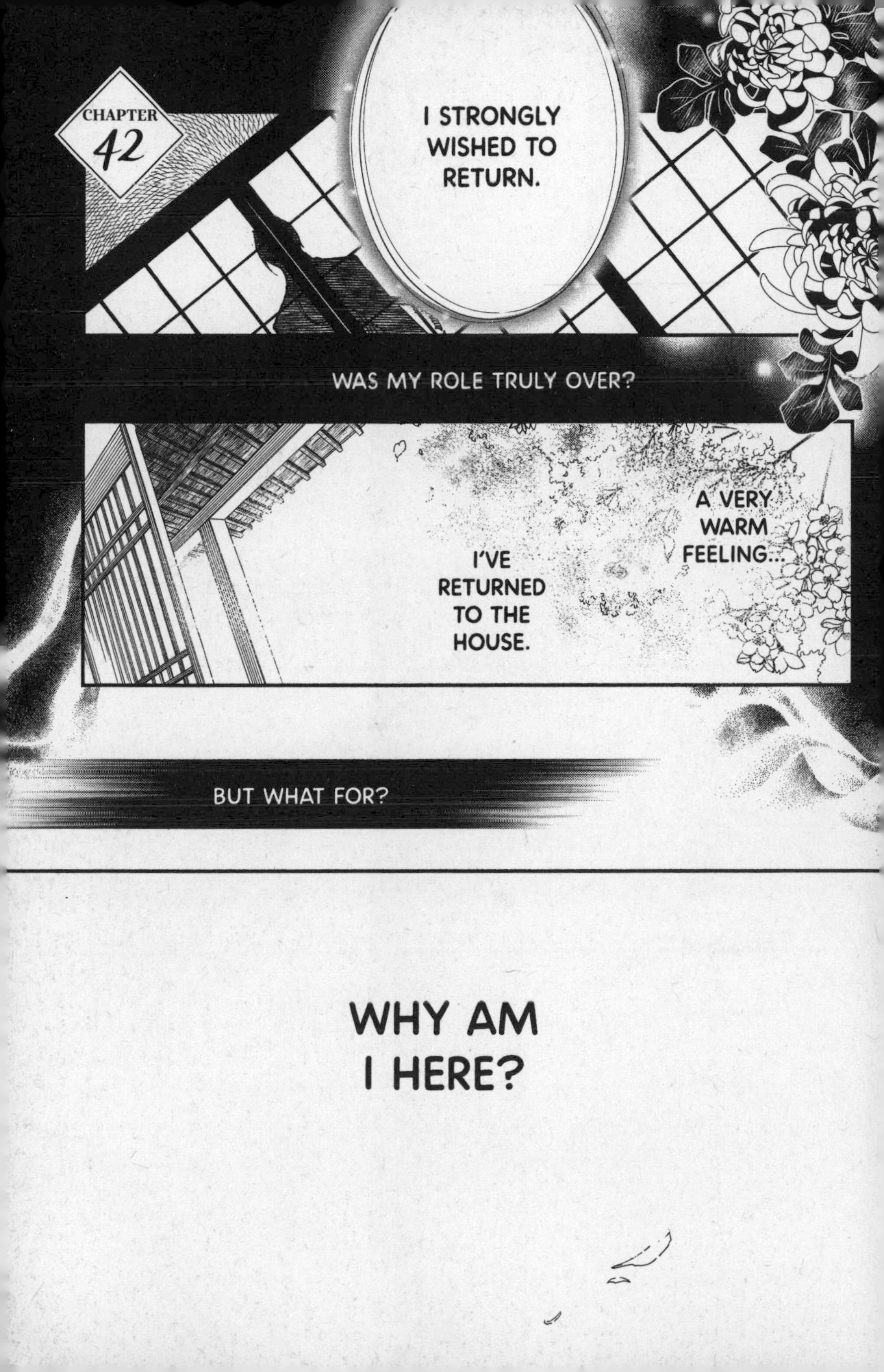
CHAPTER 42
I STRONGLY WISHED TO RETURN.
WAS MY ROLE TRULY OVER?
A VERY WARM FEELING...
I'VE RETURNED TO THE HOUSE.
BUT WHAT FOR?
WHY AM I HERE?

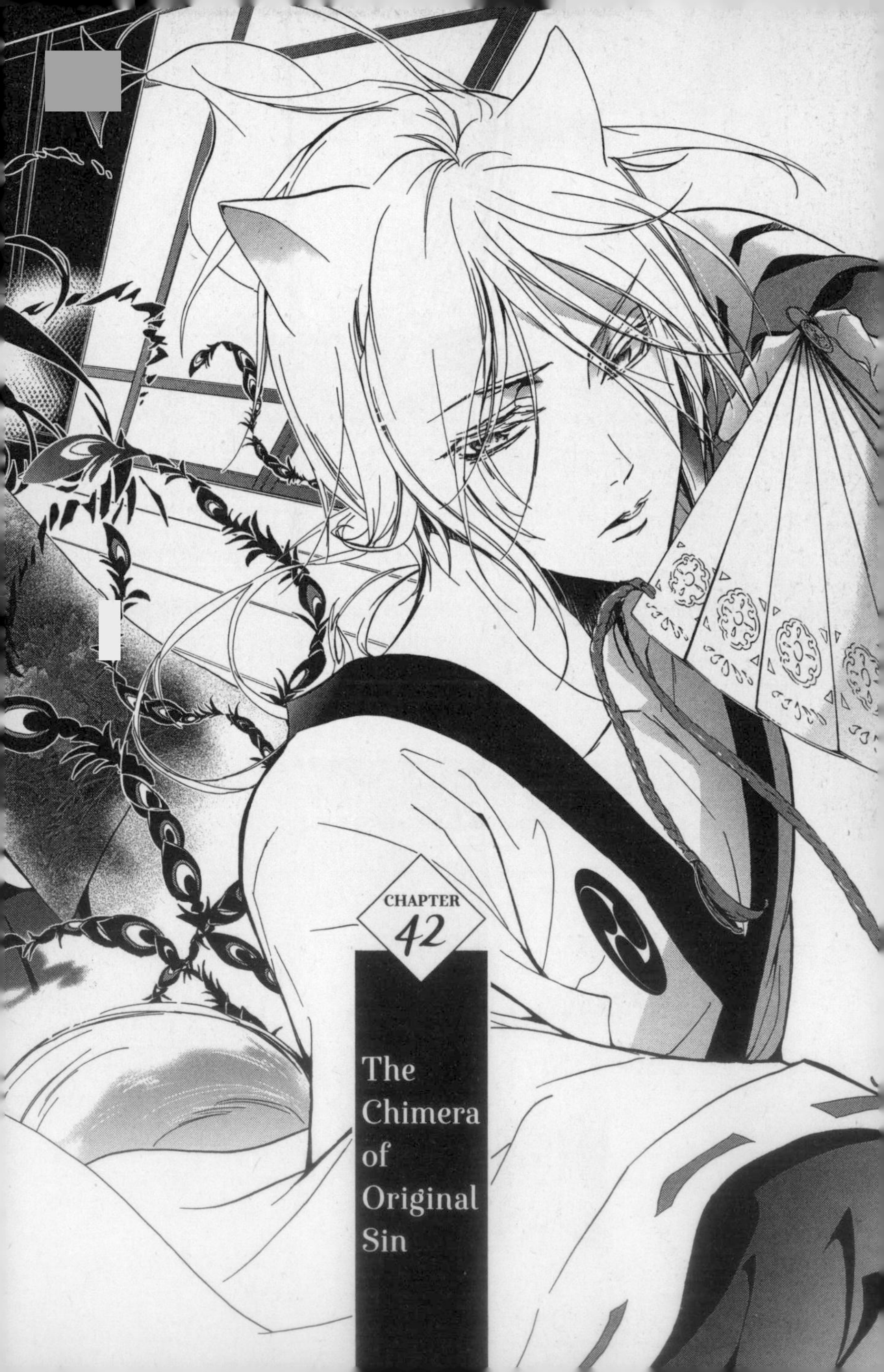
CHAPTER
42
The Chimera of Original Sin

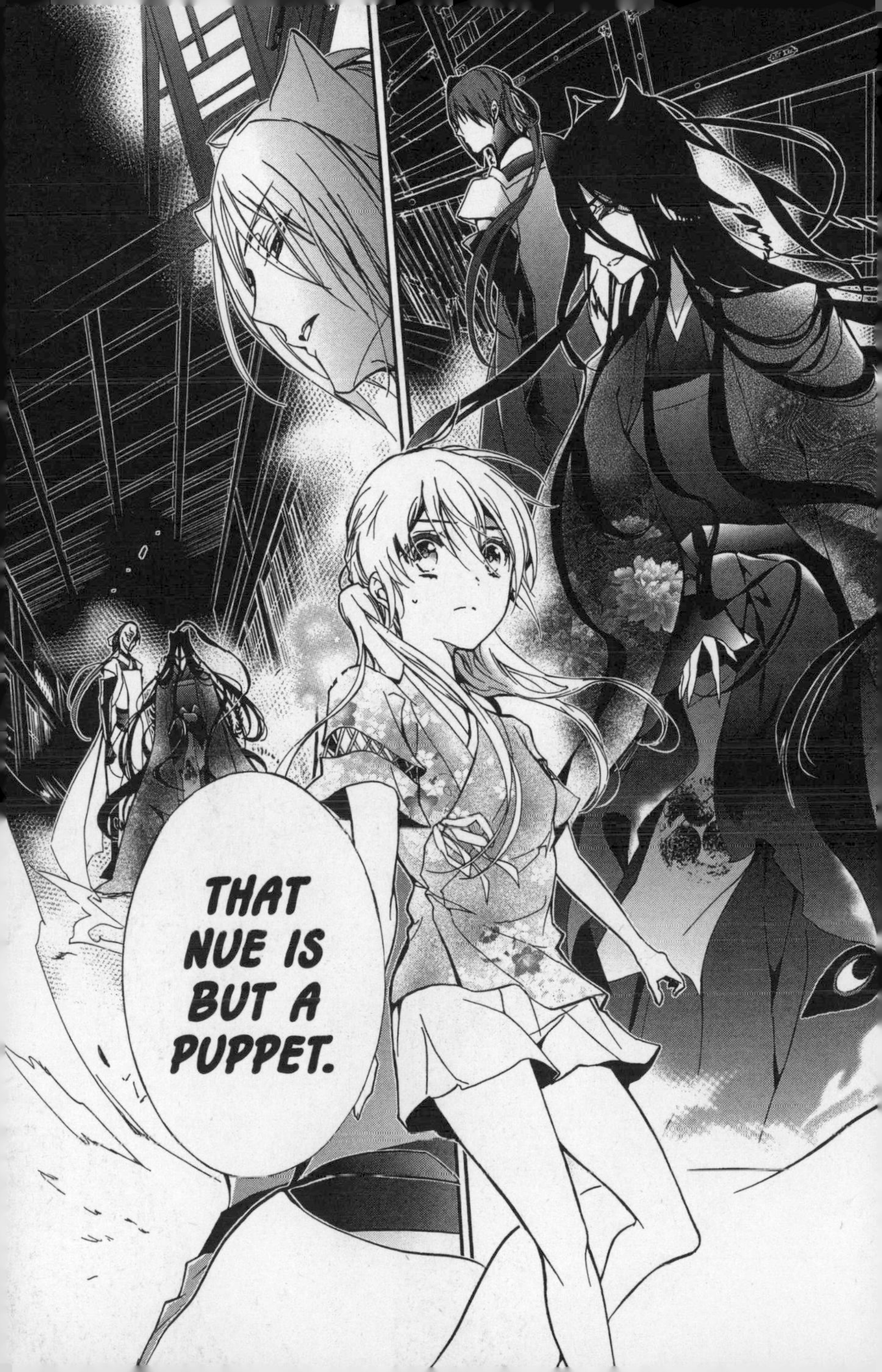
THAT NUE IS BUT A PUPPET.

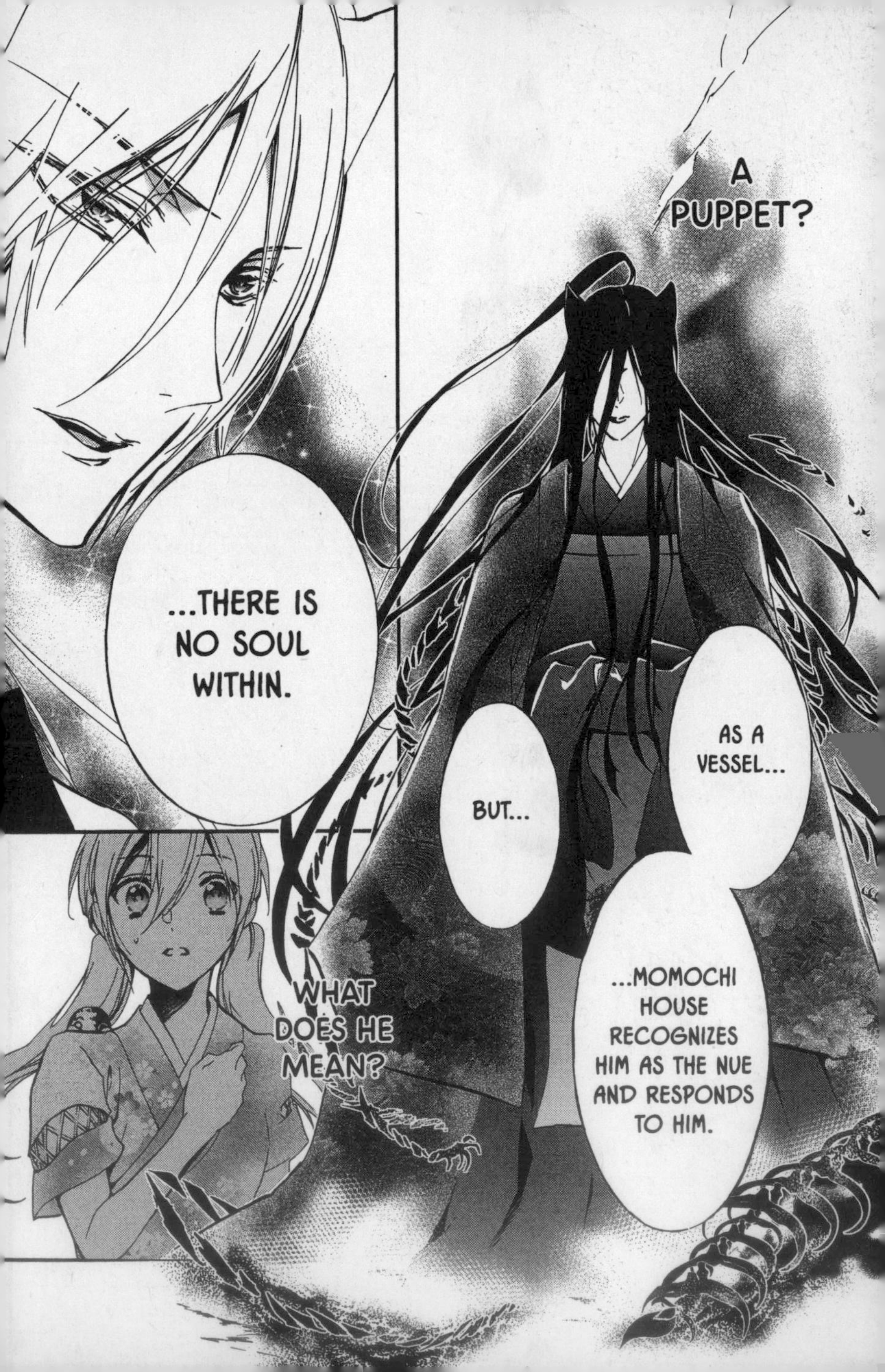
A PUPPET?
AS A VESSEL...
...MOMOCHI HOUSE RECOGNIZES HIM AS THE NUE AND RESPONDS TO HIM.
BUT...
...THERE IS NO SOUL WITHIN.
WHAT DOES HE MEAN?

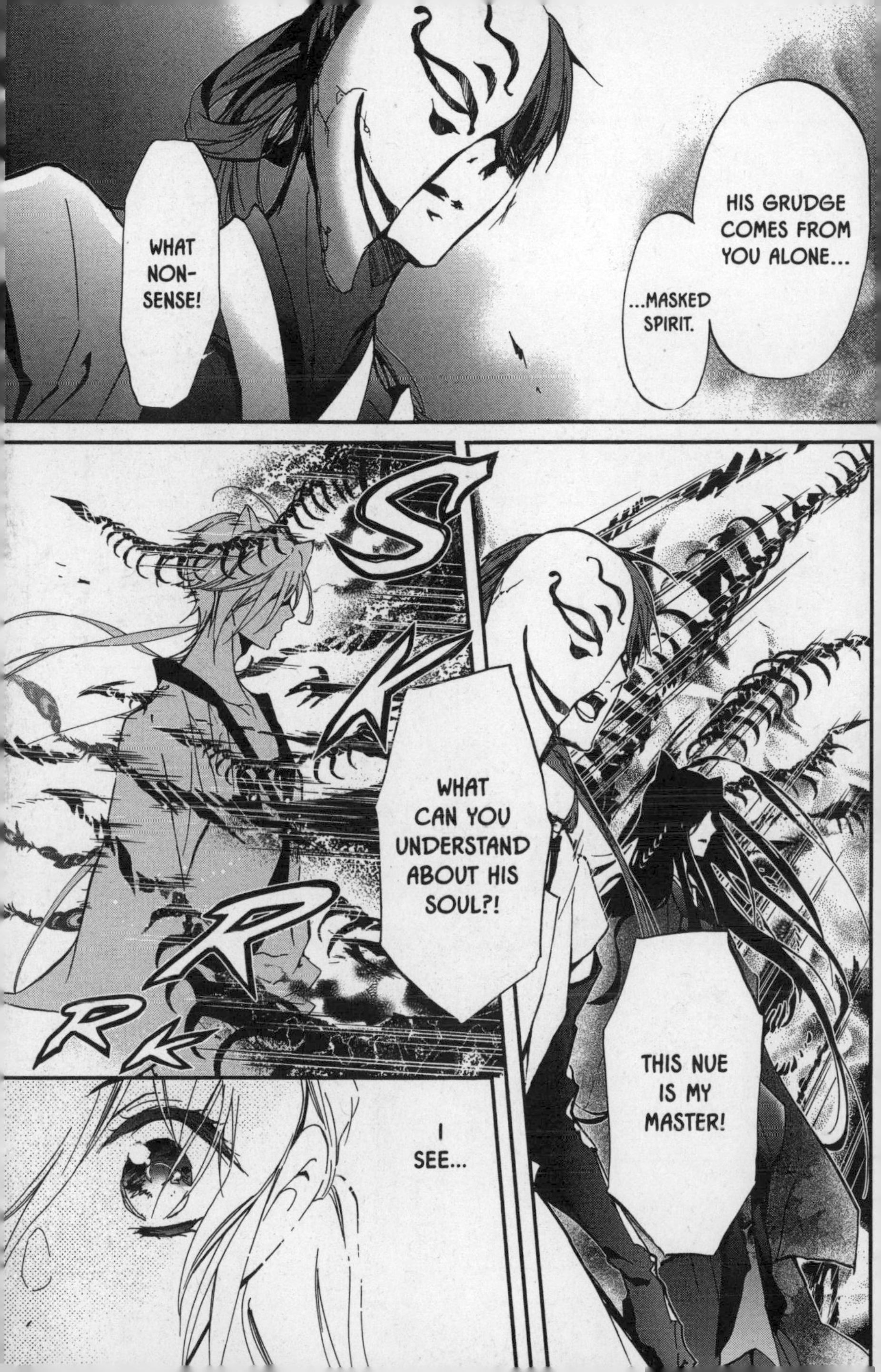
HIS GRUDGE COMES FROM YOU ALONE...
...MASKED SPIRIT.
WHAT NON-SENSE!
WHAT CAN YOU UNDERSTAND ABOUT HIS SOUL?!
THIS NUE IS MY MASTER!
SRK
RRK
I SEE...

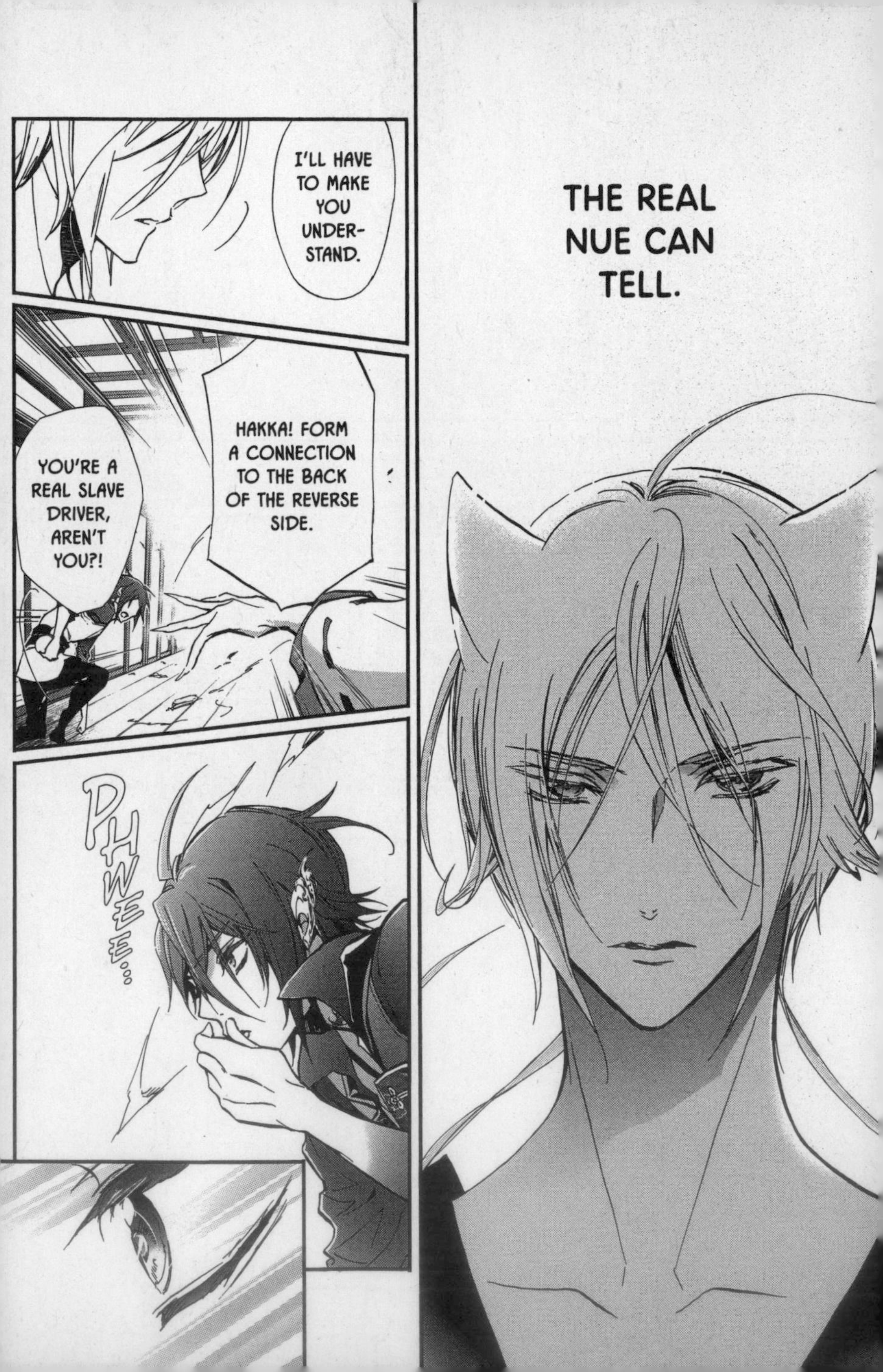
THE REAL NUE CAN TELL.
I'LL HAVE TO MAKE YOU UNDER-STAND.
HAKKA! FORM A CONNECTION TO THE BACK OF THE REVERSE SIDE.
YOU'RE A REAL SLAVE DRIVER, AREN'T YOU?!
PHWEE...

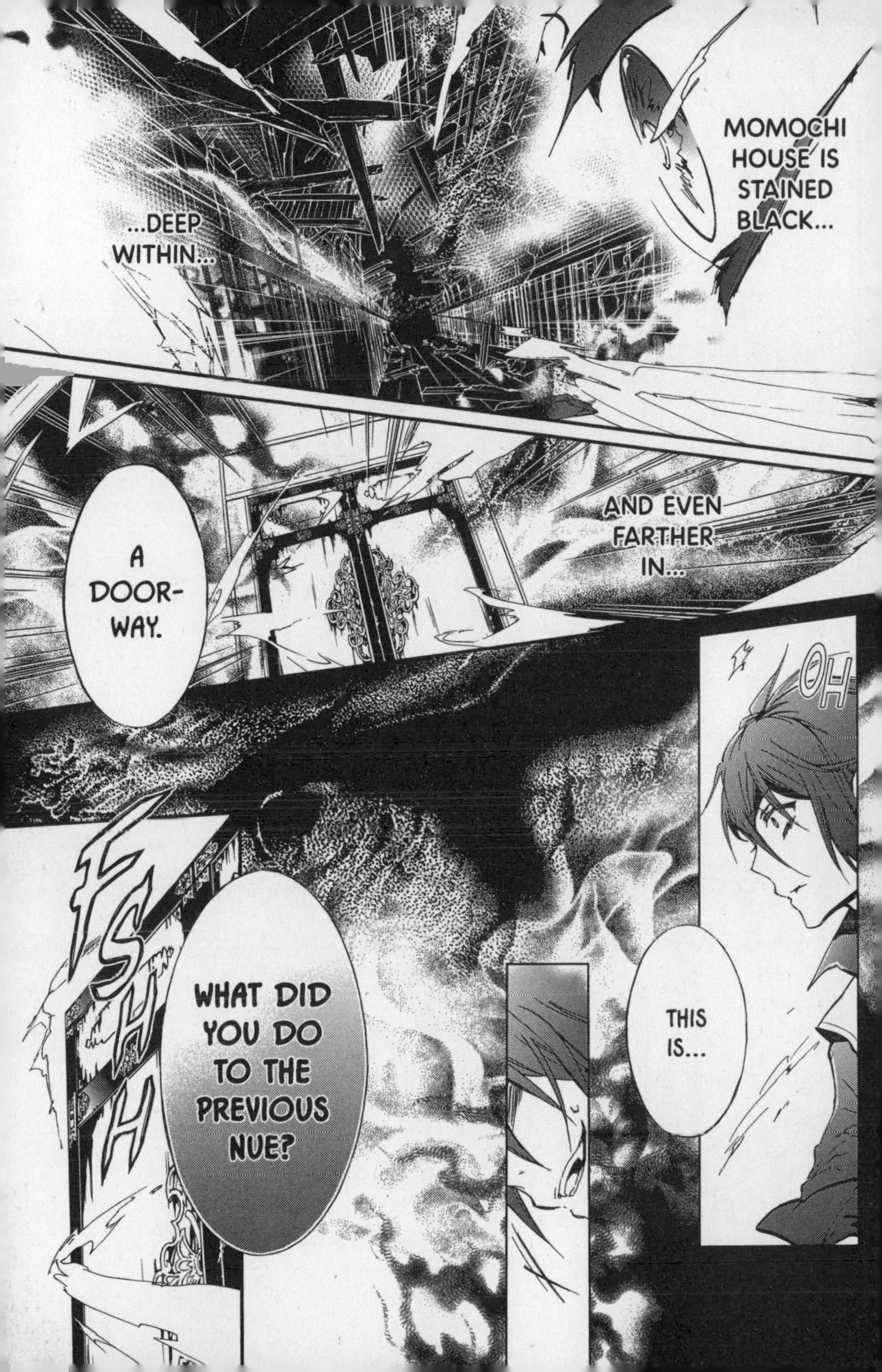
MOMOCHI HOUSE IS STAINED BLACK...
...DEEP WITHIN...
AND EVEN FARTHER IN...
A DOOR-WAY.
OH
THIS IS...
FSHH
WHAT DID YOU DO TO THE PREVIOUS NUE?

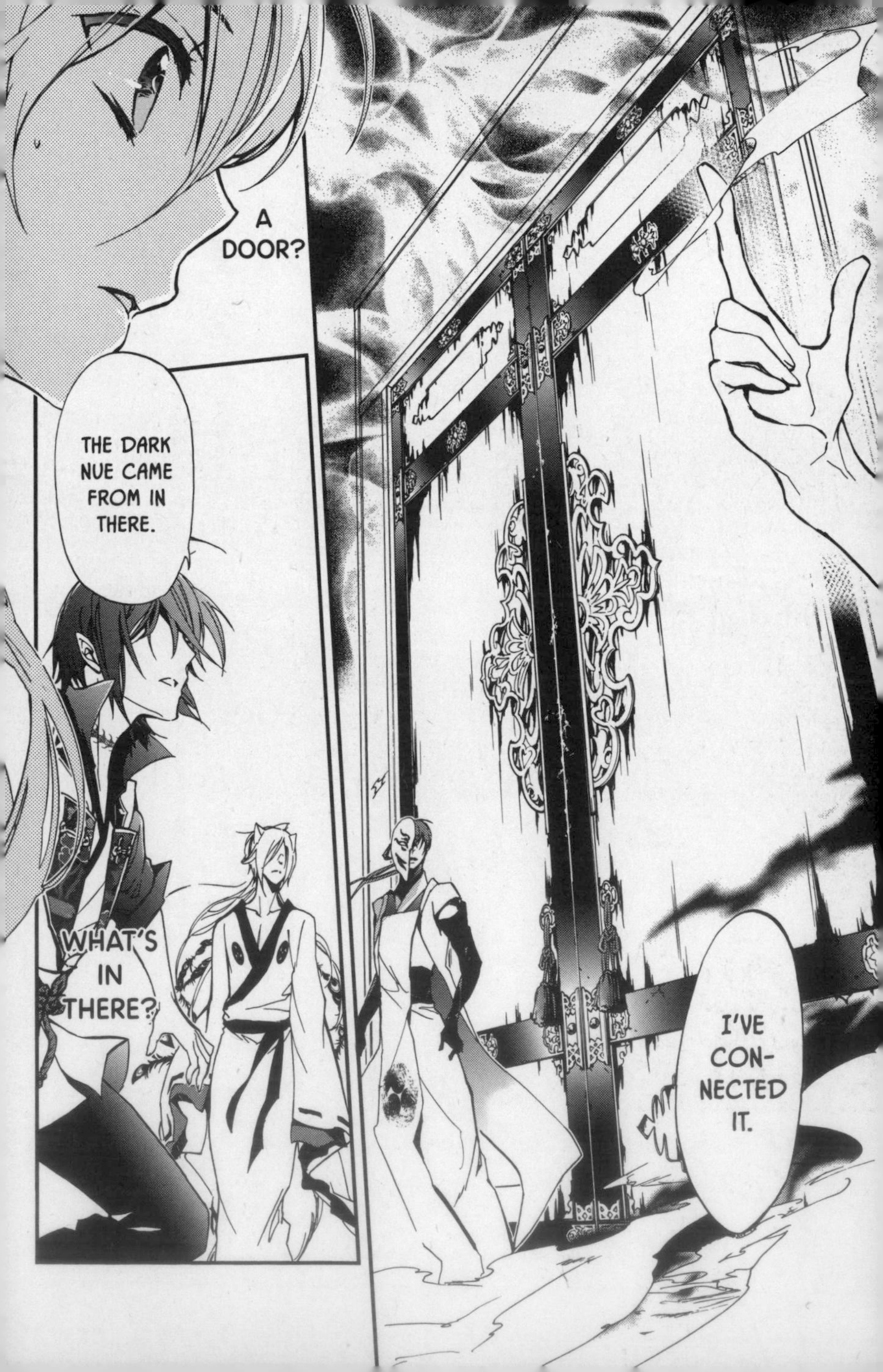
I'VE CON- NECTED IT.
A DOOR?
THE DARK NUE CAME FROM IN THERE.
WHAT'S IN THERE?

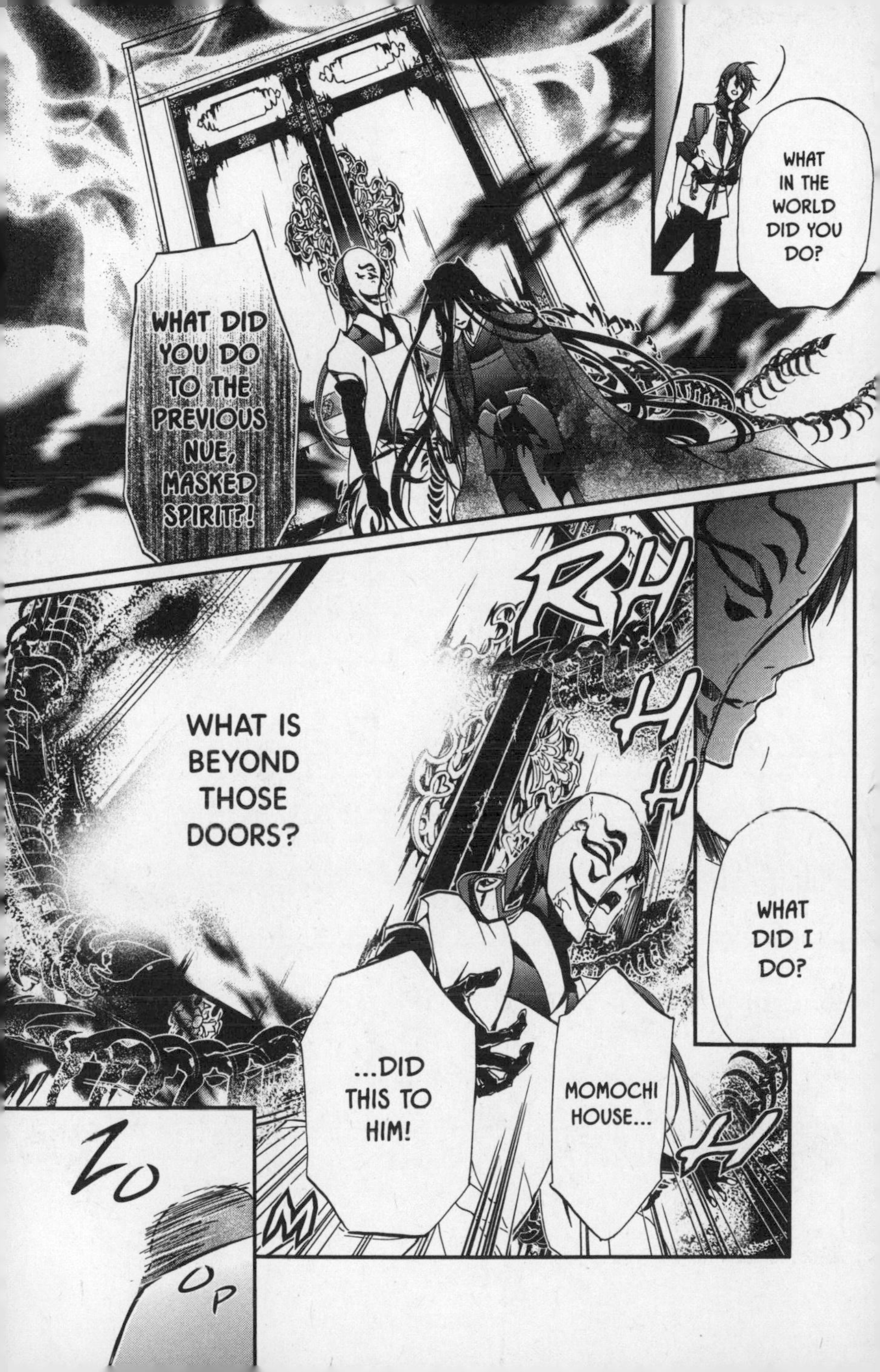
WHAT IN THE WORLD DID YOU DO?
WHAT DID YOU DO TO THE PREVIOUS NUE, MASKED SPIRIT?!
RHHHH
WHAT DID I DO?
WHAT IS BEYOND THOSE DOORS?
MOMOCHI HOUSE...
...DID THIS TO HIM!
MMM
ZOOP

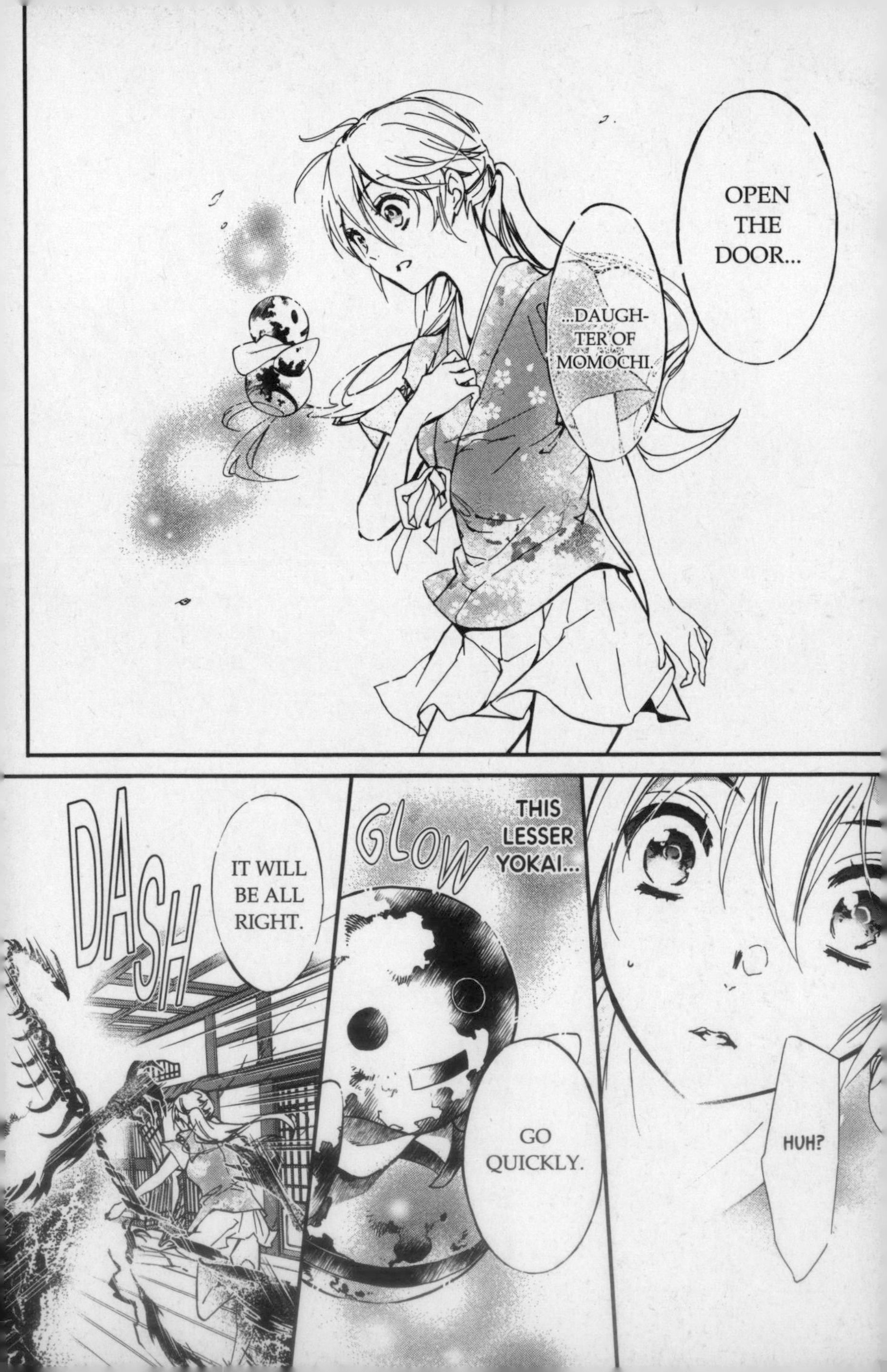
OPEN THE DOOR...
...DAUGHTER OF MOMOCHI.
HUH?
THIS LESSER YOKAI...
GO QUICKLY.
GLOW
IT WILL BE ALL RIGHT.
DASH

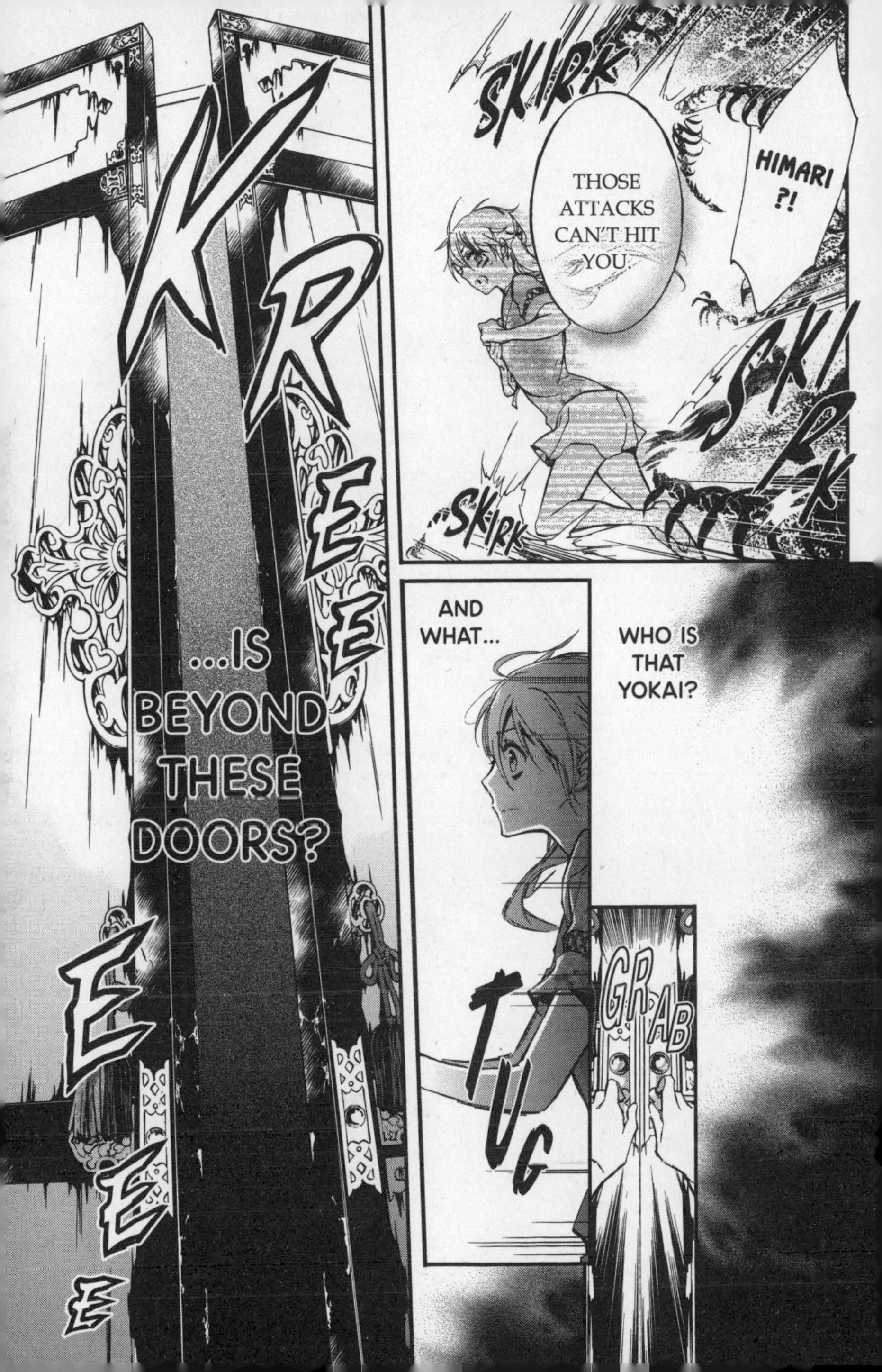
SKIRK
HIMARI ?!
THOSE ATTACKS CAN'T HIT YOU.
SKIRK
SKIRK
WHO IS THAT YOKAI?
AND WHAT...
GRAB
TUG
KREEEEE
...IS BEYOND THESE DOORS?

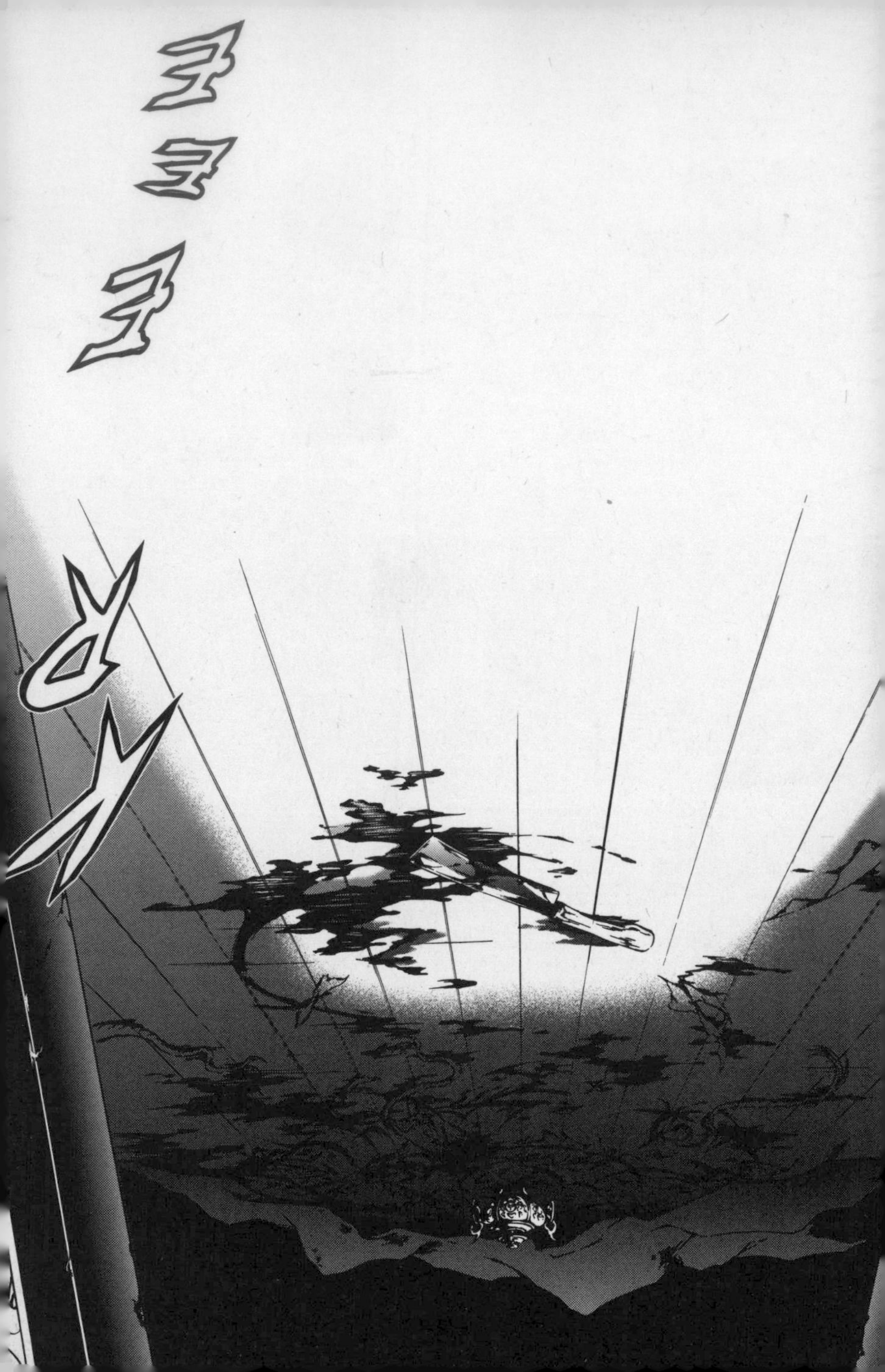

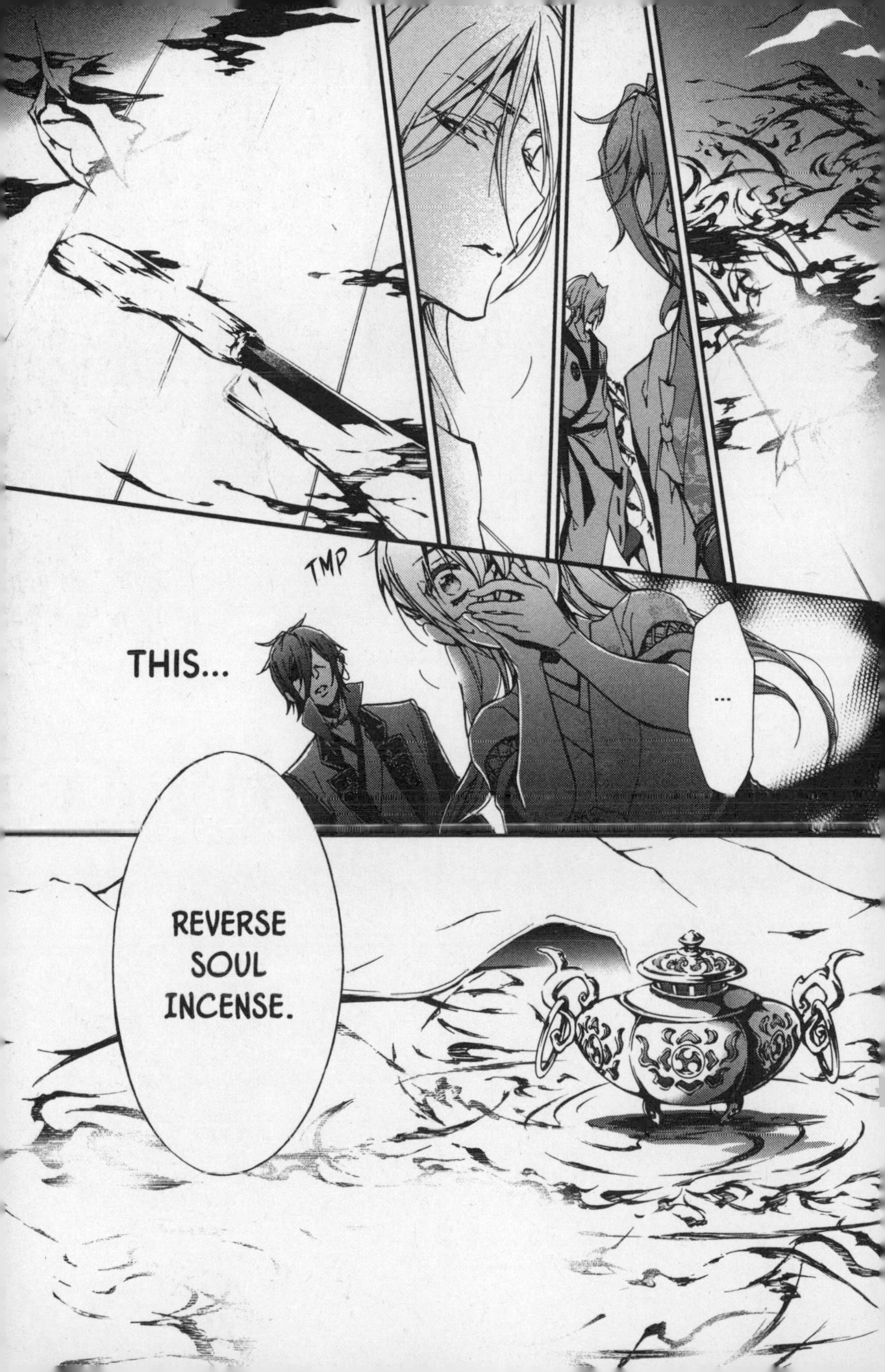
...
TMP
THIS...
REVERSE SOUL INCENSE.

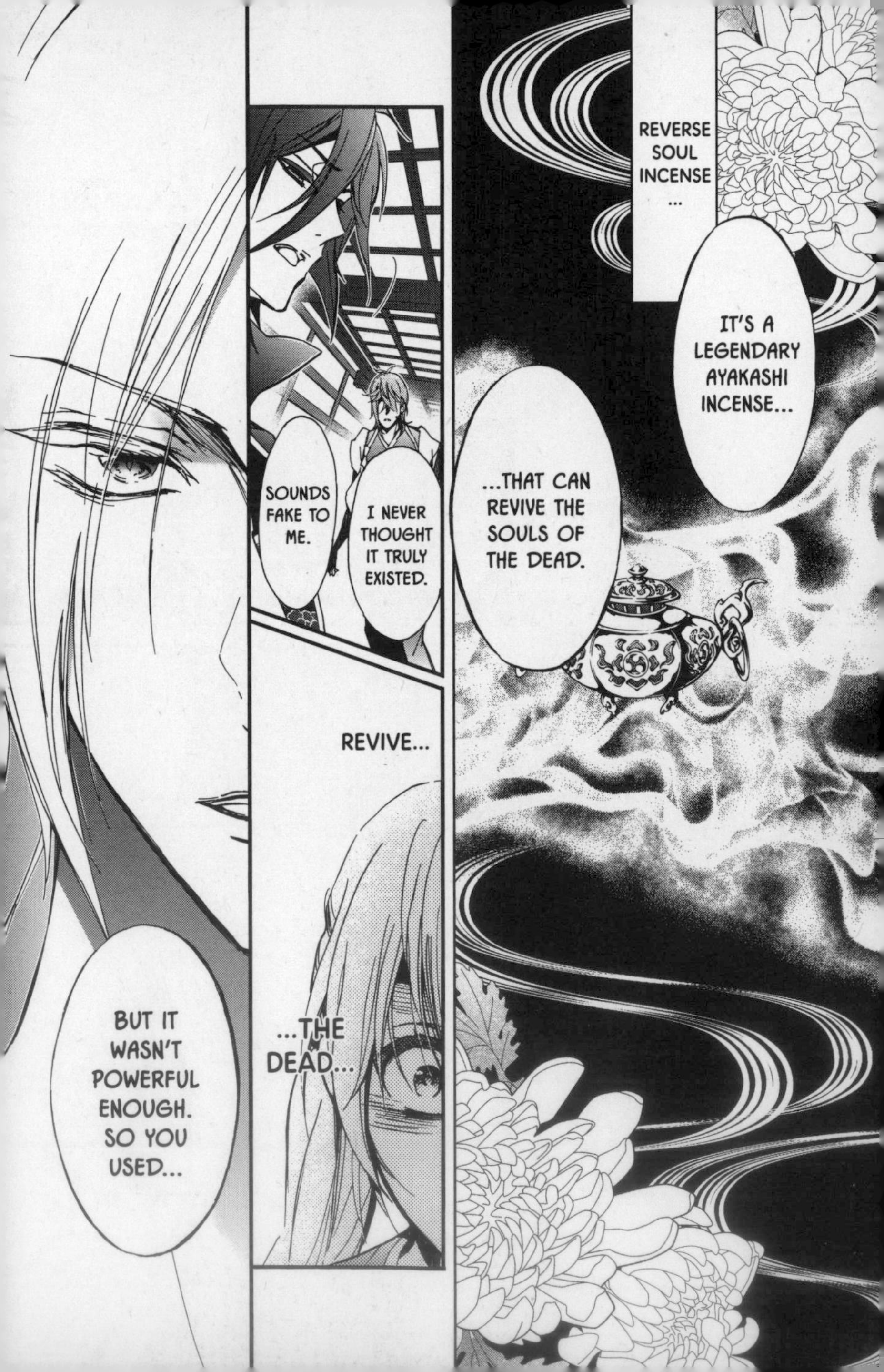
REVERSE SOUL INCENSE ...
IT'S A LEGENDARY AYAKASHI INCENSE...
...THAT CAN REVIVE THE SOULS OF THE DEAD.
I NEVER THOUGHT IT TRULY EXISTED.
SOUNDS FAKE TO ME.
REVIVE...
...THE DEAD...
BUT IT WASN'T POWERFUL ENOUGH. SO YOU USED...

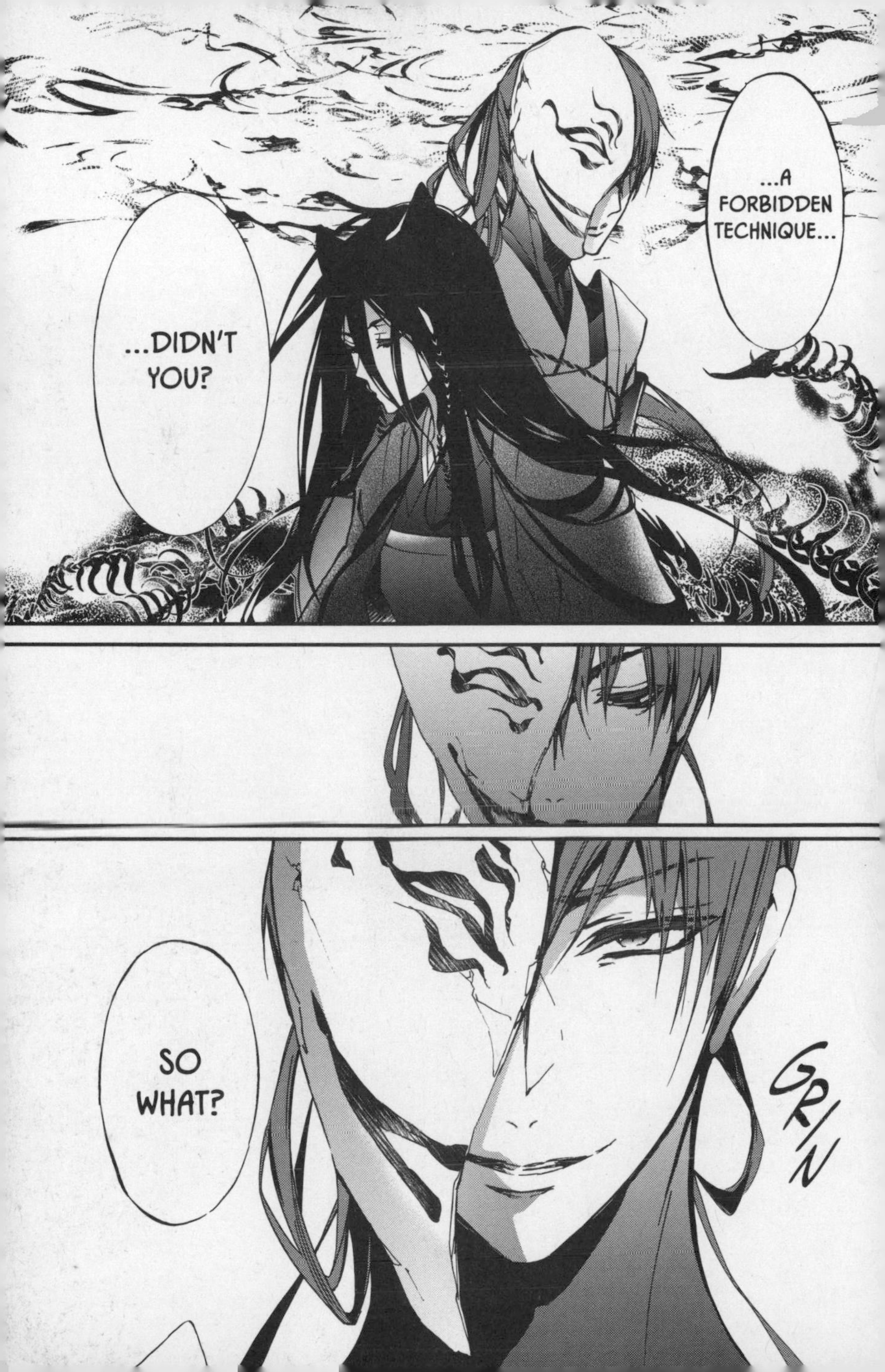
...A FORBIDDEN TECHNIQUE...
...DIDN'T YOU?
SO WHAT?
GRIN

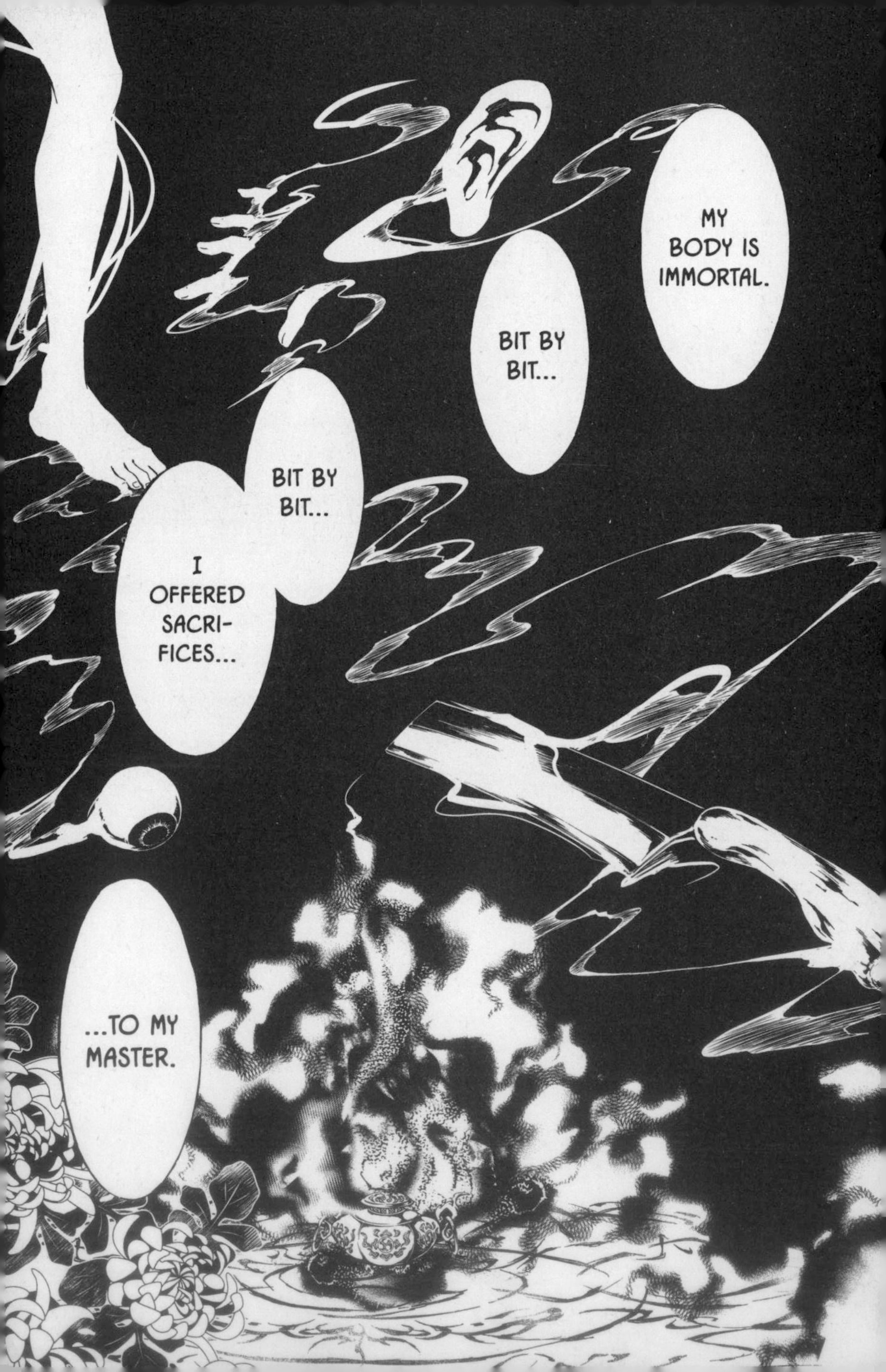
MY BODY IS IMMORTAL.
BIT BY BIT...
BIT BY BIT...
I OFFERED SACRI-FICES...
...TO MY MASTER.

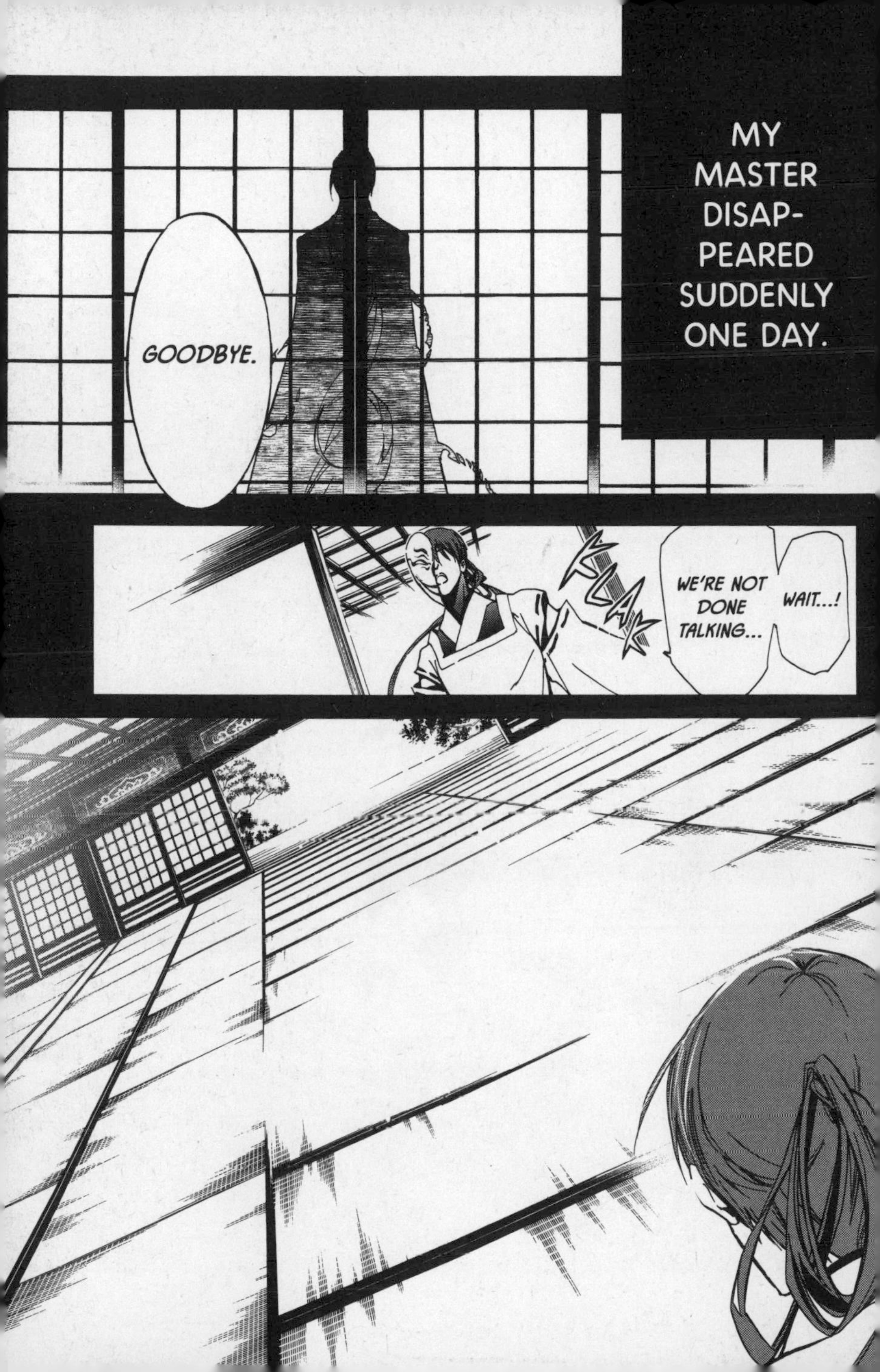
MY MASTER DISAP- PEARED SUDDENLY ONE DAY.
GOODBYE.
WAIT...!
WE'RE NOT DONE TALKING...
KLAK

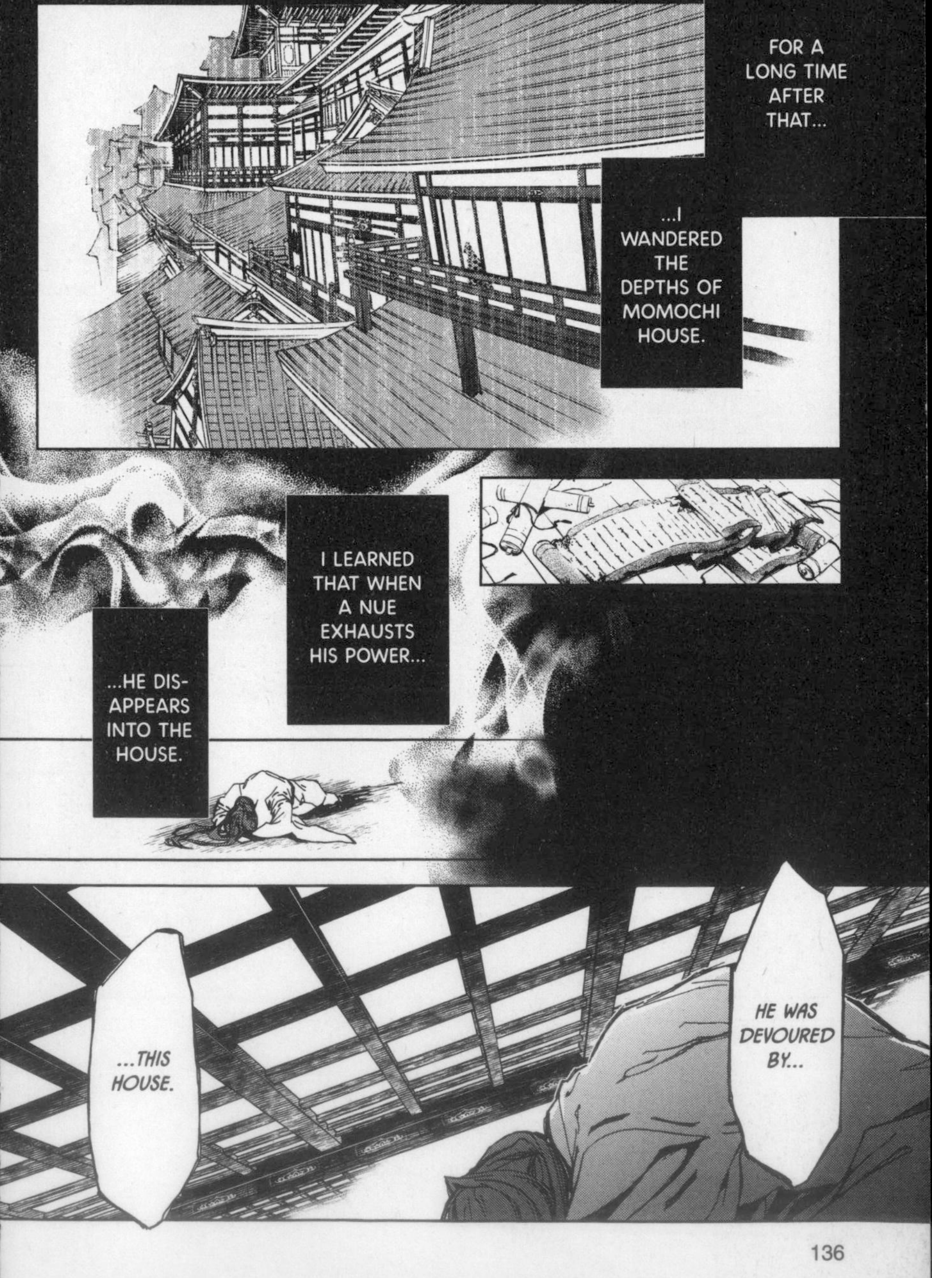
FOR A LONG TIME AFTER THAT...
...I WANDERED THE DEPTHS OF MOMOCHI HOUSE.
I LEARNED THAT WHEN A NUE EXHAUSTS HIS POWER...
...HE DIS-APPEARS INTO THE HOUSE.
HE WAS DEVOURED BY...
...THIS HOUSE.

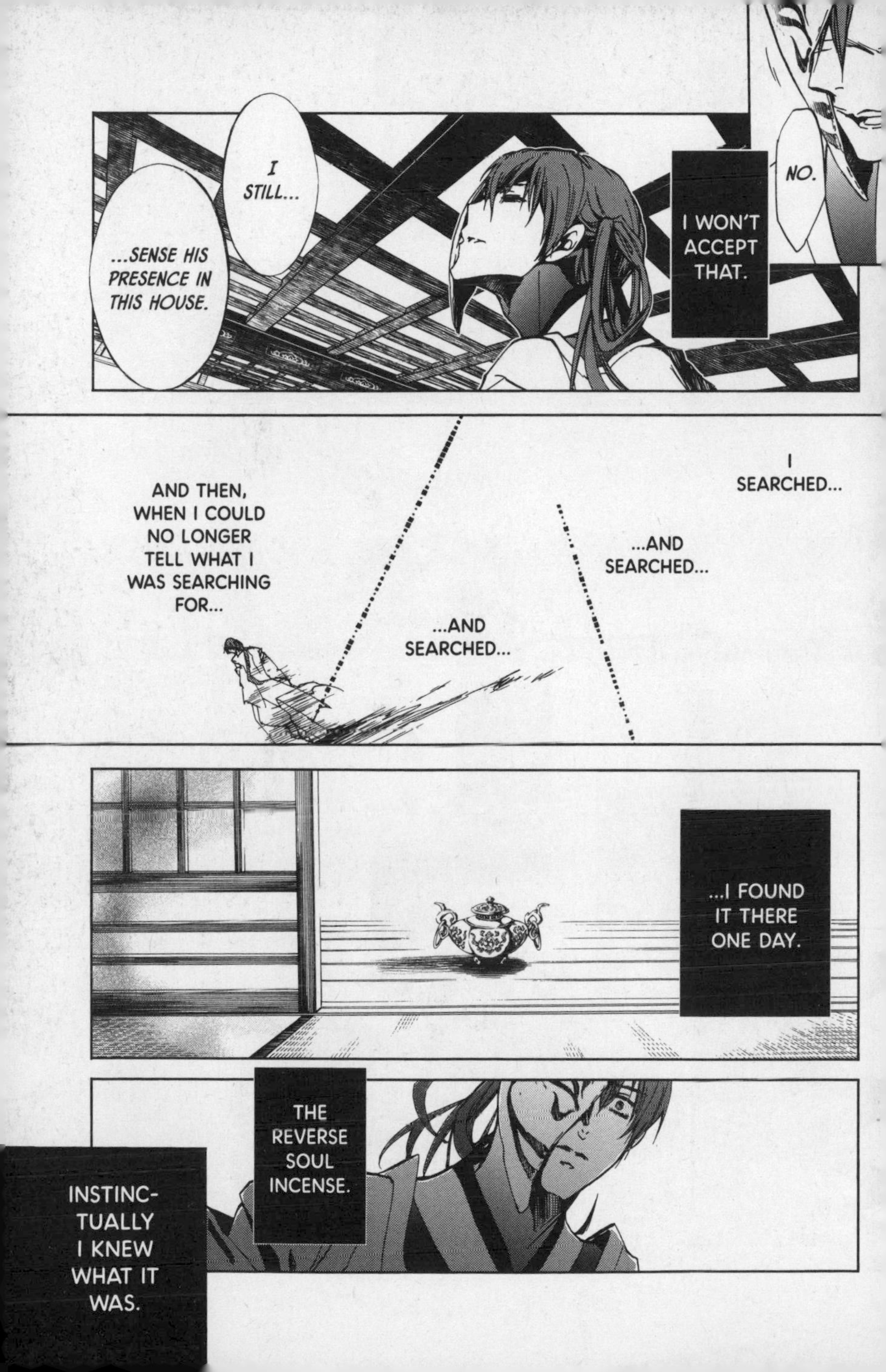
NO.
I WON'T ACCEPT THAT.
I STILL...
...SENSE HIS PRESENCE IN THIS HOUSE.
I SEARCHED...
...AND SEARCHED...
...AND SEARCHED...
AND THEN, WHEN I COULD NO LONGER TELL WHAT I WAS SEARCHING FOR...
...I FOUND IT THERE ONE DAY.
THE REVERSE SOUL INCENSE.
INSTINC-TUALLY I KNEW WHAT IT WAS.

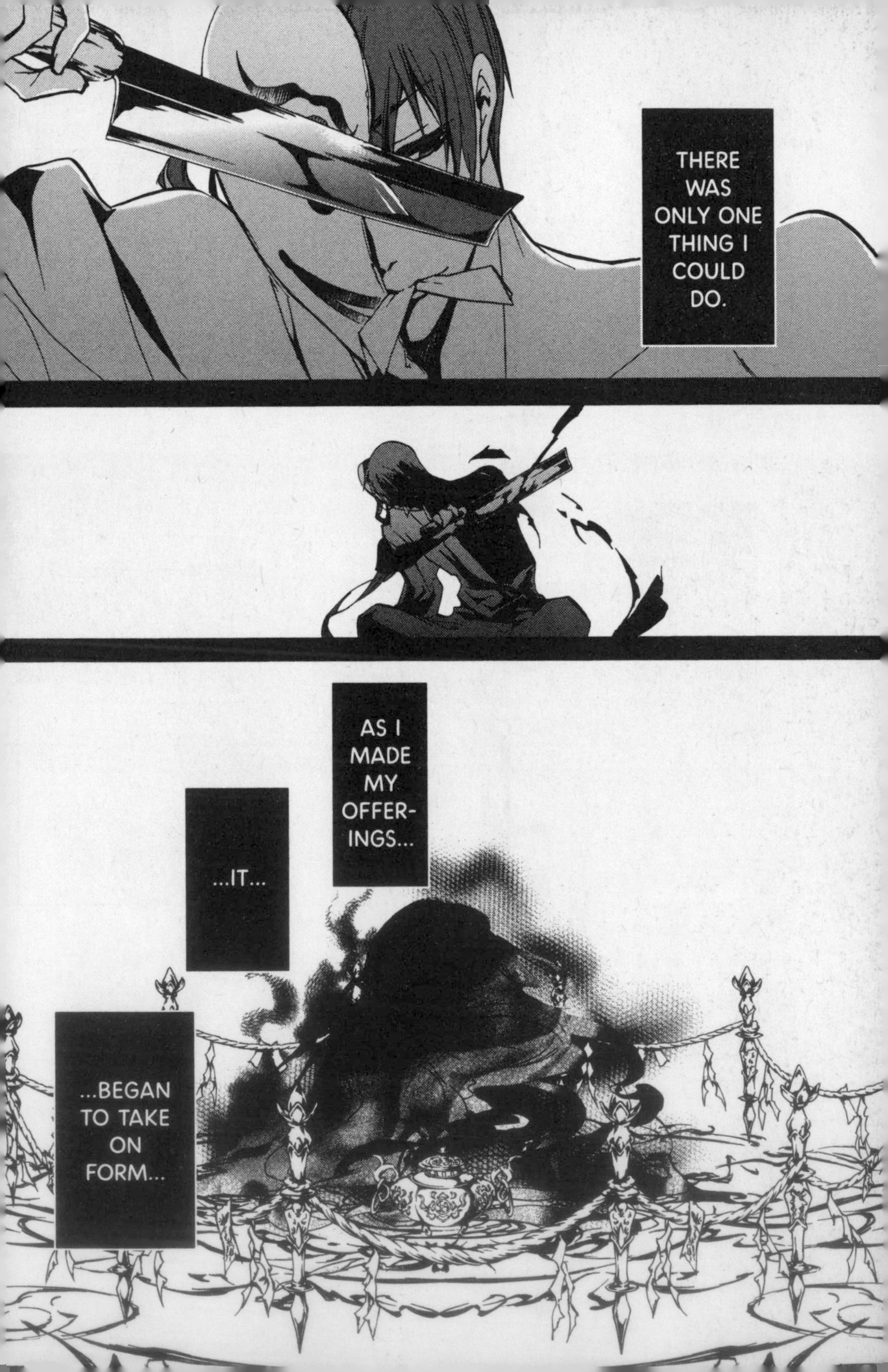
THERE WAS ONLY ONE THING I COULD DO.
AS I MADE MY OFFER-INGS...
...IT...
...BEGAN TO TAKE ON FORM...

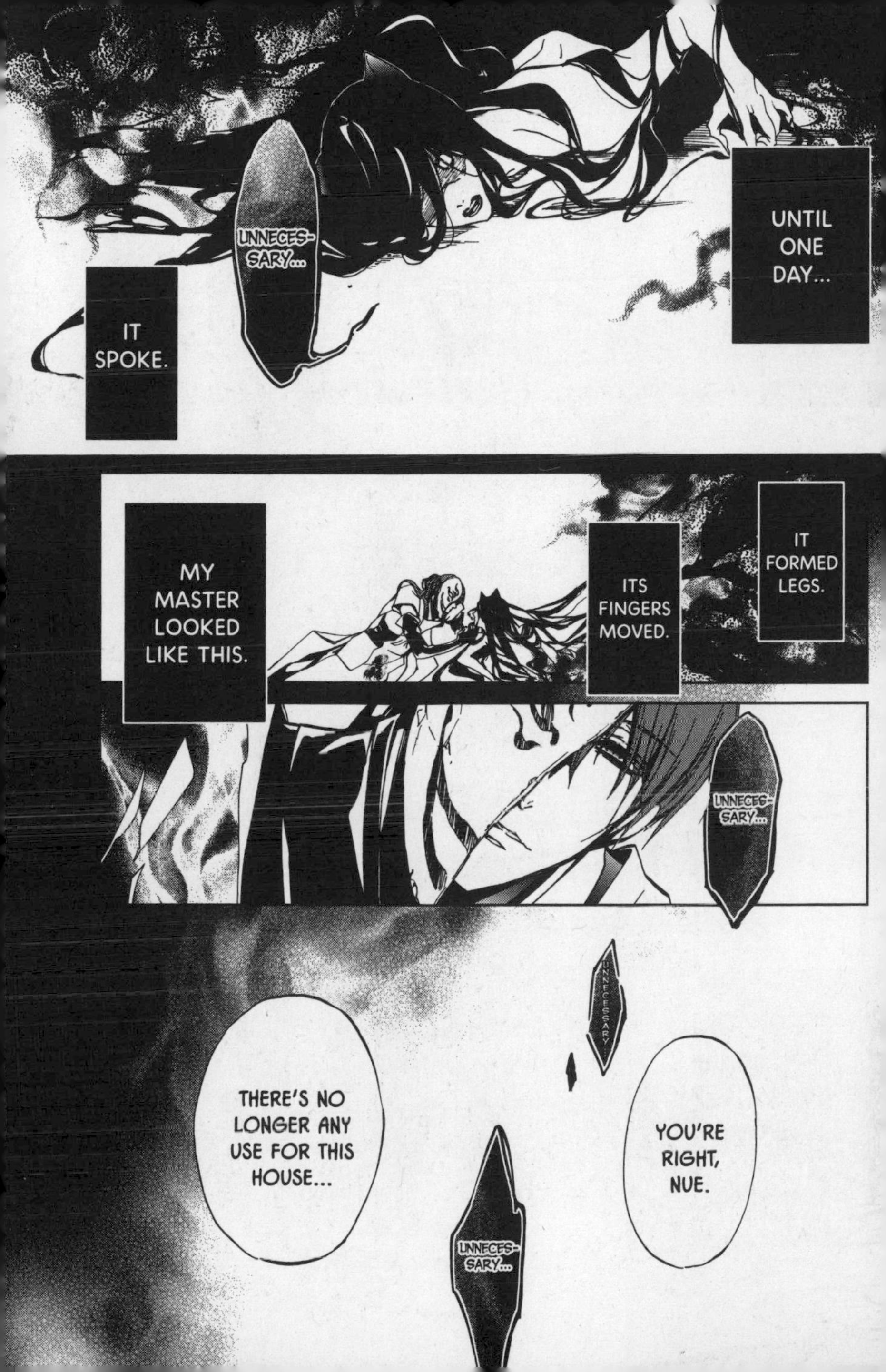
UNTIL ONE DAY...
UNNECES-SARY...
IT SPOKE.
IT FORMED LEGS.
ITS FINGERS MOVED.
MY MASTER LOOKED LIKE THIS.
UNNECES-SARY...
UNNECESSARY
YOU'RE RIGHT, NUE.
THERE'S NO LONGER ANY USE FOR THIS HOUSE...
UNNECES-SARY...

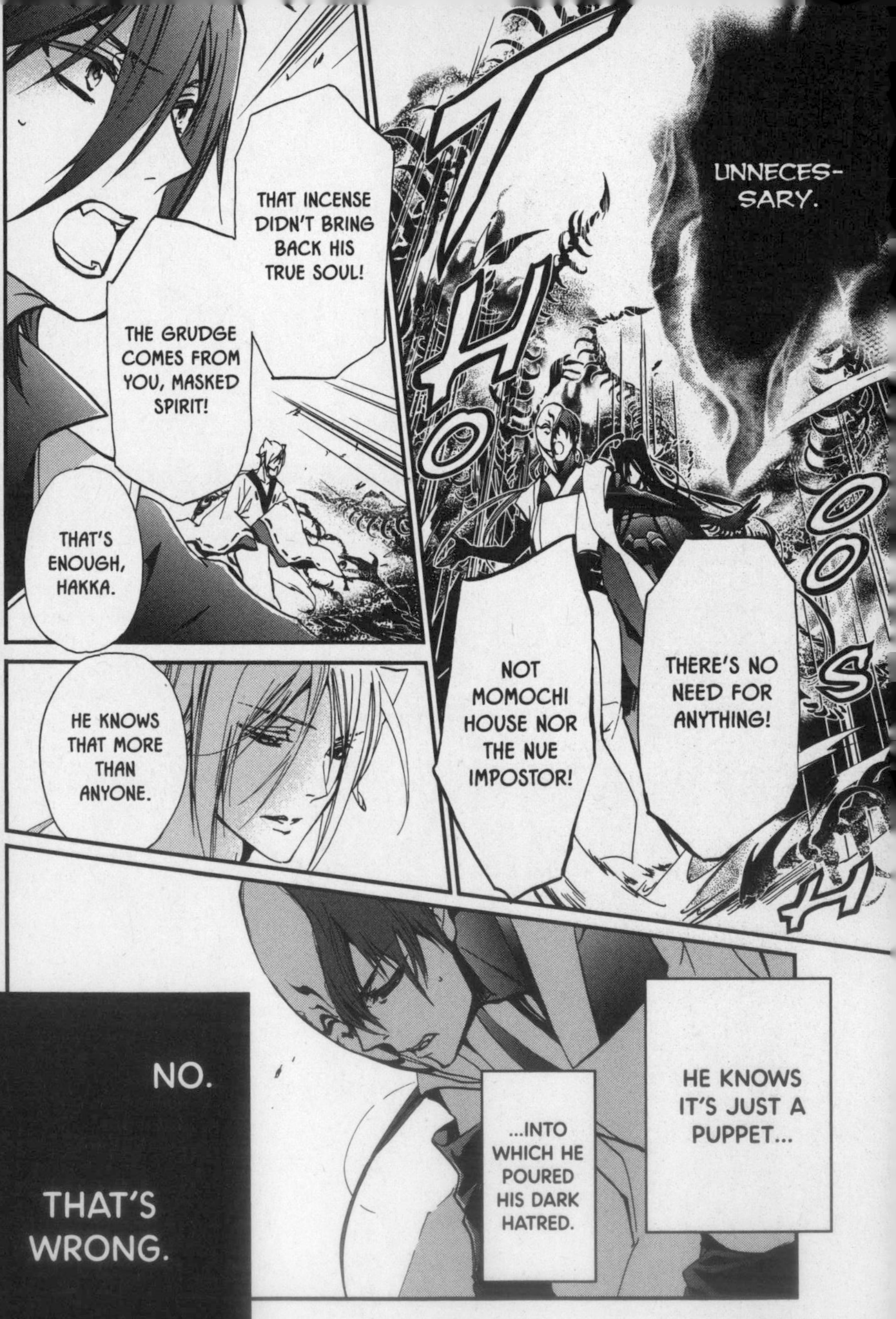
UNNECES-SARY.
THERE'S NO NEED FOR ANYTHING!
NOT MOMOCHI HOUSE NOR THE NUE IMPOSTOR!
THAT INCENSE DIDN'T BRING BACK HIS TRUE SOUL!
THE GRUDGE COMES FROM YOU, MASKED SPIRIT!
THAT'S ENOUGH, HAKKA.
HE KNOWS THAT MORE THAN ANYONE.
HE KNOWS IT'S JUST A PUPPET...
...INTO WHICH HE POURED HIS DARK HATRED.
NO.
THAT'S WRONG.

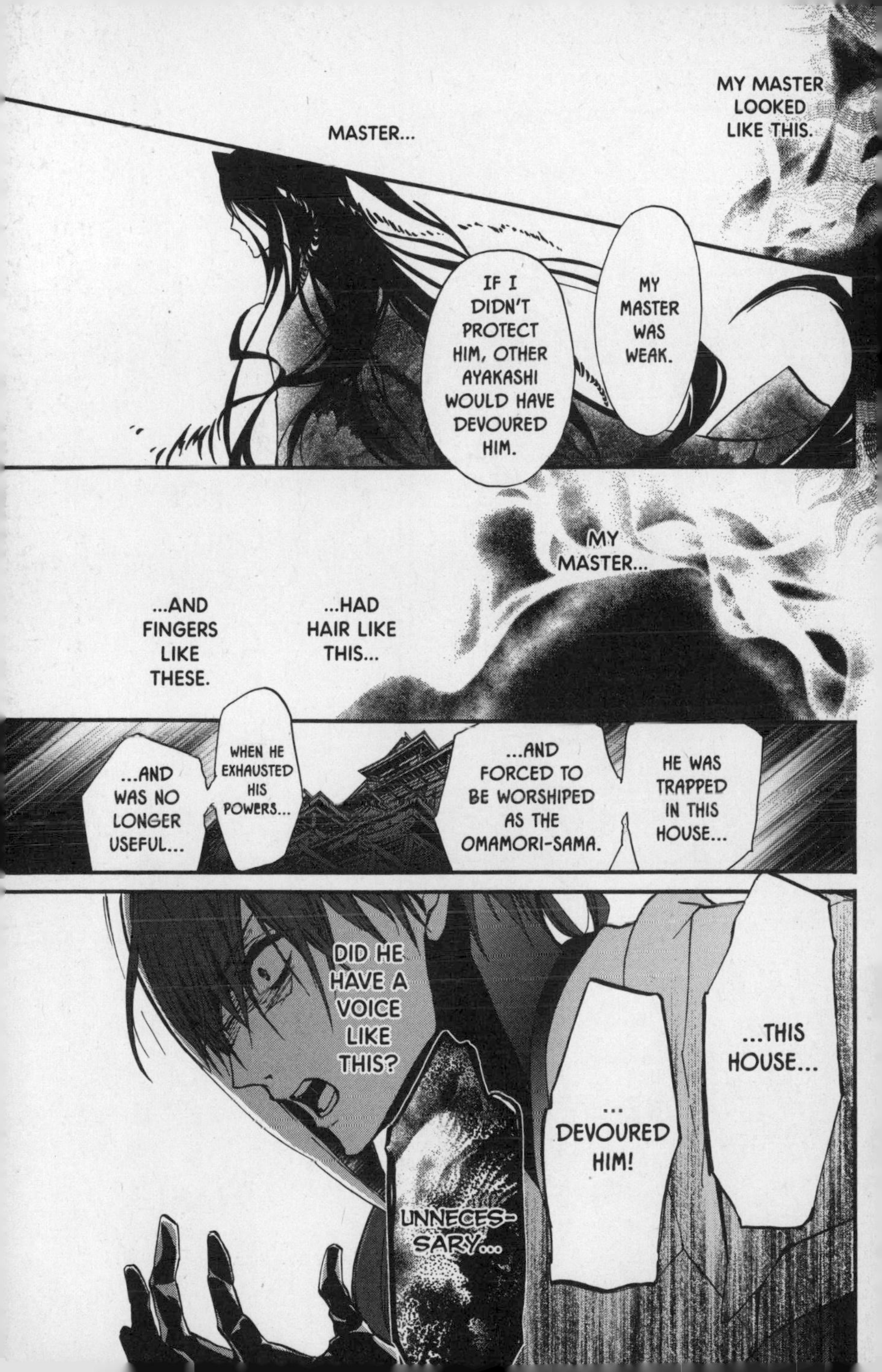
MY MASTER LOOKED LIKE THIS.
MASTER...
MY MASTER WAS WEAK.
IF I DIDN'T PROTECT HIM, OTHER AYAKASHI WOULD HAVE DEVOURED HIM.
MY MASTER...
...HAD HAIR LIKE THIS...
...AND FINGERS LIKE THESE.
HE WAS TRAPPED IN THIS HOUSE...
...AND FORCED TO BE WORSHIPED AS THE OMAMORI-SAMA.
WHEN HE EXHAUSTED HIS POWERS...
...AND WAS NO LONGER USEFUL...
...THIS HOUSE...
...DEVOURED HIM!
DID HE HAVE A VOICE LIKE THIS?
UNNECES-SARY...

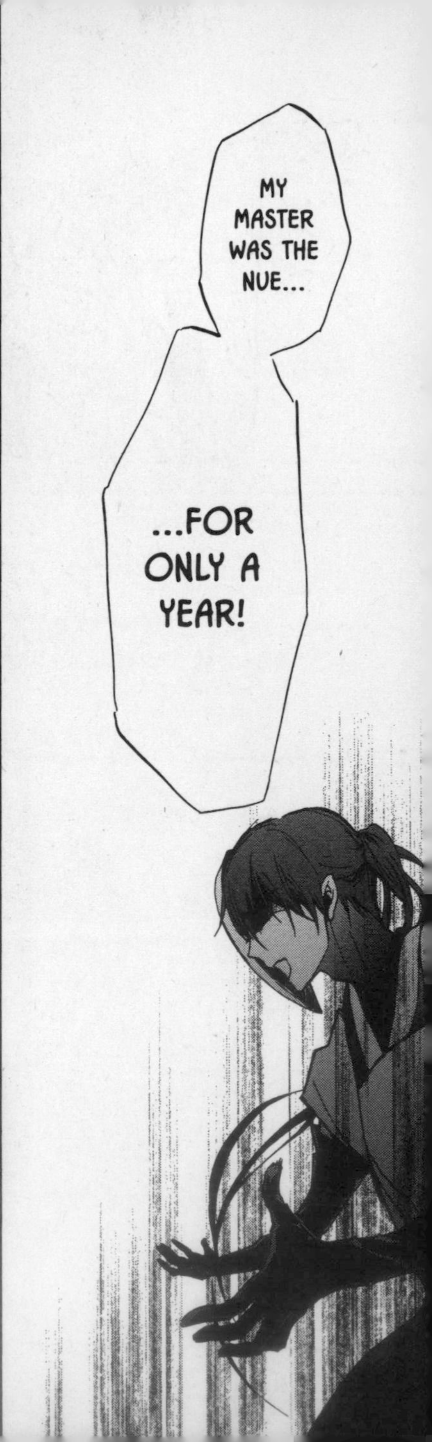
MY MASTER WAS THE NUE...
...FOR ONLY A YEAR!

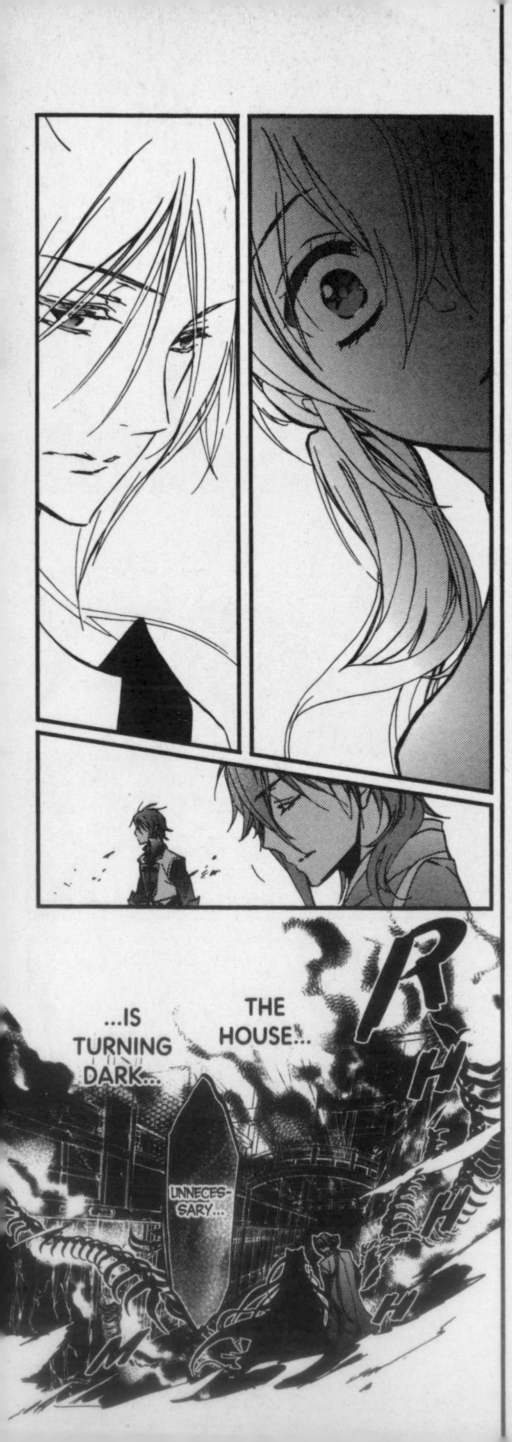
THE HOUSE...
...IS TURNING DARK...
RHHHHM
UNNECES-SARY...

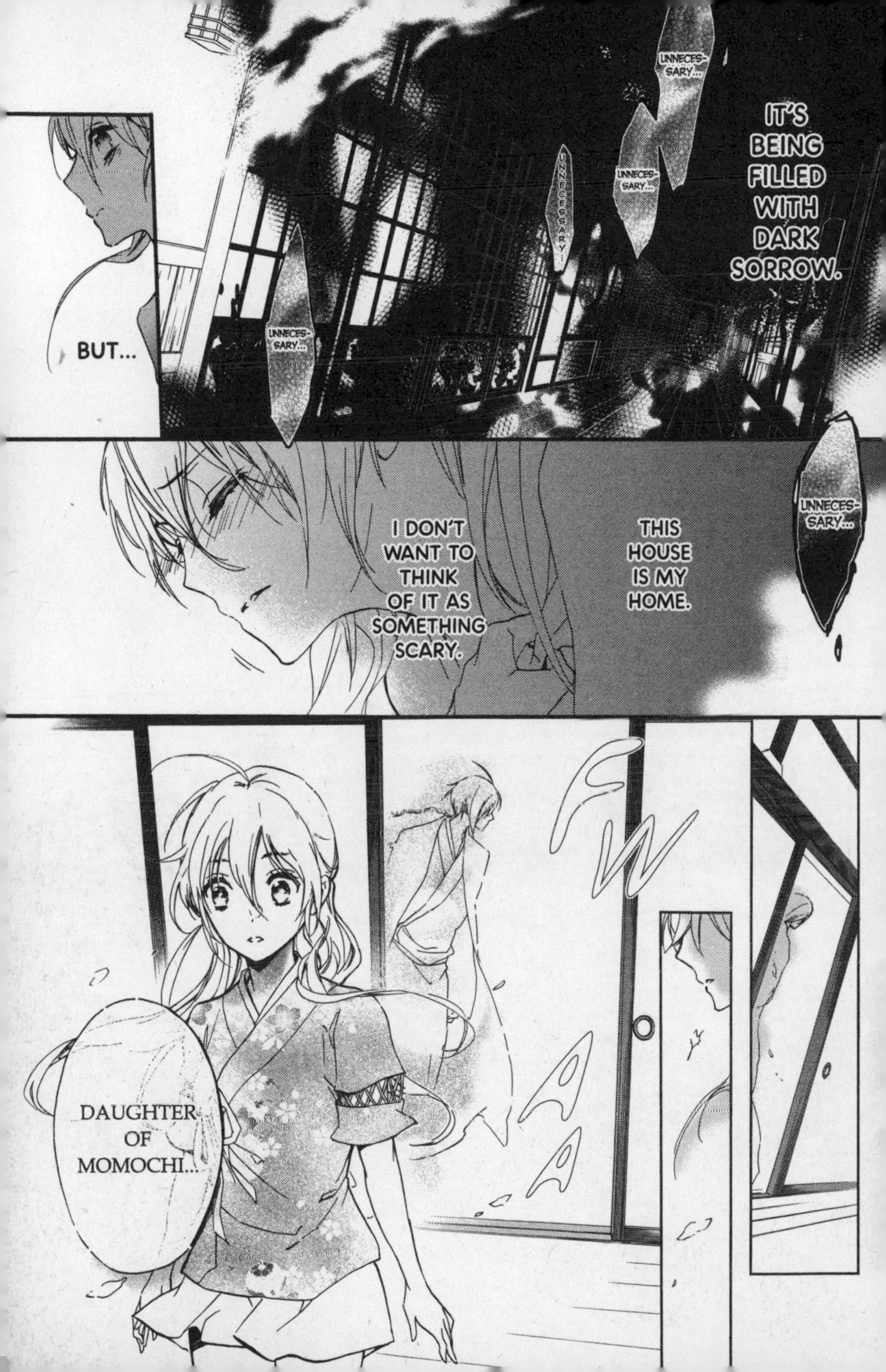
IT'S BEING FILLED WITH DARK SORROW.
UNNECES-SARY...
UNNECES-SARY...
UNNECESSARY...
UNNECES-SARY...
BUT...
UNNECES-SARY...
THIS HOUSE IS MY HOME.
I DON'T WANT TO THINK OF IT AS SOMETHING SCARY.
FWAA
DAUGHTER OF MOMOCHI...

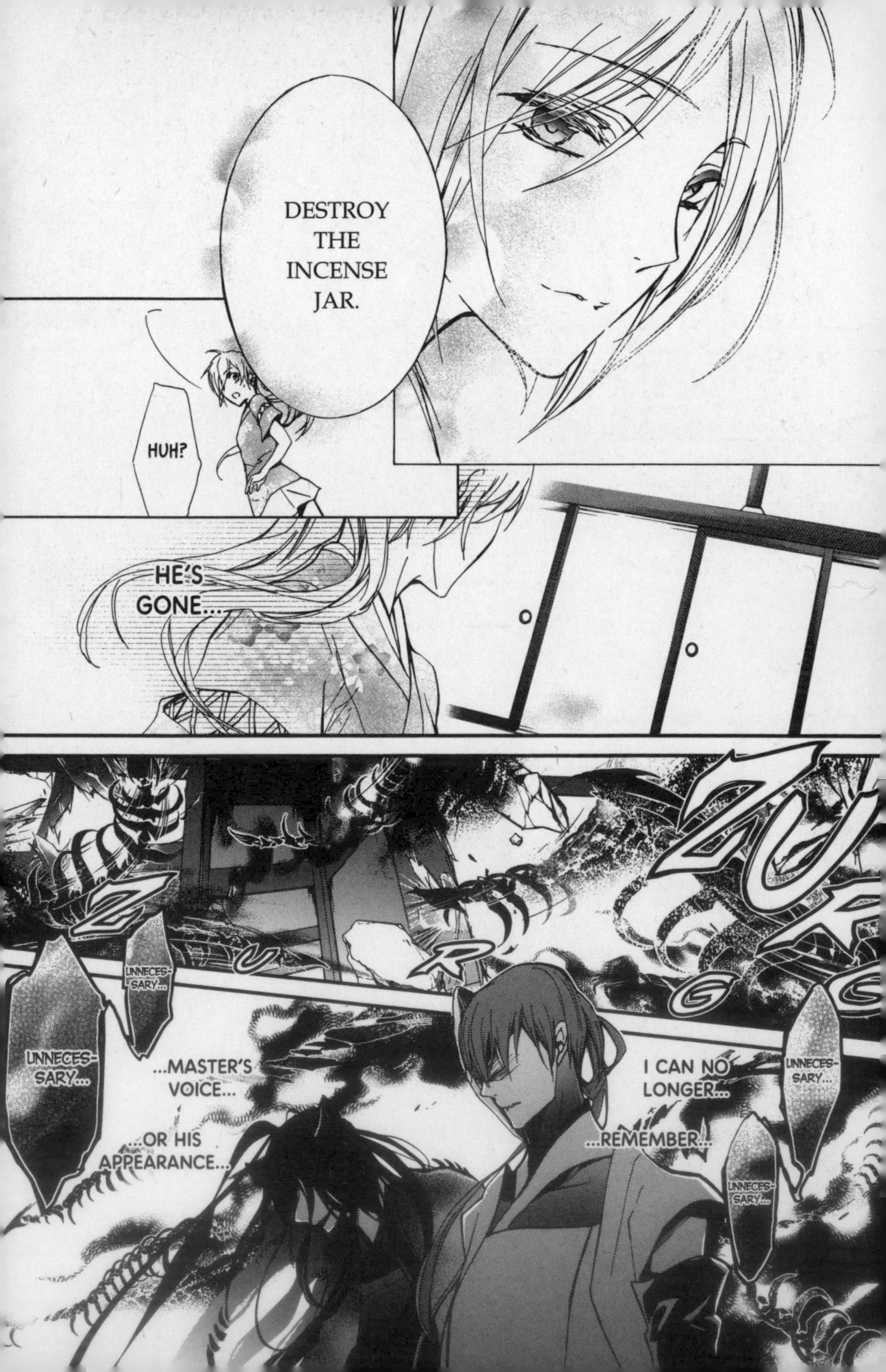
DESTROY THE INCENSE JAR.
HUH?
HE'S GONE...
ZUZUZU
GOGOGO
UNNECES-SARY...
I CAN NO LONGER...
...REMEMBER...
UNNECES-SARY...
...MASTER'S VOICE...
...OR HIS APPEARANCE...
UNNECES-SARY...
UNNECES-SARY...

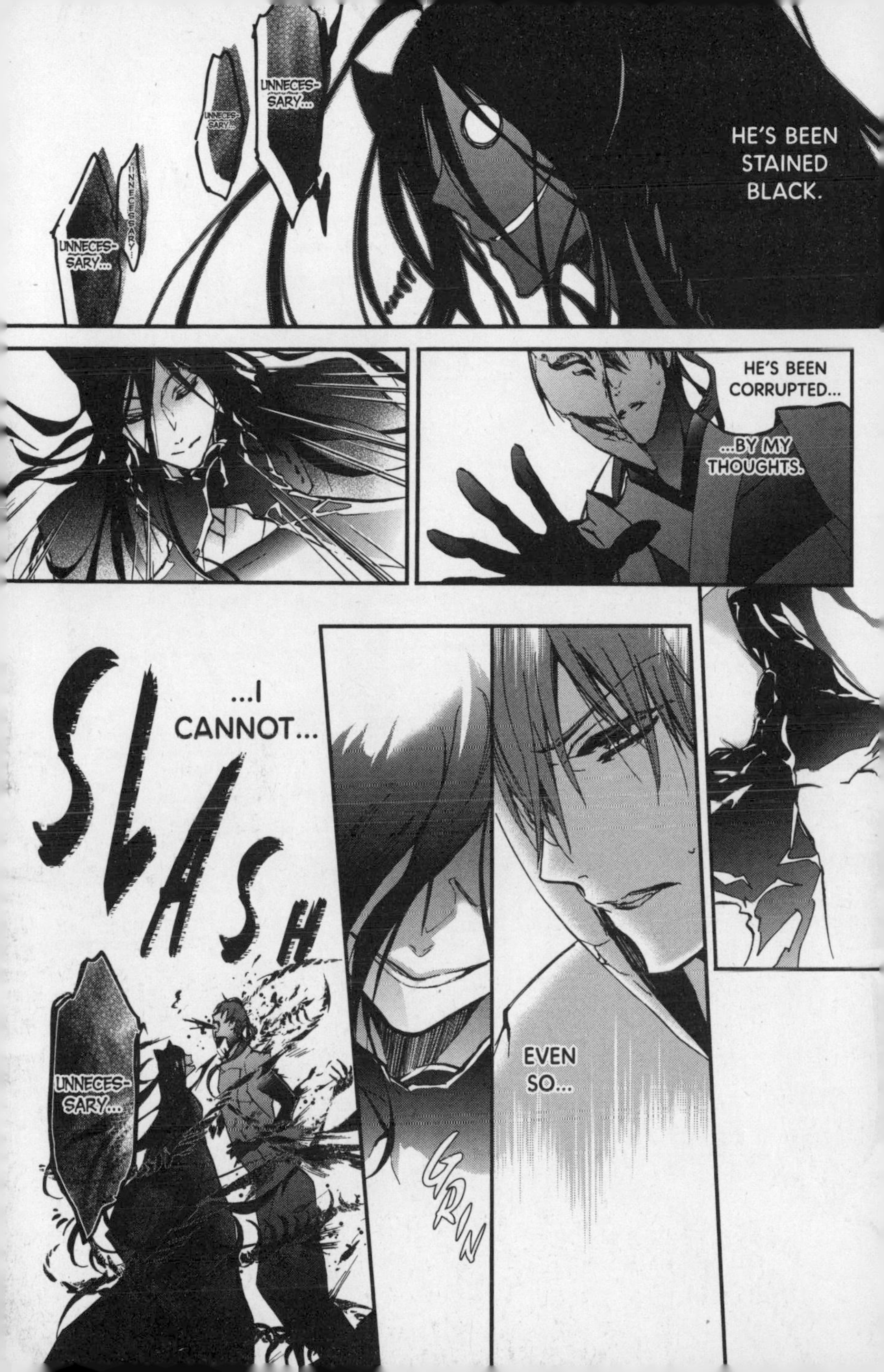
HE'S BEEN STAINED BLACK.
UNNECES-SARY...
UNNECES-SARY...
UNNECESSARY...
UNNECES-SARY...
HE'S BEEN CORRUPTED...
...BY MY THOUGHTS.
EVEN SO...
GRIN
...I CANNOT...
SLASH
UNNECES-SARY...

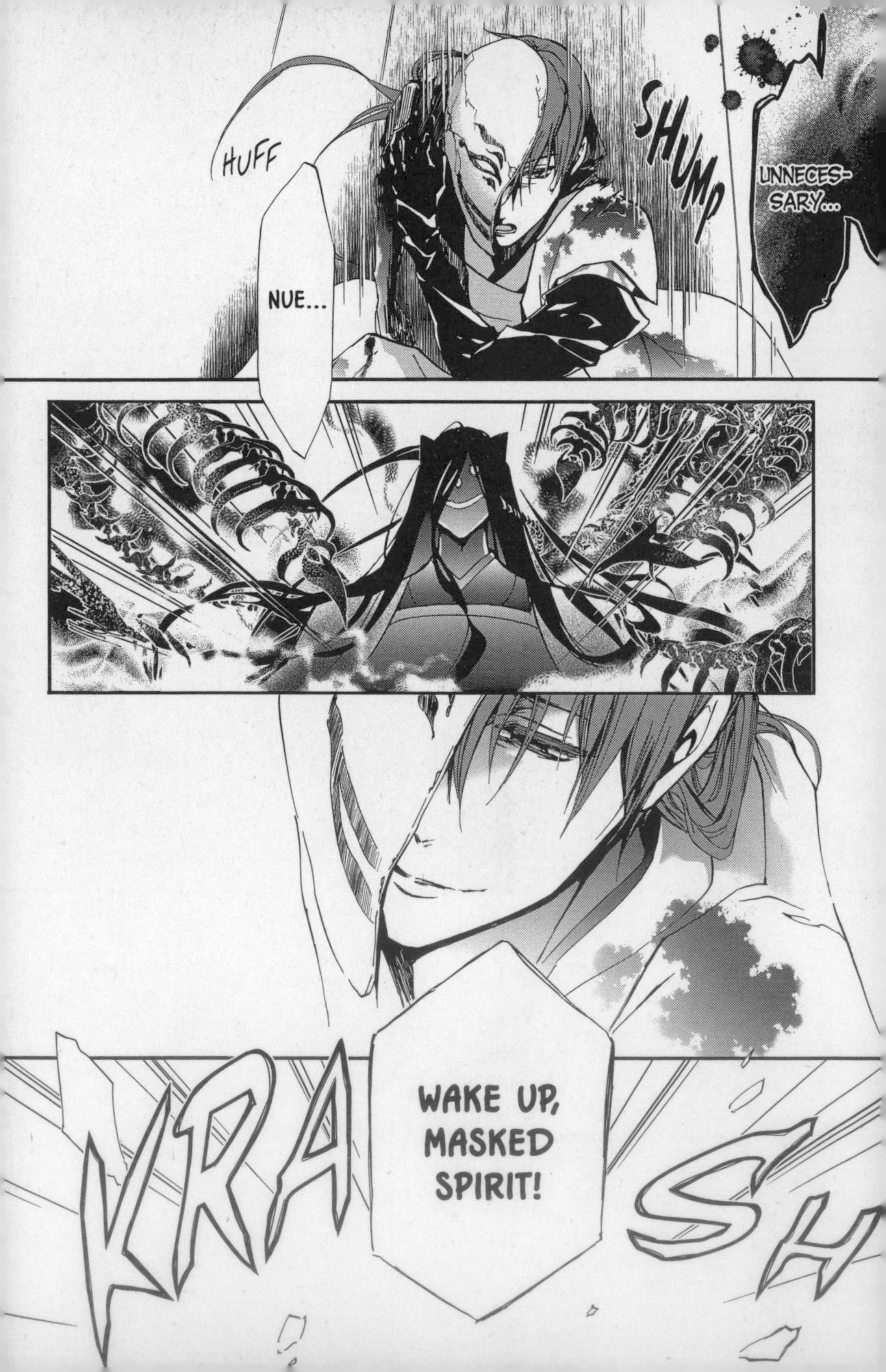
UNNECES-SARY...
SHUMP
HUFF
NUE...
WAKE UP, MASKED SPIRIT!
VRASH

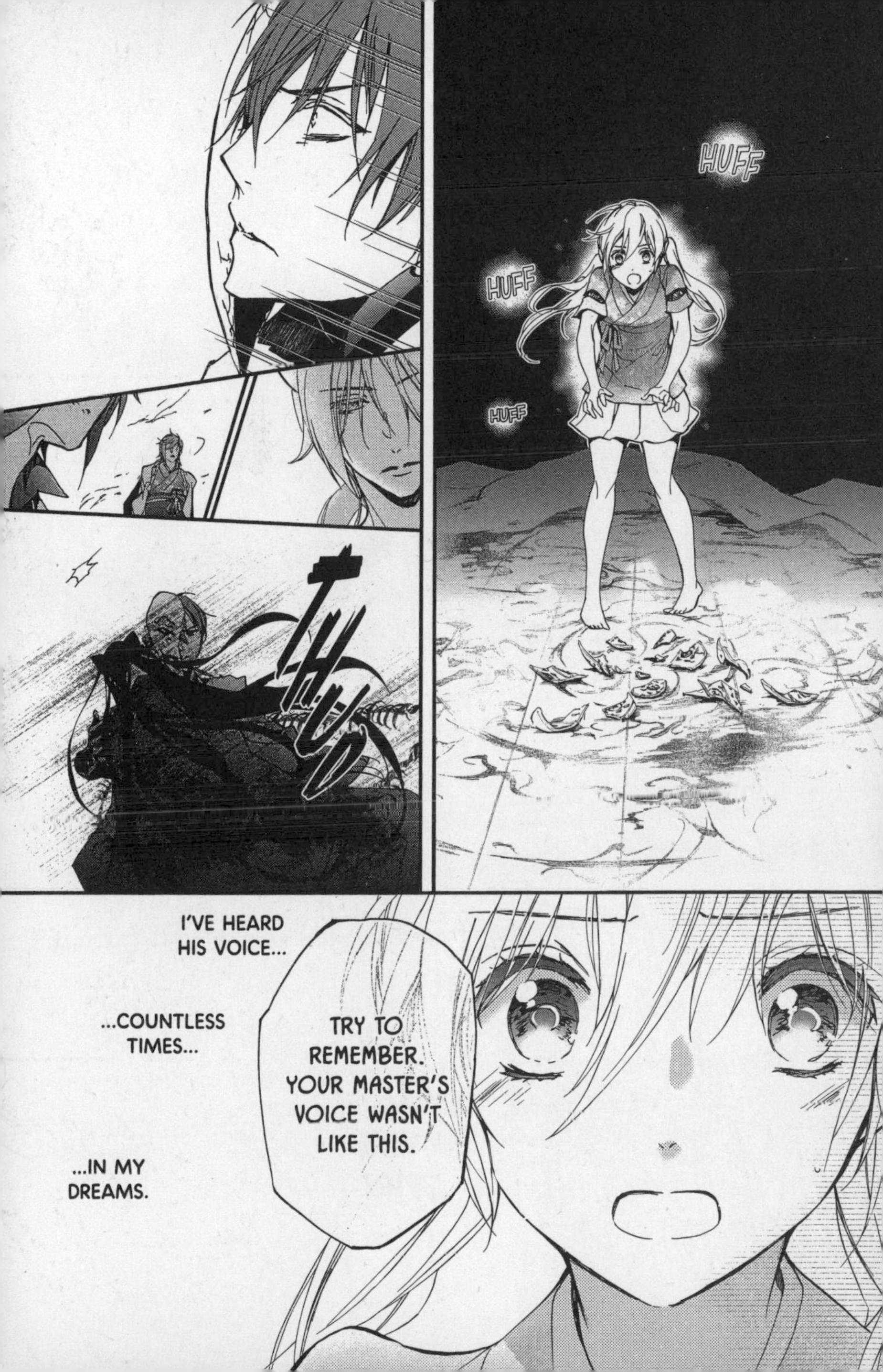
HUFF
HUFF
HUFF
I'VE HEARD HIS VOICE...
TRY TO REMEMBER. YOUR MASTER'S VOICE WASN'T LIKE THIS.
...COUNTLESS TIMES...
...IN MY DREAMS.

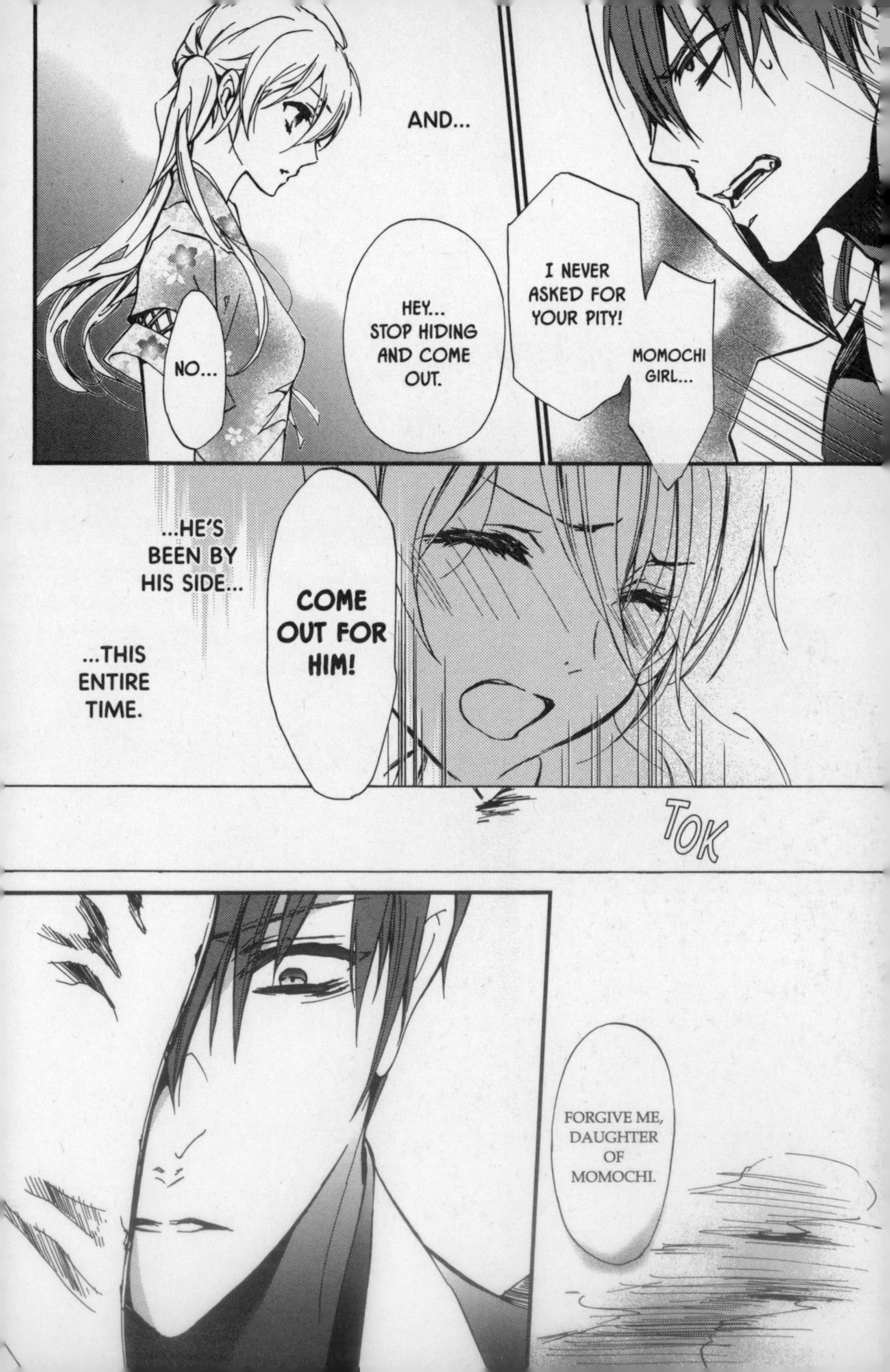
I NEVER ASKED FOR YOUR PITY!
MOMOCHI GIRL...
AND...
HEY... STOP HIDING AND COME OUT.
NO...
COME OUT FOR HIM!
...HE'S BEEN BY HIS SIDE...
...THIS ENTIRE TIME.
TOK
FORGIVE ME, DAUGHTER OF MOMOCHI.

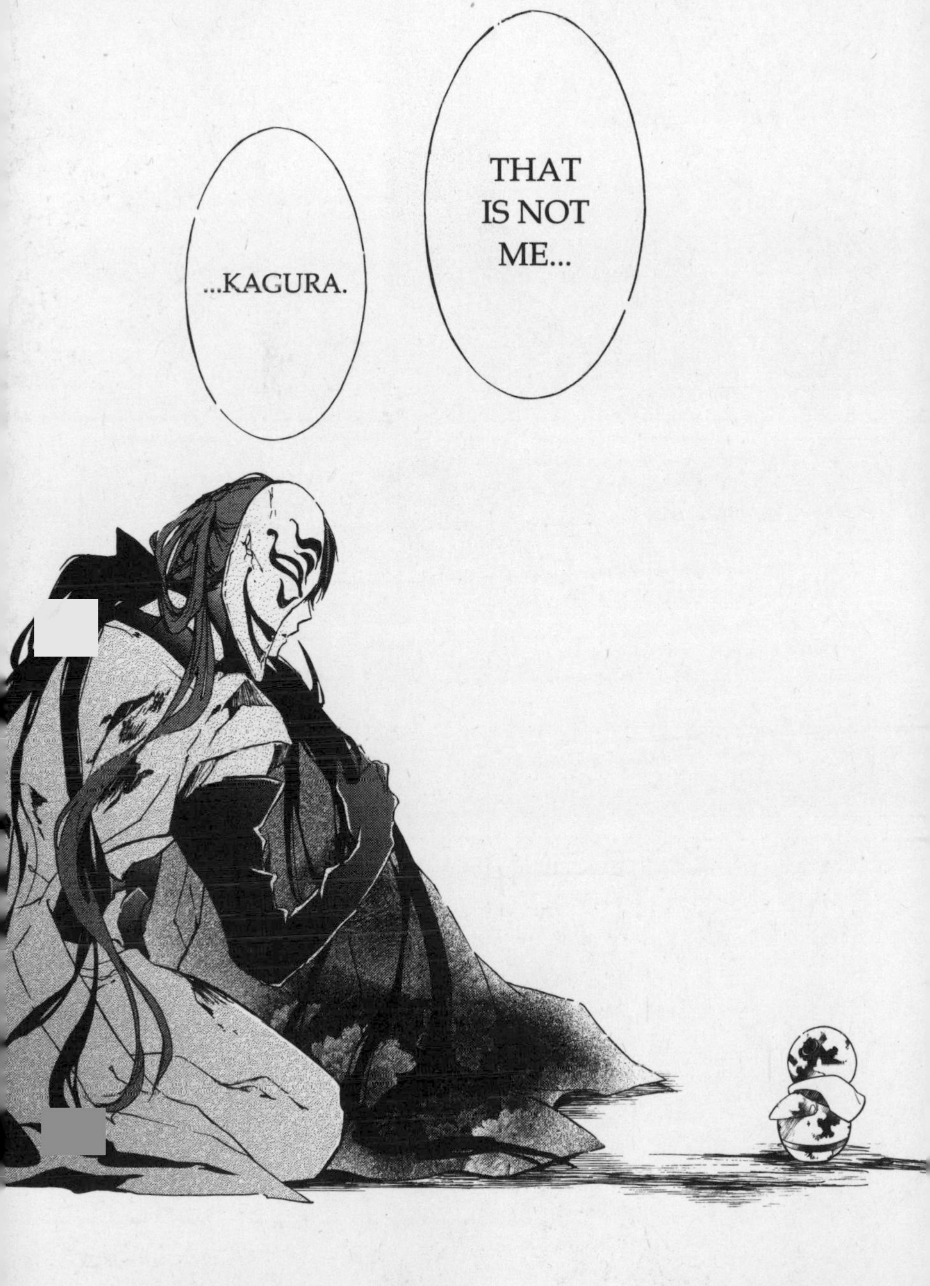
THAT IS NOT ME...
...KAGURA.

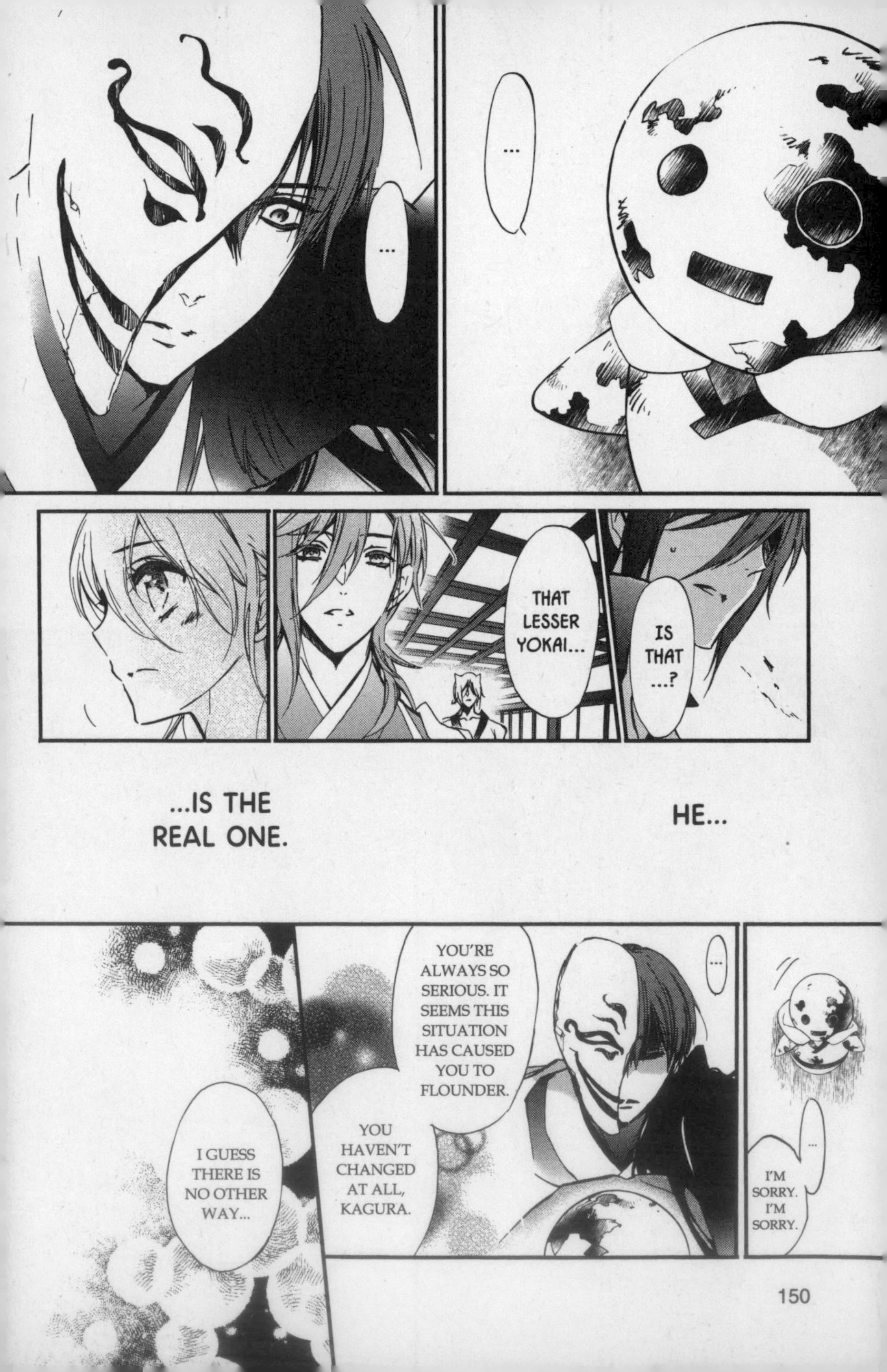
...
...
IS THAT ...?
THAT LESSER YOKAI...
HE...
...IS THE REAL ONE.
I'M SORRY. I'M SORRY.
...
...
YOU'RE ALWAYS SO SERIOUS. IT SEEMS THIS SITUATION HAS CAUSED YOU TO FLOUNDER.
YOU HAVEN'T CHANGED AT ALL, KAGURA.
I GUESS THERE IS NO OTHER WAY...

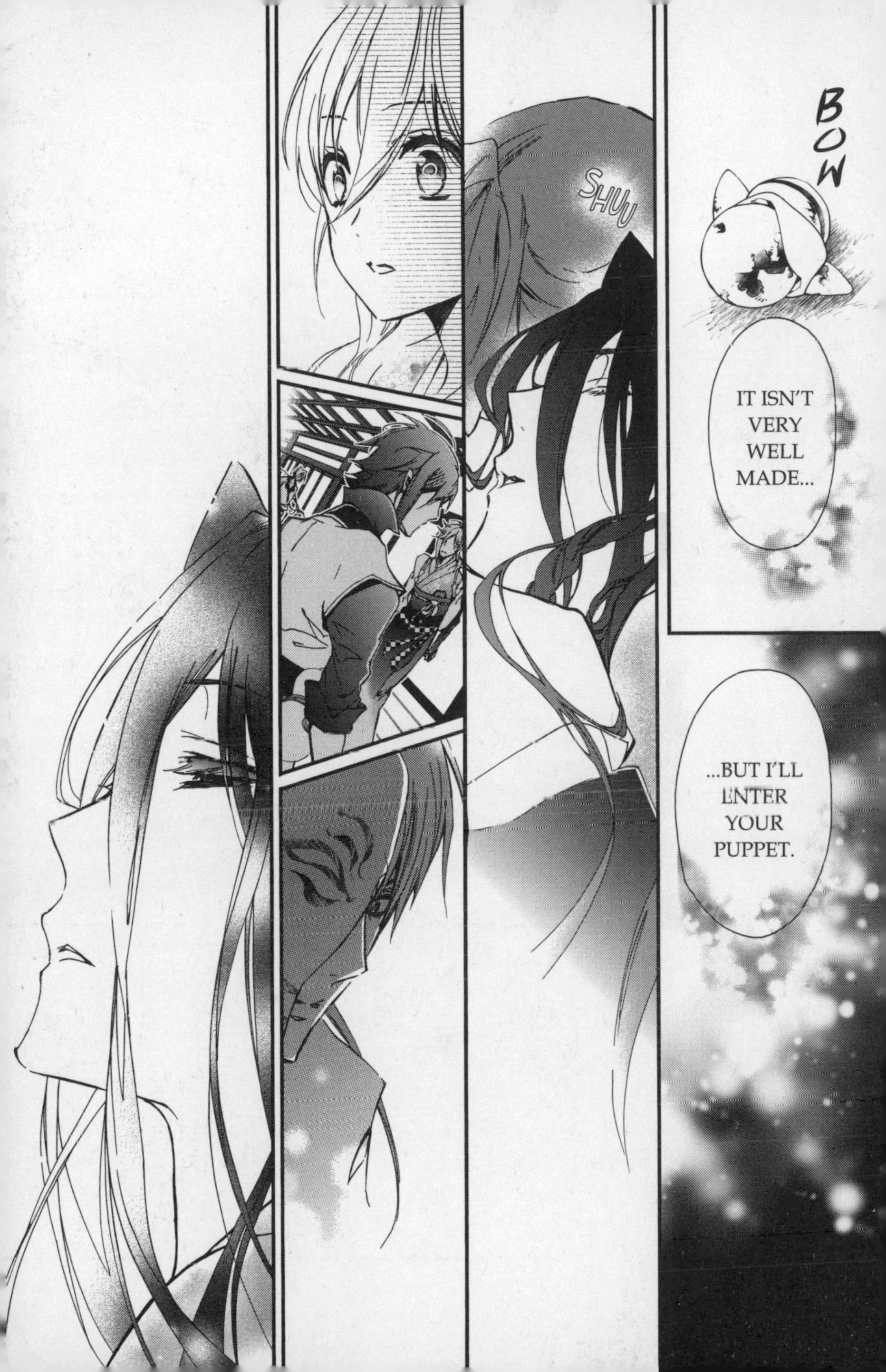
BOW
IT ISN'T VERY WELL MADE...
...BUT I'LL ENTER YOUR PUPPET.
SHUU

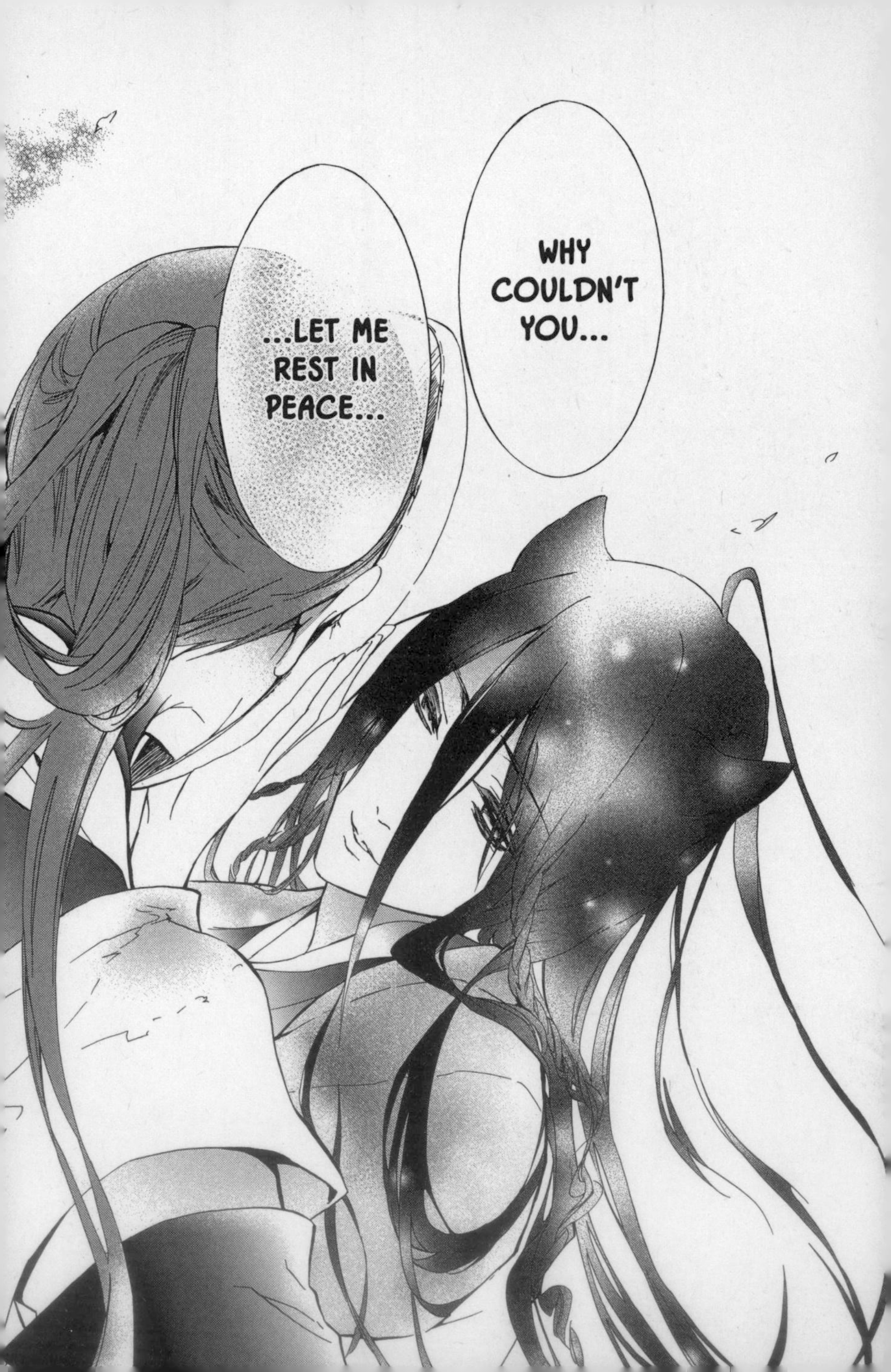
WHY COULDN'T YOU...
...LET ME REST IN PEACE...

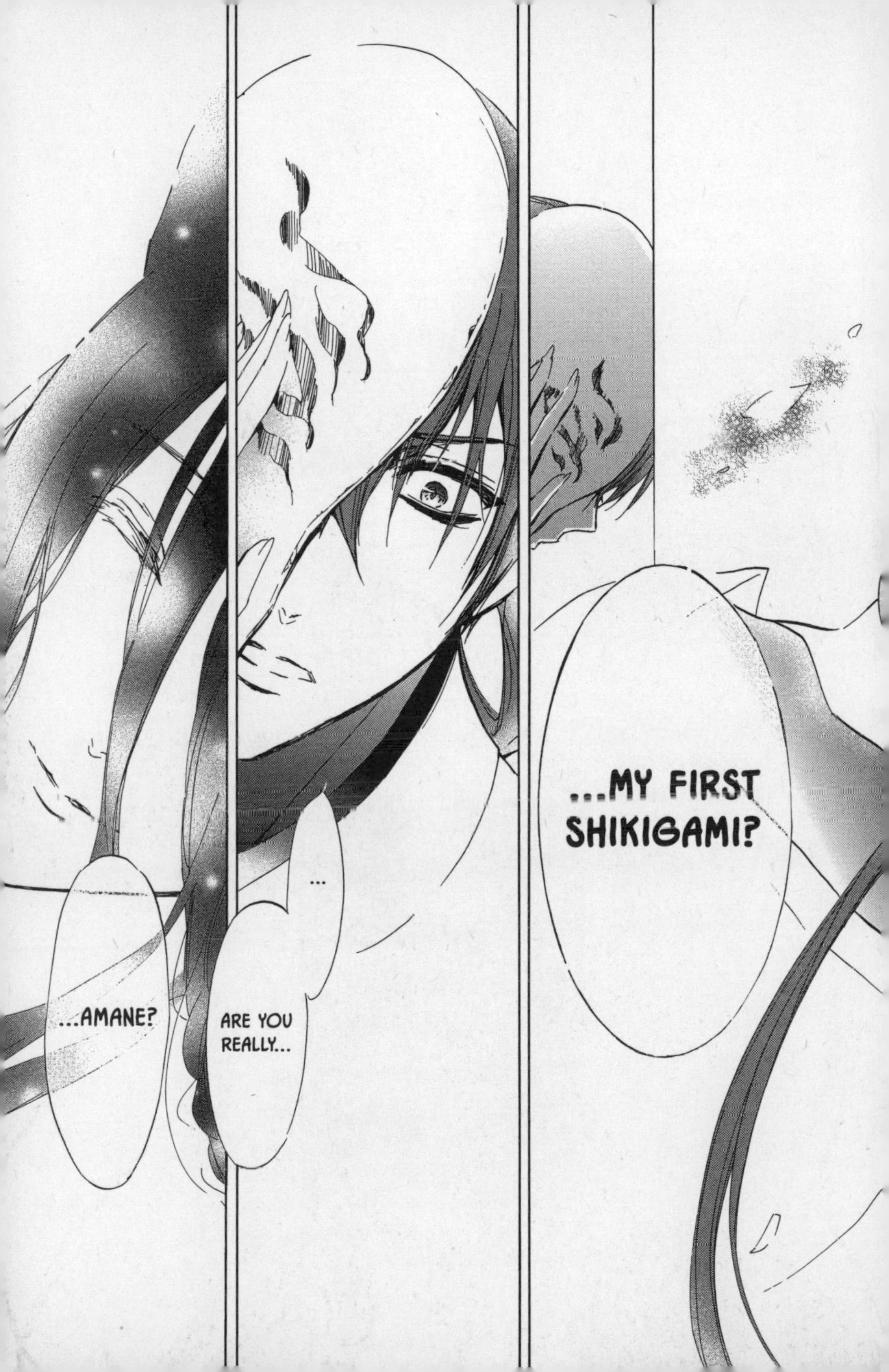
...MY FIRST SHIKIGAMI?
...
ARE YOU REALLY...
...AMANE?

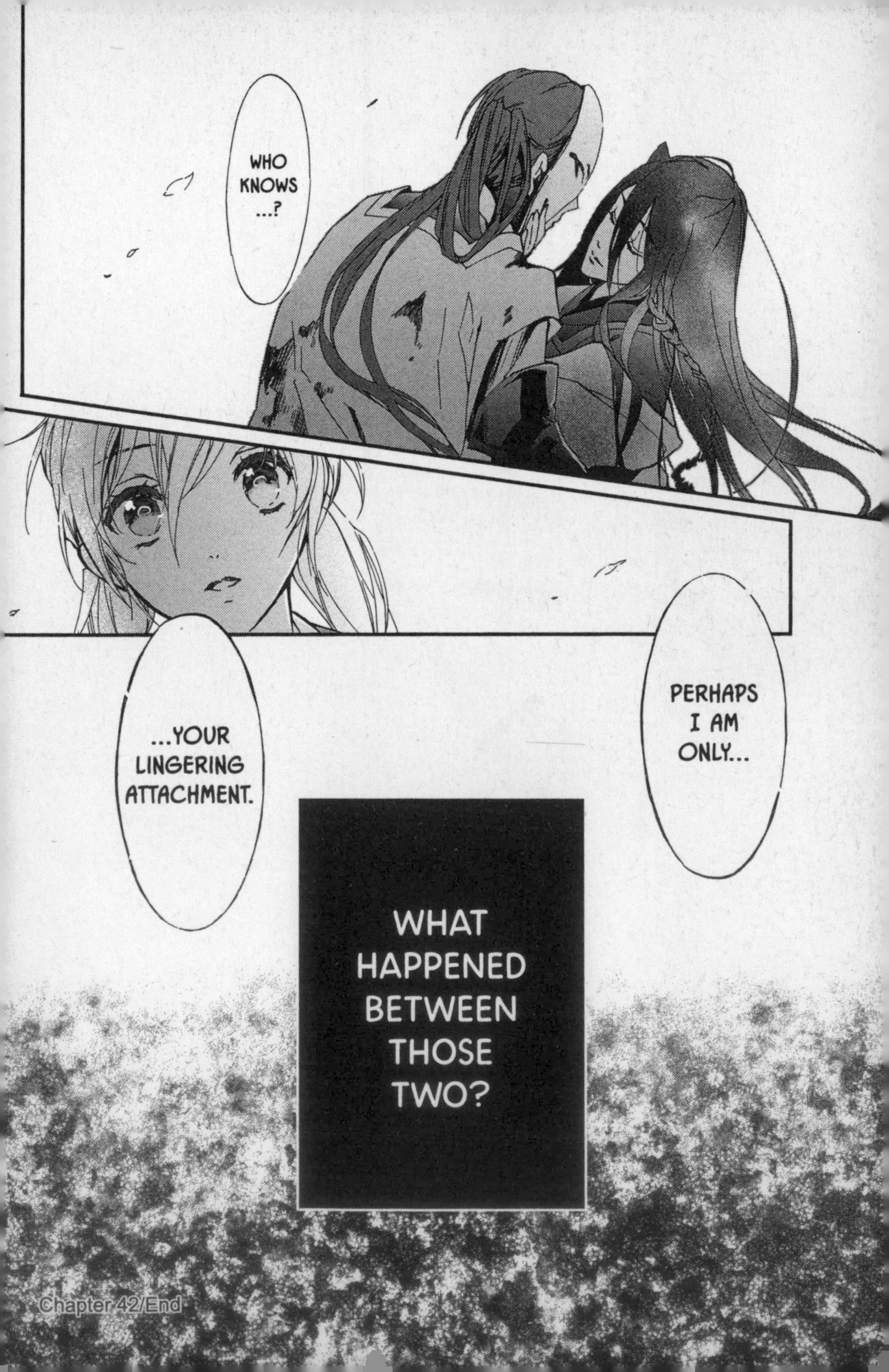
WHO KNOWS ...?
PERHAPS I AM ONLY...
...YOUR LINGERING ATTACHMENT.
WHAT HAPPENED BETWEEN THOSE TWO?
Chapter 42/End

The DEMON PRINCE of MOMOCHI HOUSE

This is volume 11. To match the world of *Momochi*, I tried to use Chinese numerals as much as possible, but I've given up on that. I'm so happy to have reached double digits! I really, really like the cover design for the graphic novel. I look forward to the designs in the double-digit volumes.

This bonus comic is something that I was too busy to upload to Twitter on Valentine's Day. This is my consolation. I uploaded my rejected rough drafts as well, so please check them out at @shouoto. Consolations are important! I don't want to have things go to waste!

I look forward to your continued support.

Aya Shouoto

Valentine's Day

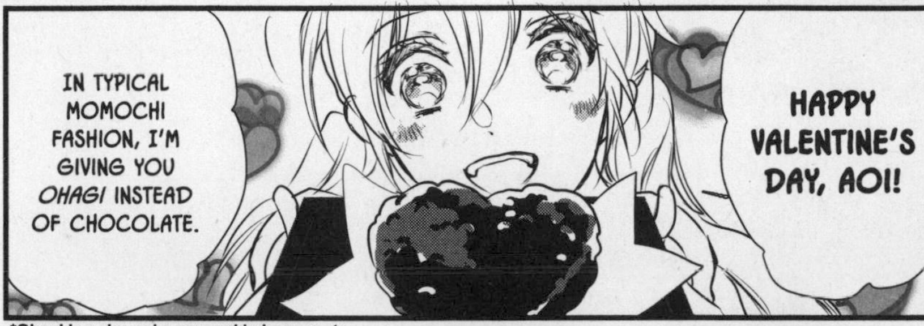
HAPPY VALENTINE'S DAY, AOI!
IN TYPICAL MOMOCHI FASHION, I'M GIVING YOU *OHAGI* INSTEAD OF CHOCOLATE.

*Ohagi is a rice cake covered in bean paste.

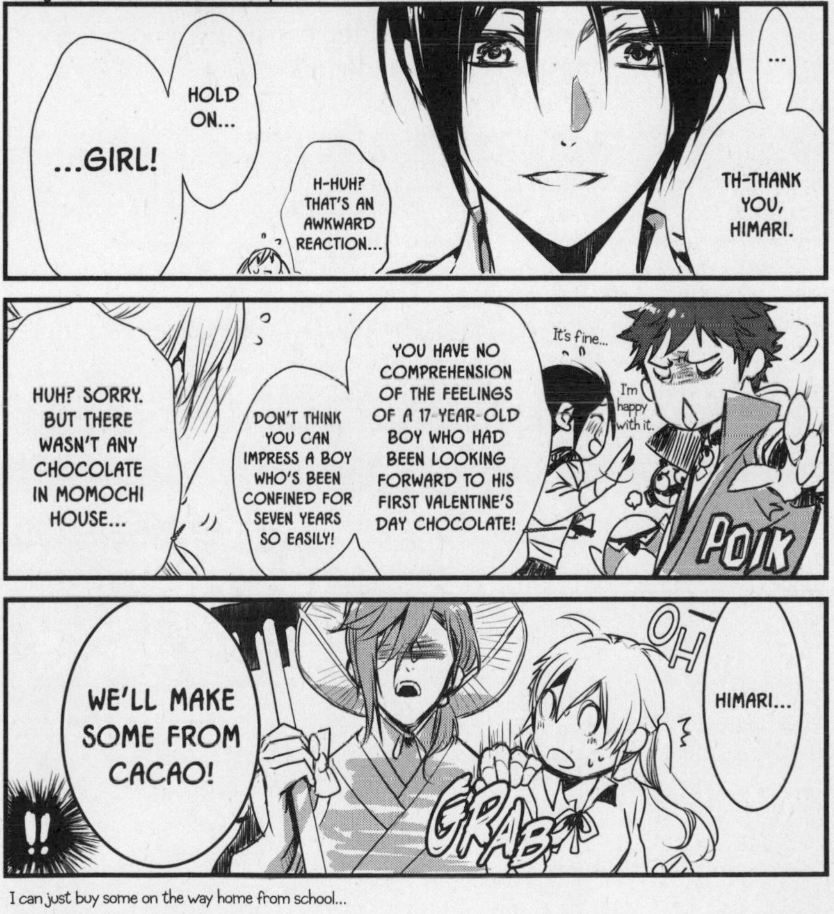
...
TH-THANK YOU, HIMARI.
H-HUH? THAT'S AN AWKWARD REACTION...
HOLD ON...
...GIRL!
It's fine...
I'm happy with it.
POK
YOU HAVE NO COMPREHENSION OF THE FEELINGS OF A 17 YEAR-OLD BOY WHO HAD BEEN LOOKING FORWARD TO HIS FIRST VALENTINE'S DAY CHOCOLATE!
DON'T THINK YOU CAN IMPRESS A BOY WHO'S BEEN CONFINED FOR SEVEN YEARS SO EASILY!
HUH? SORRY. BUT THERE WASN'T ANY CHOCOLATE IN MOMOCHI HOUSE...
HIMARI...
OH
GRAB
WE'LL MAKE SOME FROM CACAO!
!!

I can just buy some on the way home from school...

I've never had a manga series reach double digits in its volume count before. I'm so thrilled. We've been following the adventures of the cast for a long time, but I'm still building up the lore of Momochi House in my head. Whether the story is relaxing or perilous, there's never a dull moment. I'm happy that there are still many things I can share with you.

-Aya Shouoto

Aya Shouoto was born on December 25. Her hobbies are traveling, staying at hotels, sewing and daydreaming. She currently lives in Tokyo and enjoys listening to J-pop anime theme songs while she works.

The Demon Prince of Momochi House

Volume 11
Shojo Beat Edition

Story and Art by Aya Shouoto

Translation JN Productions
Touch-Up Art & Lettering Inori Fukuda Trant
Design Izumi Evers
Editor Nancy Thistlethwaite

MOMOCHISANCHI NO AYAKASHI OUJI Volume 11
© Aya SHOUOTO 2017
First published in Japan in 2017 by KADOKAWA CORPORATION, Tokyo.
English translation rights arranged with KADOKAWA CORPORATION, Tokyo.

The stories, characters and incidents mentioned
in this publication are entirely fictional.

Printed in the U.S.A.

Published by VIZ Media, LLC
P.O. Box 77010
San Francisco, CA 94107

10 9 8 7 6 5 4 3 2 1
First printing, March 2018

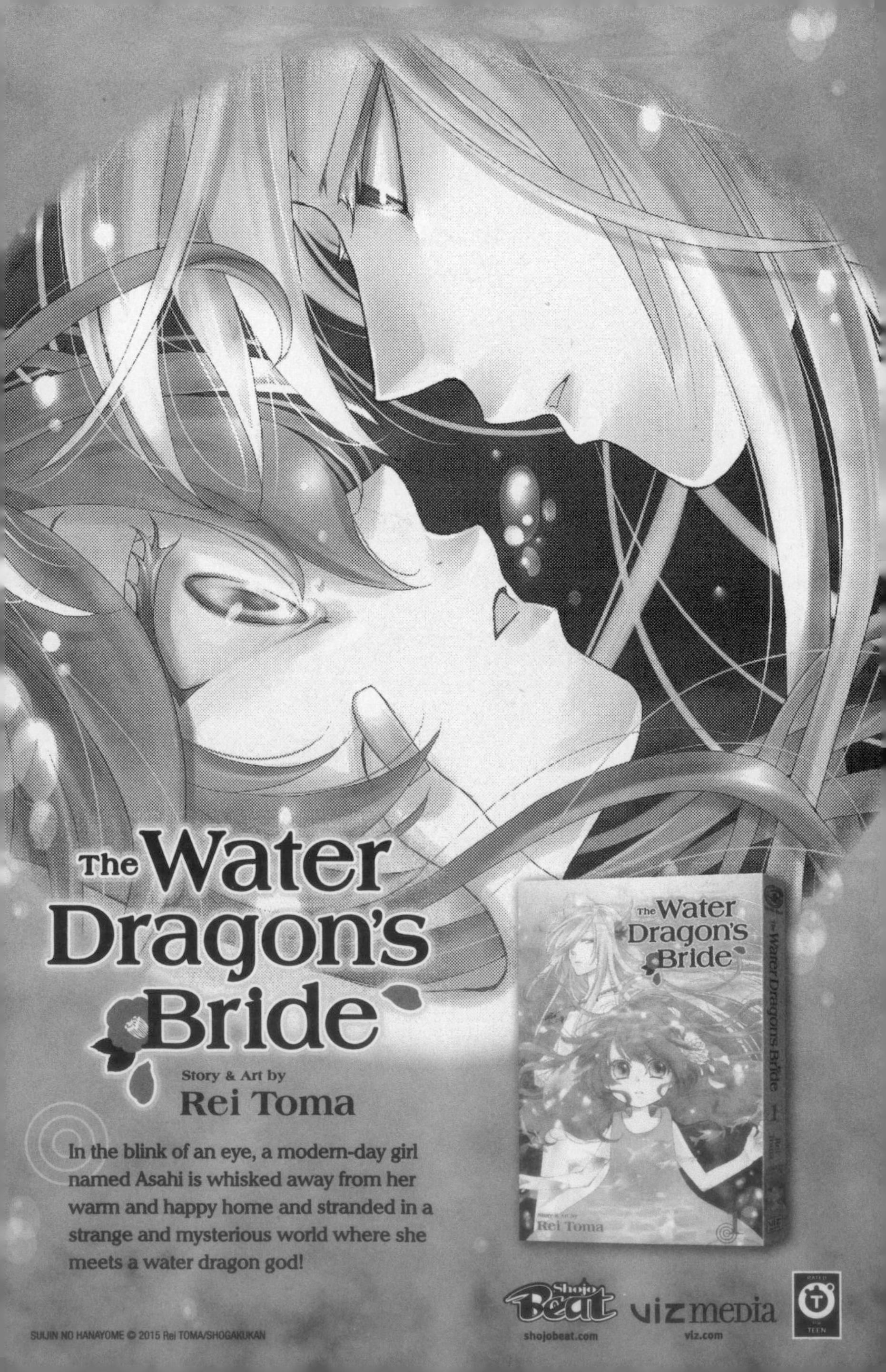
The Water Dragon's Bride
Story & Art by
Rei Toma
In the blink of an eye, a modern-day girl named Asahi is whisked away from her warm and happy home and stranded in a strange and mysterious world where she meets a water dragon god!
The Water Dragon's Bride
Story & Art by Rei Toma
Shojo Beat
shojobeat.com
viz media
viz.com
RATED T TEEN
SUIJIN NO HANAYOME © 2015 Rei TOMA/SHOGAKUKAN

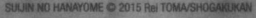

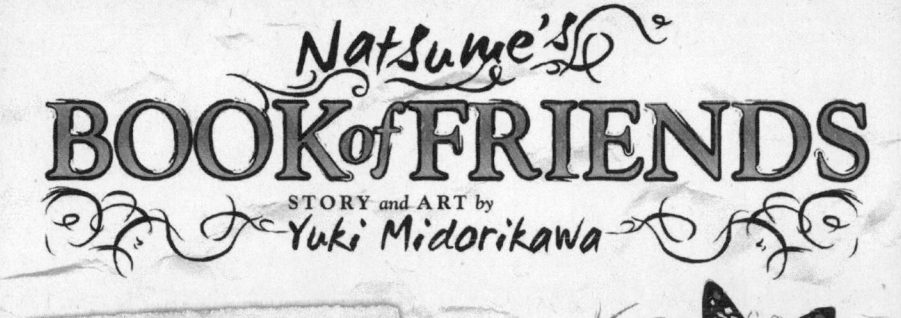

Natsume's
BOOK of FRIENDS
STORY and ART by
Yuki Midorikawa
Make Some Unusual New Friends
The power to see hidden spirits has always felt like a curse to troubled high schooler Takashi Natsume. But he's about to discover he inherited a lot more than just the Sight from his mysterious grandmother!
Available at your local bookstore or comic store.
Shojo Beat
www.shojobeat.com
Natsume Yujincho © Yuki Midorikawa 2005/HAKUSENSHA, Inc.
RATED T FOR TEEN
ratings.viz.com
VIZ media
www.viz.com

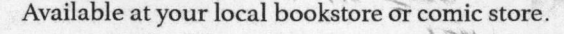

Kiss of the Rose Princess

Story and Art by
Aya Shouoto

Anise Yamamoto has been told that if she ever removes the rose choker given to her by her father, a terrible punishment will befall her. Unfortunately she loses that choker when a bat-like being named Ninufa falls from the sky and hits her. Ninufa gives Anise four cards representing four knights whom she can summon with a kiss. But now that she has these gorgeous men at her beck and call, what exactly is her quest?!

Shojo Beat

RATED T TEEN

viz media

viz.com

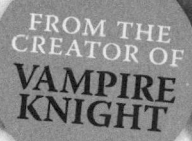

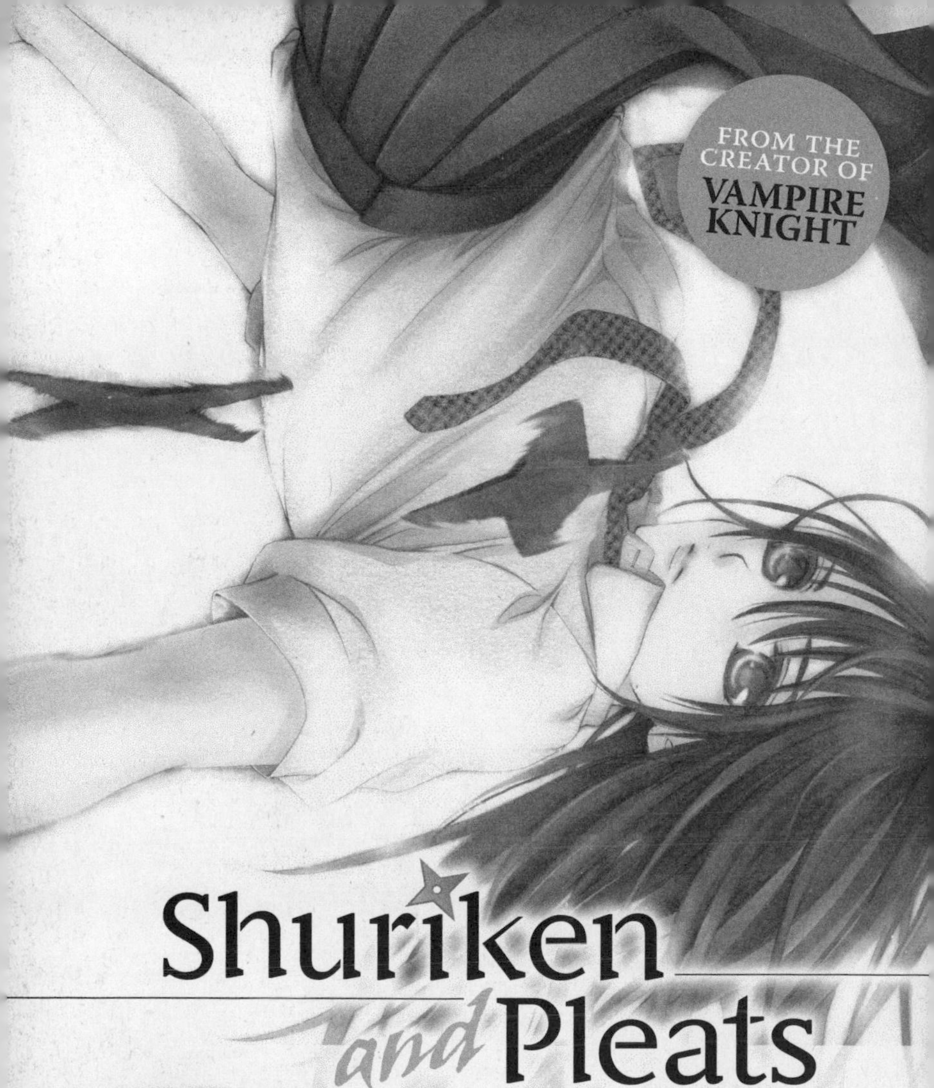

Shuriken and Pleats

When the master she has sworn to protect is killed, Mikage Kirio, a skilled ninja, travels to Japan to start a new, peaceful life for herself. But as soon as she arrives, she finds herself fighting to protect the life of Mahito Wakashimatsu, a man who is under attack by a band of ninja. From that time on, Mikage is drawn deeper into the machinations of his powerful family.

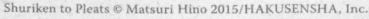

Queen's Quality

Story & Art by
Kyousuke Motomi

Fumi Nishioka lives with Kyutaro Horikita and his family of "Sweepers," people who specialize in cleaning the minds of those overcome by negative energy and harmful spirits. Fumi has always displayed mysterious abilities, but will those powers be used for evil when she begins to truly awaken as a Queen?

shojobeat.com

vizmedia
viz.com

"**Bloody**" **Mary**, a vampire with a death wish, has spent the past 400 years chasing down a modern-day exorcist named Maria who is thought to have inherited "The Blood of Maria" and is the only one who can kill Mary. To Mary's dismay, Maria doesn't know how to kill vampires. Desperate to die, Mary agrees to become Maria's bodyguard until Maria can find a way to kill him.

Bloody † Mary

Story and Art by
akaza samamiya

dreams IDOL

STORY & ART BY ARINA TANEMURA

At age 31, office worker Chikage Deguchi feels she missed her chances at love and success. When word gets out that she's a virgin, Chikage is humiliated and wishes she could turn back time to when she was still young and popular. She takes an experimental drug that changes her appearance back to when she was 15. Now Chikage is determined to pursue everything she missed out on all those years ago—including becoming a star!

Thirty One Idream © Arina Tanemura 2014/HAKUSENSHA, Inc.

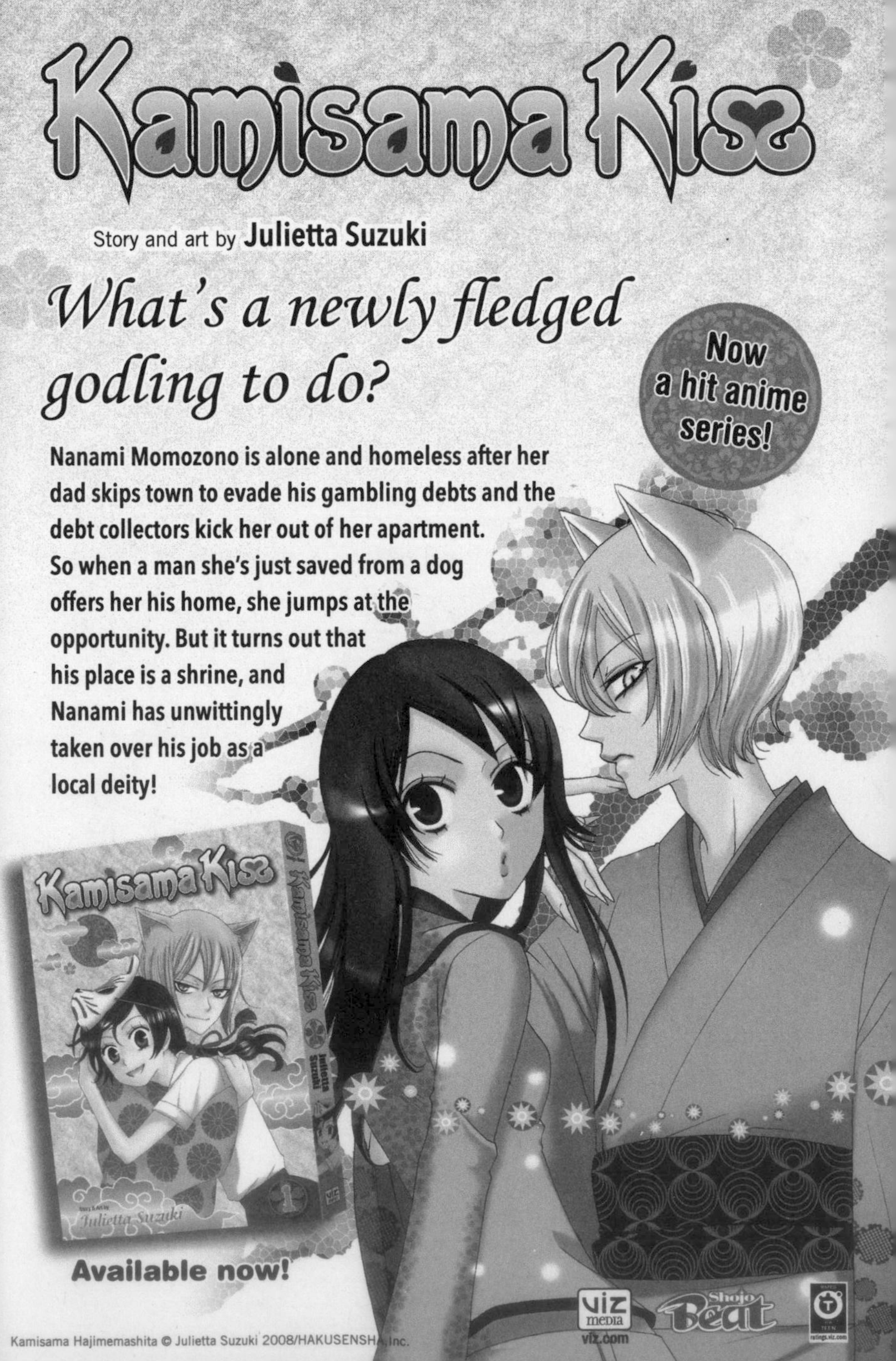
Kamisama Kiss
Story and art by Julietta Suzuki
What's a newly fledged godling to do?
Now a hit anime series!
Nanami Momozono is alone and homeless after her dad skips town to evade his gambling debts and the debt collectors kick her out of her apartment. So when a man she's just saved from a dog offers her his home, she jumps at the opportunity. But it turns out that his place is a shrine, and Nanami has unwittingly taken over his job as a local deity!
Available now!
viz media
viz.com
Shojo Beat
Kamisama Hajimemashita © Julietta Suzuki 2008/HAKUSENSHA, Inc.